L.A. MAN

PROFILES FROM A BIG CITY AND A SMALL WORLD

L.A. MAN

Joe Donnelly

Foreword by C. R. Stecyk

a genuine rare bird book
los angeles, calif.

THIS IS A GENUINE RARE BIRD BOOK

A Rare Bird Book | Rare Bird Books
453 South Spring Street, Suite 302
Los Angeles, CA 90013
rarebirdbooks.com

FIRST TRADE PAPERBACK ORIGINAL EDITION

Set in Minion Pro
Printed in the United States

10 9 8 7 6 5 4 3 2 1

Publisher's Cataloging-in-Publication data
Names: Donnelly, Joe James, author. | Stecyk, Craig, 1950-,
foreword author
Title: L.A. man : profiles from a big city and a small world / Joe Donnelly ;
foreword by C. R. Stecyk.
Description: First Trade Paperback Original Edition | A Genuine Rare
Bird Book | Los Angeles, CA; New York, NY: Rare Bird Books, 2018.
Identifiers: ISBN 9781945572876
Subjects: LCSH Los Angeles (Calif.)—Biography. | Hollywood (Los
Angeles, Calif.)—Biography. | Los Angeles (Calif.)—Social life and
customs. | Celebrities—Homes and haunts—California—Los Angeles. |
Motion picture actors and actresses—United States—Biography. | Popular
music—Californi—Los Angeles. | Rock Musicians—United State—
Biography.| BISAC BIOGRAPHY & AUTOBIOGRAPHY / Entertainment
& Performing Arts | BIOGRAPHY & AUTOBIOGRAPHY /
Cultural, Ethnic & Regional / General
Classification: LCC F869.L853 D66 2018 | DDC 979.4/94053092—dc23

For Olivia

Foreword

A RECENT BLUNT FORCE head trauma had rendered me incommunicado. My memory recall was nonexistent. The old cranial bell had become permanently rung when my skull hit the hardwood deck of an indigenous boat traversing a rigorously strict Islamic archipelago. No idea how Joe D. got my number as I then had none, but he came at me out of the void, popping up and requesting an interview about matters that had transpired decades ago. My answer was an emphatic no. The previously described perpetual mental haze prevented my willing participation in such an exercise. That wasn't much of a deterrence to Donnelly who seemed more interested in my participation than my willingness.

Somehow, eighteen years later, Donnelly is still around and still demanding answers. Through his perpetual interrogations and musings he has morphed from the aforementioned terrorist into a well-respected member of my ohana. (I realize that this could perhaps be interpreted as a classic case of Stockholm Syndrome.)

This book is a lot like that/him/then/there/now. Glad tidings from an unrelenting inquisitor. Great work oftentimes hurts as well as heals. In times like these a good read is all that really matters.

—C. R. Stecyk

Minor edits have been made to some of these pieces.

Driving Wes Anderson

Originally published as "The Road Wes Traveled"
in the LA Weekly, *January 27, 1999*

Author's note: Rushmore *debuted in New York and Los Angeles on the cold, December day that Wes Anderson and I road tripped to Texas. I was between gigs and doing some freelancing when the great Manohla Dargis, then film editor at LA Weekly, asked me if I'd be interested in a cover story on Wes Anderson, one that required accompanying the young director on his journey home for the holidays. Dargis was playing a couple of hunches. One was that Anderson, already in a precarious position after the lackluster performance of his charming debut,* Bottle Rocket, *had made a transformational film with* Rushmore. *The other was that I, relatively new in town, was the right guy to ride shotgun with Anderson while his fate unfurled in real time.*

THE DRIVER IS BREAKING the law again. Tearing like a tornado across the Mojave wastelands in a rented white Ford Explorer. Hands at ten and two. Chewing highway. Approaching his favorite speed: ninety mph. What would the honorable folks at Disney's Touchstone Pictures think?

Had they done a background check before anteing up for this buggy, they'd have known it would be like this. Wes Anderson is a recidivist. The last time he blazed through the Southwest, the law finally caught up with him in Van Horn, Texas. When the cop ran the registration and discovered Anderson had another speeding ticket besides the one he was writing, he threatened jail time. But first, he thought, let's check the trunk to see what kind of contraband this scofflaw is running across state lines.

In the trunk, the cop found a portrait of Herman Blume, the character played by Bill Murray in Anderson's latest film, *Rushmore*. The painting anchors the film's opening shot. In it, Blume sits in front of his disaffected movie family, looking like Ted Turner on painkillers. Set against a burnt-orange curtain, the Blume family portrait lingers onscreen an uncomfortable ten seconds before the curtain pulls back and the movie starts. Clearly, somebody's meant to get the picture.

"Is that that guy from *Groundhog Day*?" the cop asked Anderson.

Anderson replied that yes, indeed, the face in the painting was Bill Murray's.

"Then I went into my song and dance," he says.

The "song and dance" is that point during a pullover when Anderson humbly explains that he is a movie director on an errand of vital importance to the project. In this case, say, delivering the painting to Mr. Murray himself for approval.

"The cop ended up calling the judge at midnight, and I paid by credit card."

Then there was the time a couple years ago when a policeman in Tennessee pulled him over for doing ninety but knocked it down to eighty after the song and dance.

"The cop was really nice. He had a great accent. He thought it was really something that we were both the same age," Anderson recalls. "I thought he had some sadness about being only twenty-seven and being an authority figure."

Anderson has learned that part of Hollywood's magic is how it cools out the trigger finger of authority. The strategy in case we get pulled over, which seems like a safe bet given Anderson's preferred speed, is for me to wave the tape recorder

conspicuously and ask the officer if I can get the whole thing on record for the story I'm doing. The cop will ask what story, and...
"Then I'll downplay it, like, 'Oh, Jeez, I'm embarrassed,'" says Anderson. And the song and dance will be on.

Don't blame him for planning for the inevitable. When you drive as much as Wes Anderson does, somewhere in the John Madden range, you're bound to rack up moving violations. It's best to have a strategy. Hot chicks cry. He does his song and dance.

Today he's on the road from Los Angeles to New York, with a first stop scheduled for Amarillo, Texas. Any way you measure, it's quite a haul, but it's nothing compared to the larger journey of an artist who has come into his own. On that road, Anderson is somewhere between *Great Expectations* and *Deliverance*. There's a lot of emotional investment in how he negotiates this stretch, and not just his own. Many critics appear ready to anoint him as a favorite son. Some are even saying that *Rushmore*, just his second feature following the critically praised but largely ignored *Bottle Rocket*, marks his rise to the top of American filmmaking. *Rushmore*'s limited showing in December for Academy Award consideration earned it a place on dozens of 1998 Top Ten lists and serious Oscar hype. *Premiere* magazine has gone so far as to hail the somewhat gawky, twenty-nine-year-old upstart as the heir apparent to Allen, Brooks, Lubitsch, Sturges, and Keaton. There are, though, dissenting voices in the chorus of praise, and among the naysayers, one can sense an eagerness to lash back at whatever revenge-of-the-nerds factor Anderson's work represents, like *New Times* calling the film "self-important" or *Time* saying it "delights in itself too much."

Even though this crisp Friday in December is a portentous one—the day *Rushmore* opens for a week in New York and Los Angeles—the driver is doing his best to ignore the signs along the big journey. Audience reaction? Critical response? Backlash from the early festival fawning? Full houses? Those are the questions crashing around in the world outside the speeding Ford Explorer. For now, Anderson is relieved they are off on the horizons behind and before him. For now, his song and dance is to keep his eyes on the road and his hands upon the wheel. For now, the smaller journey, the one that will take him to Amarillo for a short rest before he drives on, is posing questions.

"Do you want a sandwich from the cooler?"

The driver pats the cooler lid with a casual grace that suggests he feels pretty at home behind the wheel of a rented white Ford Explorer. He ought to. He's been driving one on Disney's dollar since he went home to Houston for Thanksgiving.

"In lieu of In-N-Out Burger?" the passenger asks fearfully.

We are 120 miles into the trip and nearing Barstow. The digital display says we have 185 miles until empty, the voltage is good, and the oil life is 99 percent. All systems are go. We're in rhythm, which means we can stop looking ahead and start looking at each other. When you're driving fourteen hours with someone you've just met, you're going to make some silent assessments. One is that the two people onboard would probably have intimidated each other in high school. The driver unduly pegged as an intellectual snob. The passenger dismissed as a smug jock.

"No. Not in lieu of In-N-Out Burger," the driver decides. "Let's stop at the next In-N-Out!"

It's a little early for that, but when you're driving fourteen hours with someone you've just met, a roadside In-N-Out Burger, like a lot of things you thought you'd given up, has a certain siren call. It's a bonding thing.

"Hell," says the passenger, "it's twelve o'clock somewhere. We can even drive through."

"We will drive through, believe me."

A wicked grin slips across the driver's sharp face. With his round glasses and seventies shlub clothes, he looks a bit like

Mr. Rogers gone to pot, in pursuit of grease instead of grace. Soon enough, he's ordering a double-double with cheese, fries, and a Coke for the passenger; a single with cheese, fries, and a vanilla shake for himself.

"Can you put it in one of those to-go trays, please?" he says to the girl in the window.

We grab the stash and point toward Needles on Interstate 40. The colors of the Mojave—brown, blue, and fading green—clash outside the white bubble of the Ford Explorer. As we dip fries into the same puddle of ketchup, it's clear we're in this together now. To break the ice, the driver asks the passenger how he typically passes the day. The passenger admits to being in the throes of a debilitating *Beverly Hills 90210* addiction (reruns four times daily on FX). Painful admission that it is, it doesn't stop the passenger from lobbying the driver to do for Luke Perry what he did for Bill Murray in *Rushmore*—the inspired casting-against-type that earns the actor rave reviews and shines him in a new light.

"How can you miscast him? As a Mexican or something?" the driver asks.

"I suppose as a bus conductor or an airplane pilot."

"He'd just become that," the driver says with conviction. "He's such a chameleon."

Alas, ultimately Perry just doesn't have the kind of face that interests Anderson. He likes a face like that of Jason Schwartzman, the eighteen-year-old acting novice he cast as Max Fischer, the lovesick, mildly sociopathic playwriting prodigy and lead character in *Rushmore*. The actor's face becomes a billboard for teen angst and a sight gag at the same time.

"But Luke really needs this, for the indie credibility!" says the passenger, appealing to the driver's magnanimity.

Finally Anderson relents. "Okay, I think we can do that. I think we can push him through the system. Man, Amarillo is a long ways away. At the moment, we're still in California. We still have to go through New Mexico and Arizona, two of the biggest states in the US."

♦♦♦

CENTURIES AGO, A WISE man said even the longest journey begins with the first small steps. The journey of the artist might be the longest and scariest of all. On this path, the biggest step is a leap of faith: it is making the terrifying declaration, to yourself at least, that you are chosen, that you possess the tools to be an engineer of the human soul. Thanks to Mrs. Torda, Anderson began groping his way along that path a long time ago. You see, back in 1977, when Anderson's parents were getting divorced, his fourth-grade teacher, Mrs. Torda, was into experimental teaching.

"She was doing this thing where she was making everyone do these weird meditation exercises, that thing where you drop a tissue and catch it in the air, you know?" he says. "And while everyone would be doing this meditation thing, she started giving me massages. It was a little odd. It was not a thing I enjoyed. She sized me up as being extremely anxious and a problem."

Part of the problem was that Anderson was embarrassed about the divorce. He saw it as a failure—not his necessarily, but the family's. It drove him crazy. He denied it was happening and tried to keep it from everybody. Not surprisingly, the ten-year-old began verbally acting out, telling lies, running through the hallways, throwing things.

"I kept getting in trouble. I kept getting little demerits."

He also started writing—plays, of all things. So Mrs. Torda launched a program with Wes where every two or three weeks or so that he didn't get a demerit, she would let him put on another play. There was *The Christmas Escape* and also his early mystery classic *The Initial Bullet*.

"The mystery is solved because it's a doctor who has shot this guy, and they found these X-rays of the guy with a bullet in his head, and if that's not incriminating enough, the bullet has the doctor's initials engraved on it that you can see in the X-ray."

The driver is staring out at the road ahead, smiling wryly. He's a keen observer of youthful folly, especially his own.

"One of them," he continues, "was set all in cars. That was a big one, because that one, I remember, we did it for the class, then they expanded it for the lower school, and then they did it for the whole school. I was in fourth grade. Yeah, that was a big hit, that play."

The passenger looks into the rearview, stealing a reflected gaze into the driver's eyes. The past is rolling by in sequence like the broken lines on the highway.

"So, when Max says to his rival, 'I've written a hit play, what have you done?' you're speaking from your heart."

"Yeah, speaking from my heart, except I think Owen [Wilson, his best friend and writing partner] might have written that line."

"Owen's speaking from your heart."

"Yeah."

There's a long pause, as if Anderson is trying to scrutinize something ethereal.

"We did an Alamo play, *The Battle of the Alamo,* in three acts, and I was Davy Crockett. And we did *The Headless Horseman,* in which I played the Headless Horseman *and* Ichabod Crane."

"You had a grandiose sense of yourself at this time," the passenger suggests.

"Yeah, major ego, because I was"—he clears his throat—"I had a lot of insecurity, and I guess that's the way it manifested itself."

"Do you remember what kind of affirmations you got when you were putting on your plays?"

"Yeah, the affirmation of me signing autographs for people who didn't want my autograph. You know, I had a pad of paper and I was giving people my autograph. I was kind of standing there finding kids who I thought wanted my autograph and giving it to them. I was sort of feeling like I was a boy wonder."

Anderson chuckles at the thought, unaware of or uninterested in the irony.

"Well," says the passenger, "no one wants anything more in fourth grade than for people to want his autograph."

"Yeah, that's right. I tried to create a market for that."

What do you get when you pay five billion dollars to reroute the Colorado River 336 miles north and over 1,200 feet uphill to a desert cauldron fit only for rattlesnakes and scorpions, then decide the damned (literally) water is unfit for drinking but perfectly fit to be the new home of the London Bridge, which is transported and rebuilt brick by brick at a cost of more than eleven million dollars and is now the centerpiece of a town that hosts the London Arms Pub and the Sherwood Forest Nursery?

The citizens of Arizona got Lake Havasu City.

The sign in front of the Pilot gas station near Lake Havasu City doesn't say "Welcome to the Biggest Mistake in the West," but it does say "Welcome." And our gas gauge says empty. So at 2:00 p.m. and 320 miles into the trip, we stop.

During the last stretch of California, we passed a coyote on one side of the road and an attractive female hitchhiker in red pants on the other. The driver was concerned for both, especially the woman in red pants.

"Those red pants are going to get her picked up at some point," he said plaintively. "I just hope it's the right person."

Inside the Pilot station, the Chipmunks are singing *"All I want for Christmas is my two front teeth, my two front teeth."* Coyotes, singing Chipmunks, the desert, it's all part of Christmas in Southern California. No wonder Bret Easton Ellis left with a bad taste in his mouth. But the driver seems supremely untouched by it all, even the road ahead of him. He's got the air-conditioned solution. He's got books by Don DeLillo, Tom Wolfe, Robert Evans, and Roald Dahl on tape. He's got the LBJ tapes. He's got a towel in the travel bag. He's got the Pixies, Rolling Stones, Elliott Smith, and his best friend's girlfriend (Sheryl Crow) on CD. He's got a cooler full of sandwiches and chocolate-chip cookies. For the time being, he's got the world at bay.

The characters populating Anderson's movies are the same, existing in a heightened, insular world of their own making. In *Bottle Rocket*, the three friends at the film's core barely come in contact with anything or anyone that could be mistaken for life as most of us know it. When they do, the outcome isn't good.

"There's never a world, there's never a real world that they're involved with," Anderson explains. "They're doing their own thing. It looks kind of like this." He waves at a flat, brown field outside the window of the Ford Explorer.

In much the same way, *Rushmore* focuses on the emotional lives of the kids orbiting around Rushmore Academy, particularly Max's schoolmates. Adults, for the most part, aren't allowed in the game unless they play by Max's rules. When they don't, there's trouble.

"The thing I always think about with these movies, I always think a lot about Charlie Brown," he says. "You know how in Charlie Brown, in *Peanuts*, they are in their own little world? There's only a group of kids. It has a mood all its own."

By focusing on this alternate reality, Anderson turns his camera into a microscope and his movies into lab studies. What's under the glass, to a large degree, is the sustainability of friendship and the things people do when friendships are tested. Max in *Rushmore* and Dignan (played by Owen Wilson) in *Bottle Rocket* are the Charlie Browns of these little worlds, where things go awry when a storm blows into the emotional harbor of friendship.

"Both these movies are about friendships that get put through weird tests and that are renewed, kind of, you know? That are broken up and renewed, especially if you go through some big things together," he says, "like me and my friends who all did *Bottle Rocket* together. Our lives are so different from what they were when we started being friends."

◆◆◆

WHEN WES ANDERSON AND Owen Wilson started being friends, they were a couple of kids lollygagging through the tail end of college at the University of Texas. They met in a playwriting class and eventually became roommates. A mutual love of movies and writing proved to be a creatively combustible combination. In time, an idea for a quirky fourteen-minute short became the first installment of their eventual first script, *Bottle Rocket*. When the film was made, Owen and his brother Luke's offbeat, charismatic performances landed them on the Hollywood hot list, winning them high-profile movie gigs and Sheryl Crow and Drew Barrymore, respectively. Things changed, all right.

Even though Wes, Owen, and Luke presently live together in a ramshackle Tudor in an unfashionable part of LA, Anderson seems to understand it's never going to be the same among the three amigos. The ride from Texas to Hollywood is over, and now that they made it, they're certain to go in different directions. They already are. Each is looking for his own home. It's hard not to wonder if the themes in *Bottle Rocket* and *Rushmore* are Anderson's way of addressing the fear that the real world will impinge on his friendships.

"Yeah," he says, "I mean, it happens. That's the way it happens. But I don't feel like we're, right now I feel like our…" He searches for the right words, hands staying tight at ten and two. "The friendship that gets the most strain is the one between me and Owen. And I feel like that's as strong a friendship now as it's ever been, and we still have several movies we want to do together. And I just sort of feel like it's not something that I feel worried about right now."

When Wes Anderson idealizes himself, it is as an artist. He sees himself in a loft in New York, perhaps, with space and light and crazy hair and a breeze through the south-facing windows and the burnished reflection of creativity, emotion, and connection bouncing back off the page through his round glasses and into his shy eyes. Something, he says, like Nick Nolte's character in "Life Lessons," Martin Scorsese's contribution to *New York Stories*.

"That would be something to aspire to," he says almost wonderingly.

Anderson's next steps along the larger journey were little forays into the life he began envisioning for himself. In high school and into college it was time to try on the identity of an artist for size.

At St. John's, the prep school Anderson attended in his hometown of Houston, where much of *Rushmore* was shot, he withdrew from the center stage he had provided for himself with the plays and began focusing more on writing.

"Short, like J. D. Salinger short stories," he recalls. "At that point, I sort of felt like I was going to be a writer. Just a story writer. A novelist or something. But I was also doing little movies at the same time. Then the movie stuff just started to take over more and more."

During college, Anderson made creative use of the University of Texas's curriculum policies, engineering his course load so that almost all his credits were earned in independent or conference classes. The loose schedule gave him and Owen Wilson time to mine Austin's cultural resources.

"We never had any money, so it was kind of limited. There was just a lot of hanging around and reading and going to movies. I was always doing some research. You know, they have this incredible humanities research center called the Harry Ransom Center."

All he could bring into the Ransom Center was a piece of notebook paper and a pencil, but once he was inside, a world populated by artists, writers, and filmmakers was his to explore. Some of us spent the better part of our college years pouring beers over our heads. Anderson spent hours researching F. Scott Fitzgerald, Francois Truffaut, and others who would become his cultural heroes.

"I was interested in those people and just as interested in their lives as I was in their work," Anderson says.

The driver drifts off, and Amarillo is too far away for the passenger to pursue him. Conversations need rest stops, too. Inside the rented Ford Explorer, it's basically inert. The miles roll by unheralded except by the digital miles-to-empty reading on the truck's display panel. Finally, the shrill ring of the car phone interrupts the sound of wheels turning. It's Anderson's brother Eric in D.C., petitioning Wes to come home for Christmas or New Year's or something like that. When the phone is handed to the passenger, Eric picks up where the conversation about college left off, telling of going through old stuff at their father's house and stumbling upon a box of about twenty post cards Wes sent Eric from college. He says the post cards were bursting with enthusiasm for films and books and the lives Wes was discovering.

"They were the most vibrant things," Eric says. "They just got me excited about anything to do with movies and writing. That was my artistic education."

It wasn't long before Anderson's exploratory steps became more determined. He began using the local cable-access station's equipment to make and air what he calls "little, short, stupid little movies." This enabled him to develop basic skills and to hone his eye for the endearing idiosyncrasies of the people in his world. Starting with his landlord.

"That was the main thing," Anderson says, "this landlord documentary."

It all began when he and Wilson, who were roommates by now, started to battle their landlord over his refusal to fix their window cranks. To illustrate the gravity of the issue, Anderson and Wilson staged a break-in of their own apartment. They took some stuff out, messed the place up a little, and called the police, blaming it on the broken window cranks. When the police and the landlord arrived, the landlord said it looked like an inside job. The police didn't take it too seriously, either. Things then escalated to where the guys stopped paying rent, and the landlord tried taking some of their stuff as collateral.

"We ended up moving in the middle of the night, and he hunted us down with a private investigator," Anderson recalls fondly. "I went to meet him, and I proposed doing this project."

Amazingly, the landlord agreed to fund the documentary, which would run on the access channel, ostensibly to promote Carl Hindler Properties.

"He believed in, like, death penalties for drunk driving, burglary, and he had this pet snake that died and that he had given mouth-to-mouth resuscitation, which didn't work. I said, 'Well, what was the snake's name?' And he said, 'Ah, we didn't really give it a name, we just called it baby, or snake.' And I said, 'Uh, well, what did you do with the snake after it died?' And he said, 'I have it in the freezer in the back. I'd like to take it to a taxidermist.'"

Anderson continues with his head slightly nodding and a smile escaping. It's as animated as he's been since In-N-Out. "I asked him, 'Have you ever used a lawsuit as a method of doing business, as a way of pressuring people to get what you want?' And he said, 'All the time. We use it all the time. And we're always winning, always winning major settlements.'

He had this sailboat in his driveway. He liked to just go out and sit on the boat, but he never got the boat in the water. The boat was not seaworthy."

Welcome to Wes Anderson's movie milieu, where friends apply nasal breathing strips or dress in yellow jump suits to do armed robberies, as in *Bottle Rocket*. Or where a sophomore preppie who looks like a discombobulated teen version of Superman-era Christopher Reeve tries to build an aquarium on school grounds to express his love for an older woman, as in *Rushmore*. Or where, as with the landlord, peculiar individuality is exploited for humor but never derision.

"I didn't do the documentary in a way that was meant to look bad," Anderson explains soberly. "I just thought he was a funny character, and I would just try to make it a truthful portrait."

Given all that *has* happened, the passenger is curious about what the hell the driver thought was *going* to happen when he and his friends started cooking up those fourteen-minute installments of their pet project, *Bottle Rocket*.

"You know, we were hoping we were going to become huge and all that stuff," he says matter-of-factly. "I mean, our ultimate hope was that people are going to see the movie and everybody's going to love it. That kind of thing."

"So, you literally had this naive idea, 'Hey, let's make a movie with our friends and we'll just throw everybody in it, and we'll tell our story, and the world will love it'?"

"Yeah, more or less."

◆◆◆

REMEMBER WHEN YOU WERE like that? When you and your buddies had your own language, your own style, your own way of looking at things—your own world in the larger universe? And you thought to yourself: if we could just capture this, this magic, how cool would that be?

That's what Wes Anderson and Owen Wilson thought during that senior year at the University of Texas, when they were hanging out and doing the landlord documentary and the *Super 8* films about themselves and their friends. They finally made the declaration: We want to make movies, and this thing, this thing that is *us*, that's gonna be our bottled lightning.

So Wes and Owen went to work on *Bottle Rocket* with a manic determination. It would start with a staged break-in, an inside job. They wrote a 330-page script. They moved to Dallas, where Owen's older brother Andrew worked at an advertising agency and could supply sixteen mm film, cameras, and a crew. They cast themselves and friends. And they made the first fourteen-minute installment. It wasn't about them, per se, but it did represent how they saw themselves at the time. And it worked.

At least to the degree that in 1994 screenwriter/indie kingpin L. M. Kit Carson passed the short on to producer Polly Platt, who passed it on to writer-director James L. Brooks, who badgered Columbia Pictures into coughing up five million dollars for the feature-length version. It would have the same cast—Owen and Luke Wilson in the lead parts, Robert Musgrave as the third wheel, Kumar Pallana as the incompetent safecracker—and the same director, Wes Anderson.

"And you felt totally assured in your ability to do this?" the passenger asks.

"Yeah, because there's never any time to have too much self-doubt anyway," Anderson says with the distant tone of someone who is stifling a post-traumatic-stress flashback. "And also, I was of the opinion that we were going to make this thing that everyone was going to love. But at that point I was operating under total naiveté."

"Why'd you think it was so special?"

"I don't know. Just because it was *our thing*. I mean, I had nothing else. Our whole lives were dedicated to this; it was a thing that meant something to us. It was based on our own ideas, and we thought they were different from other people's ideas, and it was just what we were stuck on."

When Anderson speaks of *Bottle Rocket*, it's as if he's talking about a first love. There's tenderness for what it was, for how it opened up new worlds, but there's also disappointment for everything it didn't turn out to be.

"I was just so personally excited about what it was going to be that I thought, 'Wait until they see this.' That's why I was so blindsided."

What blindsided him was the audience reaction at test screenings in Santa Monica prior to the film's release in early 1996.

"When we had our first test screening, and it was a disaster, I was just in shock, because I always felt like people were going to..." Anderson hesitates, his voice hinting at the distress he felt. "I had it in my mind that people were going to like it. I didn't realize it was a strange movie that only certain people were going to like and a lot of people would hate. And that was the situation.

"We just thought we'd blown the whole deal, kind of," he continues. "I kind of always felt like if the movie's a disaster, well then, okay, it'll be harder to make the next movie. It'll be very hard. There are a million ways to do it, you know? But it was sort of an awful time."

I mean, Owen wanted us to go into advertising at one point, and he says he investigated joining the military, which I didn't know."

Anderson turns and looks directly at the passenger. It's his grandest physical gesture in at least three hundred miles.

"You know," he says, "I could be a trucker."

For a long time now the vistas have been numbingly spare and redundant. Interstate 40, the more efficient if less resplendent replacement for old Route 66, goes on in a monochrome Southwestern blur. We're not sure where we are on the map, but it feels as if we must be halfway to Amarillo. To combat something like the doldrums, driver and passenger down large colas and a gigantic bag of peanut M&M's. Then we agree to take advantage of the driver's access to ambush the notoriously inaccessible Bill Murray with an unsolicited call. Beneath road-weary giddiness at the prospect of interrupting him at home is the notion that this might not be a good idea, that if Murray is not up for it, the wind could go right out of our sails. Then what'll we do? But the sugar and caffeine prevail, and the driver dials the secret number.

After Anderson briefs him on the situation, Murray seems eager to talk. It's clear he likes the idea of a couple of guys driving into the night with a fairly absurd destination in mind. Amarillo? Why Amarillo? Because that's where Anderson made his first stop the last time he drove to New York, and it worked. Weirdly enough, as Murray warms up to the car phone, the passenger gets the idea the actor wouldn't mind riding shotgun on this trip.

"Is what you see with Wes what you get?" the passenger asks, looking over at the driver, who has resumed looking straight ahead.

"No, no. I don't think what you see is what you get with Wes. You get much more," answers Murray. In the background is the excited pitch of the family pool tournament we've taken Murray away from. "He looks like R. Crumb's old drawings of himself. He looks like he's going to be outraged, like he finally sees what's really wrong with you, and then the horror backs off and the beauty comes through."

Murray goes on to say that what made the *Rushmore* shoot work for him, besides the quality of the material, was Anderson's ability to stress the positive. "Wes could find the good content in whatever you were working with. That made it easy. It freed you up to work."

His wife's sharp cue having hastened an early departure from the action, Murray peppers the conversation with droll commentary on the tournament's progress. It isn't hard to place him there as Blume, off to the side in a tux, cigarette dangling from his lips, a spectator in a tournament of his own making, tossing peanuts to the family retriever in a small act of resignation and rebellion.

It is suggested to Murray that his characterization of Blume has an elegant, spiritually wasted quality that suits the actor.

"I was feeling the elegance of my own spiritual wastedness. I was feeling how all the touchstones of wealth and privilege are slippery," he says. "Those emotions are not far from anyone's home if you've lived a little. Some days I came home and I felt a little sore. I felt like I'd been cooked a little."

What about Anderson? Has Murray seen something in him that might not be apparent to the casual observer, or even the fourteen-hour one?

"He's very good at what he does, but don't be afraid to ask him if he needs a Band-Aid or some change, things you generally ask of people who look like they're in worse shape than him," Murray says in a way that makes you unsure how serious he is. "A Band-Aid, yeah, I think a Band-Aid. There's some cuts there."

"The first night we were on the shoot, he gave me three pairs of socks," recalls Anderson, after Murray hangs up. "Two are still in my bag."

◆◆◆

DARKNESS WRAPS AROUND THE rented Ford Explorer like a blanket as we drive into the plains of eastern New Mexico. We made it from the kiln-baked landscape of the low desert to the higher elevations of pine trees and snow on the ground and moonlight reflecting off mountain silhouettes. And back down again. The driver was right, Arizona and New Mexico are big, but at last Amarillo seems within reach. It's not that far from Tucumcari, and Tucumcari is not that far from here. The driver is ready for the home stretch. Ever since he stopped flying two years ago, he's used to putting these miles on a day.

"Wes won't characterize it as a fear of flying, but more as a love of the open road," explains Owen Wilson, calling from Los Angeles. "Once my mom asked why he won't fly, and Wes replied, 'Nobody knows.' That's become the standard answer."

It's the third or fourth time in a matter of minutes that Wilson has called. He and Anderson are involved in a minor squabble regarding some advice Anderson is giving Wilson that Wilson probably agrees with but doesn't necessarily want to hear.

"That was the smooth-things-out conversation," Anderson says of Wilson's latest and most conciliatory call, "which then becomes the general criticisms, the 'Okay, I agree, *but here's your big problem.*'"

Anderson is chuckling. "We're like an old married couple. Never go to bed angry."

Outside the Explorer, the *Rushmore* hoopla is steamrolling. In fact, the car phone has been ringing off the hook all afternoon and into the evening with reports from the openings in Los Angeles and New York. The larger journey seems to be catching up with us.

"We had two guys who were either on hallucinogens or laughing gas," buzzes Randy Poster, the film's music supervisor, from New York.

Übermanager Geyer Kosinski had a stool pigeon at the LA opener who phoned in a report. Kosinski phoned Owen with a report of that report, and then Owen called Wes with a report of the report of the report. The report? Only front-row seats for latecomers. Spontaneous applause when the credits rolled. And this from a typically blasé LA matinee crowd. Word on the reviews is overwhelmingly positive, too. The *New York Daily News* says it's "the best and most beautiful movie of 1998." The *New Yorker* can't keep the smile off its face. In *The New York Times*, Janet Maslin says...well, who the hell ever knows what Janet Maslin is saying, but it seems really good.

The passenger wants to know how this makes the driver feel.

"You're the next big thing. Does that rattle you?"

"Do you think that's right? I don't know if that's right."

"Film critics are building altars to you in their offices."

"Yeah, but did you read Kenneth Turan's? Turan's wasn't that great."

"How do you know? I want to talk to someone who knows this."

"Barry Mendel [*Rushmore*'s producer]. He can read it to you. Okay, I mean Turan's review is not the greatest review ever. It's not terrible, but he says, like, he says something like... he didn't like Max."

"He didn't like Max?"

"He didn't like the character. Not the performance, but the character."

"All right, but you're being hailed. You're being praised. You're being compared to Buster Keaton. Are you skeptical?"

"No, I'm not skeptical. I mean, I like it. It doesn't feel that great, but it feels good."

"Why doesn't it feel that great?"

"Well, I don't know."

"Are you like Max in that you think, 'Hey, I should be making what's being called the best American movie of the year'?"

"No, I wouldn't say that. I'm actually in good spirits. But the reviews, bad reviews, I think, make you feel horrible. And, like, Turan's review does not make me feel very good."

"It doesn't sound that bad."

"It's not that bad, but it just has a tendency to, like, draw everything into that. You sort of look for the worst and sink to that level."

"Well, I could be sitting in the car with the Woody Allen of the next generation. How do you think I'm supposed to feel?"

"Well, you gotta know that it's hundreds of miles to go tonight, so I don't care who you're sitting in the car with, you're not going to feel that good."

"Yeah, I don't know how I'm supposed to feel, either."

"I actually feel pretty good. I wish we had some more daylight, but aside from that, I think we're doing pretty well."

"That's what I mean, you're keeping your eye on the project at hand, but I'm trying to talk about, not your place on this road to Amarillo, but your place on this road of life."

"Right. The road to, uh, the road to Mulholland. The road to Fifth Avenue. Well, in terms of that, I can't say that I feel ecstatically happy about it. The thing is, we really don't have any sense of what level of attention the movie is going to have when it really comes out, you know?"

Anderson should be forgiven if he's a little wary of the warm embrace being extended to him and *Rushmore*. He heard it from the movie people before with *Bottle Rocket*, although not on this scale. Then, when *Bottle Rocket*, which refers to low-impact fireworks, lived up to its name at the box office, the experience left him thinking there were "lots of people hating that movie that we don't know about."

Rushmore, however, is different in important ways. Even though it clearly shares the same tender heart and skewed sensibility, the film is the product of an examined life—mostly Anderson's—whereas *Bottle Rocket* was a snapshot of a particular moment. It's a short distance between Max Fischer, the hurting adolescent who is trying to find the right balance of insecurity and bravado, and Wes Anderson as a boy.

"It definitely couldn't be more personal. *Bottle Rocket* was about our behavior at the time. This is about our lives and backgrounds and all that family stuff," Anderson admits. "When I talk about the story, I talk about it as something we did together, but there's a tremendous amount of personal connection with me."

Indeed, when Anderson speaks of the paradoxes of Max Fischer's tenure at Rushmore Academy, it sounds as if he's talking about himself in Hollywood.

"Max wants to lead everybody, but he wants to do it in a way that uses this whole establishment, kind of," he says, obviously getting a charge out of divining his and Max's character. "But he has his own ideas about things. He's just not a conformist, but he hasn't, like, reconciled himself with the image he wants to have, you know?"

Of course. For men and for artists, that's something that happens a ways down the road, on the larger journey. And that's if you're lucky. Meanwhile, even as his much-hoped-for film opens on both coasts, the driver is moving farther into the anonymous middle of America, where for a few days, anyway, he won't have to reconcile anything. The passenger suggests it's kind of symbolic.

"Now that you mention it," says the driver, "it sounds a little psychological. Like something's happening, and I don't even know what I'm doing."

Morning Becomes Electra

Originally published as "Please Don't Squeeze the Carmen,"
Bikini, *April 1997*

Author's note: In the mid-nineties, I worked for RayGun Publishing, the iconic and irreverent indie-publishing concern started by Marvin and Jaclyn Jarrett. For a few years, RayGun was a West Coast arbiter of cool. Bikini magazine, which I'd eventually edit, was its tongue-in-cheek pop-culture title.

In its day, RayGun was a thriving den of underpaid creativity. The famed designer David Carson made his first impressions there. Johnny Knoxville cut his teeth at Bikini and journalist Alex Wagner got hired straight out of college. Many excellent journalists, novelists, screenwriters, and top-notch photographers gained their footing at RayGun during what seems now like a looser, more creative time for magazines.

For a while, I was kind of the starlet-interviewing stunt guy. The conceit being that I'd stand in for the reader on something approximating a "date" with the likes of Shannen Doherty, Jenny McCarthy, Carmen Electra, and others I'm forgetting. They were all good sports and none were easily dismissed. I managed to dig this one up and it seemed as fitting an ode to that era in my life as anything.

MY DEAR READER, BY the time you have reached these words, I trust that the cover teaser, the table of contents, and the headlines will have sufficiently clued you in on the general premise of this article—my "date" with Carmen Electra.

But, of course, this wasn't just my date, reader; it was our date. I was merely chosen to represent you, to go in your place, as Carmen would've been understandably overwhelmed, perhaps even frightened, had several thousand of us descended upon the appointed romantic rendezvous spot, flowers and candy nervously clutched in our sweaty palms. I had to be the guy. I had to be you. And even now, long after the fact, I can feel the weight of your hopes and dreams as you suffer paper cuts turning the pages to arrive at this point and find out how our date went.

I would like to tell you that we fared well, that we got to something real, that we fully transcended the self-aware beauty and layers of image-making that separates us from America's MTV-anointed object of adolescent adulation. And at times, I thought we did…but the thing about first dates is you can never quite tell what's really going on inside your date's head…the gleeful laughter could well have been nervous, the broad smiles may have been forced, the warm parting perhaps nothing more than sheer relief. During our "date," reader, I did not think so. But when a concerned publicist greeted me on the phone "the morning after" with reports of a nervous Carmen thinking she'd perhaps "gone too far," I had to wonder which way it was for Carmen…and for us.

I'm sad to report, reader, that this was probably our last date with Carmen. But I'm not sure whom or what is to blame. Were we but gristle on her grill as she burns down the road to phenomenondom? Or, was she simply a doe-eyed innocent caught in the headlights of the image-making machine? Maybe we just weren't such a hot date. I'm confused, reader, and all I can do is invite you to watch the accident unfold and then crawl with me through the debris in search of clues…

So, like my editor said, it would be cool if we had, y'know, a date and we talked about dates and stuff. Do you like dates?

Carmen Electra: Not blind dates, no.

No? Actually, I was…

…because, I wouldn't want to go out with someone I don't know and be stuck with the whole night. I think that would be miserable.

I was talking about the fruit.

I'm sorry?

The fruit. I was talking about the fruit. Y'know…dates.

Oh, the fruit. I don't like those either.

Can you hear the clunk as clearly as if you were there? You see, reader, God made a face to let you know he could be deadly serious about beauty and he put it on Carmen Electra. So, when confronted with this face as she strode into Geoffrey's seaside restaurant in Malibu—carrying her lithe, compact, and curvaceous body like all the world was a runway—I thought a cornball joke like the one above might help break the ice. Bad move? Shall we go on? Or, have you had enough already?

So, when was your first date? Can you remember your actual first, nervous-perspiration date?

I can remember in kindergarten, having crushes on boys.

Oh, definitely. I think I had my first orgasm when I was in first grade.

I think I had mine on the school bus when I was twelve. By accident.

Really, the bumps?

Yeah, tight jeans. The Calvin Kleins. We wore them so tight, you'd have to use a hanger to get them off.

I remember. I was alive then. Did you know what was going on?

I had no idea. I just thought it was the most amazing feeling I'd felt in my life. Everyday, I sat on the bus, I'd try to repeat the same thing, but it wouldn't happen again.

You couldn't find the right spot...

Hey, now, you may be thinking, it's a little early in the date for this kind of talk—and maybe that was our mistake. But why wait, reader? Any first bite could be poison and if we hesitate, there are things we could all go to the grave not knowing. Besides, the restaurant is empty but for Carmen, me, and the staff. We are sitting in the corner of the patio, overlooking the dark sea. A heat lamp the size of the Olympic torch lights our menus and warms our faces. Are you with me now? Carmen takes to the bread with extreme prejudice while I nervously eye the dinner napkin still resting under her cutlery. Cumulonimbus swells offshore, pregnant with an impending monster. Maybe I shouldn't have asked her to order for me...

Carmen: Are you a vegetarian?

Pretty much, but I do shrimp and fish and stuff like that.

How about the fettuccini with shrimp, tomatoes, and spinach?

Good choice.

Waiter: Good choice.
(Still no movement on the napkin.)

We are all shaped by our experiences. Does anything have ore to do with who we are now than who we were when we were five? When Carmen Electra was five, Jimmy Carter was in his second year at the White House and the idea of taking a herd of American hostages was just hatching in the nether regions of Ayatollah Khomeni's fundamentalist mind.

Somewhere in Cincinnati, Ohio, Carmen was quantum leaps ahead of her kindergarten classmates in terms of self-realization. She knew she wanted to be a star, but she didn't know how— whether it would be from dancing or singing or what? She might have known something else, though.

Carmen's mom put her in dance classes and her teacher saw talent. She won her first dance contest, at five, prancing around to Rod Stewart's "Do Ya Think I'm Sexy?" Did she choose her weapon at that moment?

The following years were spent honing her dancing and singing skills at The School for Creative Arts until the ninth grade. Then, she decided she wanted to trade in a little of the practice that kept her busy until 9:30 p.m. every night for the possibility of making out with someone under the bleachers, of having people talk about her in the hallways, of riding shotgun in the Z28 IROC, of a normal adolescence. Did it get normal enough for us, reader, to have some common ground?

I bet she got good grades.

Did you date the captain of the football team?

No, I dated a rapper in our high school.

Oh, yeah? That's even cooler, right?

[Laughing.] Yes, exactly.

Was it Vanilla Ice?

No…did he live in Cincinnati?

I don't know. I think Texas, or something. So, tell me about high school. I want to know all about your history of high school dating. What were your best dates and worst dates? I'd be hard-pressed to remember three dates.

Yeah, what's a good date in Ohio?

You'd meet at McDonald's, right?

Yeah, we'd meet at Pizza Hut and run out without paying. Eat and jump in the car. So, I can't really say I had a good date. That was, like, exciting. It was fun. It was fun to go to King's Island. That was the big amusement park.

As she drains her third Coke, reader, I can see Carmen from further away than the tabletop that separates us. I see her off in the distance at a place few of us will ever reach, the place of earliest childhood fantasies realized by the age of twenty-four. The wild-fame welcome wagon at the door, wiretap hidden inside the bouquet of roses, an army of tabloid grubbers in the bushes. Cocked and loaded in the media's pinball machine. It looks scary to me, and I think to myself that one could easily negotiate that brink of bigness with less grace than Carmen.

Where does she go when it looks like a steep drop? Is it back to Ohio, to the amusement park where she performed in the magic shows and got sawed in half? Is she up there alone, or are we with her?

When we resume the date, Carmen tells me that she never sleeps with anyone on the first date. I'm not so convinced this is a good rule to live by and I bet her the man she marries will be the first one she does sleep with on the first date because he will be unlike the rest and she will know it immediately. But other fundamental differences are now rearing their ugly heads...

So, you're a spaghetti slicer, huh?

Yeah, I don't like to twist. It messes up my lipstick.

So, uh...

Who knows, maybe you're the one for me and we'll have sex tonight. (Laughs.) Just kidding.

I don't think so. I don't think we are a good match.

No?

I mean, maybe, but…you haven't put your napkin on your lap yet…and it's making me nervous. (I try to cover up by saying I'm kidding.) I'm just kidding. (Unfortunately, I'm not.)

I'll do it for you.
(She knew I wasn't kidding.)

Maybe the odds were just stacked against us, reader.

Despite all the innuendo, despite the celebrity pictorial in Playboy, despite the fact that sex may be the most potent weapon in Carmen's arsenal, she has been with only four men. It's hard to compete with that level of selectivity. Another thing working against us, reader, is the whole name thing. Carmen seems to go for men with hooky marquee handles. There's been a "Shan Sparks," who took her to the junior prom; a "Craig Carrington," who deflowered her admirably late in the game for a modern girl, and don't forget the recently departed "B Real" of Cypress Hill. "Prince" is another name she's been linked to professionally, if not romantically. Let's admit it: "Joe Donnelly" or _____ (fill in your name here) might just fall a little flat.

What do you look for in a guy? How do you feel about a sky-blue pickup truck? Is that something you look for in a guy?

No.

Oh, then, we're definitely off.

I like a person who is a good time, who can have fun under any circumstances, someone who is adventurous. Life is short, and I like to enjoy each day.

What would it take to get you to even think twice about me?

Well, we'd have to take a drive to the Mercedes dealership and buy me a new car, and then to a jewelry store to buy me a new Rolodex, and then, we'd be off to a good start.

Really?

[Laughing.] I'm just kidding.

You wouldn't settle for a guy with a big heart and a small paycheck?

I have.

You have, but those days are behind you.

[Laughing.] All behind me.

What about looks?

I'm into exotic-looking men with an edge.

That sort of takes me out of the picture.

I like a man who's in touch with his feminine side.

I'm back in!

And who's not afraid to express himself and doesn't have a caveman complex. It's hard to find the two.

Well, for a man, I'm all woman.

You're every woman and more?

I'm so much woman.

Do you like to dress up in drag?

I have. Well, just with my ex-girlfriend. I've, like, worn her underwear and shit.

Makeup and stuff, too?

Well, I thought putting on her stockings and G-string was a good start [laughing]. You know, actually, she's done me up.

Yeah, she liked it?

Unfortunately, I think I liked it more.

That's what I'm talking about, you know? Just have fun. I've gone out with men who are just afraid of everything and are too conservative and it's no fun.

I think of Carmen, the terrible beauty, terrorizing boys to men with her beauty and brashness. She told me how she used to like to go to the playground with her tight jeans on and check out the boys. What has she done to us? Or, reader, what have we done to her? Did she merely recognize early on that we've turned the world into a sexual food chain where she can always come out on top? Certainly, there's no denying Carmen swam like a shark in these waters as a five-year–old prancing in that contest to her more recent stint as a dancer for the Erotic City shows at Glam Slam.

I have a theory, reader, about what keeps us on the horizon, about what could even keep her apart from Singled Out's hormone-charged masses with whom she needs to connect in order to assume the mantle of pop-culture phenom as deftly as her predecessor, Jenny McCarthy. It is the specter of sexual objectification that I fear has haunted Carmen since she became self-aware. You see, Jenny McCarthy chutzpah-ed her way into Playmate of the Year and nude, internet icon, and she seemed as relieved as we were when Singled Out returned her to her natural place as the somewhat dorky, tomboy, babe-next-door.

Carmen, on the other hand, appears to come by her sex appeal more honestly. She exudes a more sophisticated sensuality that would probably work better on the big screen than on MTV's giddy dating-game show, where it's understood nobody's going past second base.

As opposed to Jenny McCarthy, you have this more sophisticated and real sensuality and sexuality, to me anyway…

Well, thank you.

I wonder if that will change the dynamic of *Singled Out* at all.
Hmmm.

You, you're dark and actually sexy. She's kind of this cartoon character. You know?

Well, that's probably why MTV picked me, because we really are different. I know they were looking for someone who is really different than Jenny because there's only Jenny McCarthy. It would be ridiculous to bring someone in to be her.

What are you going to do? You're not going to bop guys around and kick 'em and punch 'em and stuff?

Well, sometimes I do because there's, like, a hundred contestants and I'm in control of all of them and the show is a really fast show. I don't have time to say, "Here, honey. Come over here."

Are you going to use sex as a weapon the way Jenny used her hands and fists?

I have thought about that. What's going to be my weapon…?

The plates are cleared. We are both stuffed and drowsy. The heat lamp is threatening to singe our eyelashes. Carmen ordered well. The taste of fettuccini with shrimp is still on the tip of my tongue, but, reader, I can't for my life recall how it looked on the plate. At this point, I was deep inside the crystalline eyes of Carmen Electra.

In no hurry to leave the place, I ordered coffee and nothing else mattered. None of the other stuff that keeps us apart. I wanted to wade into that deep pool, splash in its warm waters, and then plumb its depths, because, reader, it was at this point that we finally saw Carmen stripped clean of the industry manipulation, naked before us, and it was still her eyes that captured our imagination. Ten more minutes in the lotus land of Carmen's eyes and we would have been spinning back to Ohio, to her senior year, and we would have asked her to the senior prom and she would have said "yes" and it would have been the first great date of her life. I know it. And I think she might, too.

So, um, you want me to come back and watch some movies with you?

I thought you said you didn't like me.

I'll do anything for you. I'll admit it. I'm in love.

Yeah, yeah. Like I believe that.

I thought you said you didn't like me.

I said it because you said it.

You said it first.

Nuh-uh, you did.

Oh, really? I didn't say I didn't like you.

You said you wouldn't date me and I said I wouldn't date you either.

I was kidding. You meant it.

I was kidding, too. [Laughing.] How do you know I meant it?

Every interview is a date and every date is an interview. It's all cat-and-mouse disguised as seduction and charm. At this point, reader, you are probably wondering…why? Why the morning-after regrets? Why the call back ASAP from the worried publicist? Just when things started to look promising, you want to know… where did we blow it?

Well, to be quite honest, we spoke of things not revealed here, things that in the morning light perhaps revealed as too raw, too intimate, or too prurient to attach to Carmen the commodity.

The nervous follow-up call concerned these things, said freely, but, alas, poor reader, Carmen isn't completely free. She's pinned to the slide and her image is under the microscope. She has more to lose by closing the distance between us than we do. So, if things were said the night before that could bring about repercussions from the handlers, who could blame her, or them, for burning a little rubber and putting the miles back between us when the day broke.

And you know what, reader? I say, let's give the girl some space. Carmen has worked hard and she deserves the chance at whatever pot of gold lies at the end of this rainbow. If she loves us, she will come back. If not, she never did. But, maybe we shouldn't count ourselves out...

Would you ever go on another date with us...er...me, I mean?

I would. [Laughing.] I had a good time. At least you didn't ask me the same boring questions...

So, dear reader, do as I have done: however hard it may be, start to see other people—but keep your eye on your call waiting. Next time the phone rings, it just might be Carmen calling.

Lou Reed Laughs Last

Originally published in Ray Gun, *1998*

Author's note: A straight-up interview is a suspicious pick for a collection of profiles, but I thought I'd include this one because, well, it's Lou Reed. It's also a vestige of the predigital phase of my "career" when I'd had the good fortune to interview many interesting people such as Ray Charles, George Clinton, Jack Kemp, and others, but not the good sense or energy to hold onto hardcopies of those pieces over the many years and many moves.

Reed had been a hero of mine since I was a young man. I'd long imagined meeting him and that we might even be friends (can you tell?). Some of my colleagues at RayGun, though, tried to warn me off with their funny and frightening tales of having suffered his wrath for one faux pas or another.

Reed was eating a ham and cheese sandwich in a London hotel room when I reached him by phone. I can't remember what I said to break the ice, but he started laughing and then choking. He managed to spit out "call me back" before hanging up, possibly to get a Heimlich. I figured I'd blown it, but Reed answered when I called back. From a continent and an ocean away, at least, he seemed like just the kind of person you'd want for a friend.

ATTEMPTING TO SUMMON UP Lou Reed's place in the pop pantheon is a fool's errand. It leaves one straining for overheated metaphors. How about we just say that ever since

The Velvet Underground and *Nico* deconstructed rock 'n' roll in 1967 with droning feedback, viola squeals, down tunings, odd meters, and songs about scoring, fixing, bondage, nihilism, and mortality (while the rest of rock was, at it's most adventurous, dallying in a blues-structured, hippie daydream), Lou has been the Lewis and Clark of our rock 'n' roll explorations. While piloting the Velvets, and, during a prolific solo career that spawned landmarks such as the glam prototype, *Transformer*, the unforgiving rock novel, *Berlin*, the tortured confessional, *The Blue Mask*, and the righteous social commentary of *Street Hassle* and *New York*, Lou plotted a map followed by two generations of rockers and rappers who, when they come home to roost, park it in Reed's driveway.

Simply put, he made modern rock a viable medium for addressing the uncomfortable, the difficult, the honest, the frayed nerves and despairing souls—real-life stuff the form had mostly swept under the rug or spoke of in code before Reed and the Velvet Underground put a soundtrack to the complexities of adult life. He's been our mirror, and he didn't just hold it up lyrically, he also found a way to capture the sound of how we felt at our most vulnerable. If Warhol made fine art pop, then, perhaps, Lou Reed made pop music fine, taking it places where the pen and the paintbrush dared to go.

"Lou Reed brought rock 'n' roll into the Avant-garde," said David Bowie. "He supplied us with the streets and the landscape and we peopled it."

And, of course, he damn near did it in a commercial vacuum. Though he's been anointed with Dylanesque critical acclaim, and while hundreds of better-selling bands regard Reed as a Rosetta Stone for "alternative" music, commercial success, aside from modest hits such as *Transformer* and *New York*, has largely eluded him. Not that it matters, Reed was always going for more than the big bucks, and this summer we get to see one of his masterworks, *Berlin*, being rereleased with royal treatment while PBS's American Masters debuts *Lou Reed: Rock And Roll Heart*. Dire warnings to the contrary, when we tracked Lou down at a London hotel, he was relaxed and ready to laugh.

◆◆◆

So, you know, we're doing this interview for the *Ray Gun* "Pop 50" issue—our assessment of the fifty most influential people in pop culture at this time—and Andy Warhol is on the cover. I wonder if it surprises you that the influence of you and Andy and the Velvets continues to be so profoundly felt today, and may actually be reaching some sort of critical mass [A massive Warhol retrospective would come to LA, his spiritual home, just a few years later].

Lou Reed: Umm…astonished is how I feel about it.

Have you thought about why that may be so?

Well, I always thought that Andy was great, *fantastic!*, as he would say, and I've always thought the Velvet Underground was really something superb, but things were ignored for so long that, speaking for myself, I'm just happy to be able to be out there playing, and I many not have an accurate reading of the way things are. Put it that way.

How about the rerelease of *Berlin*? Twenty-five years later it seems like people are finally ready for it. Has that been pleasing to you?

Well, I'm so in love with the *Berlin* album. I mean, I always was. I was actually just talking to a friend about it. I mean, I can't listen to it, but I never listen to my own stuff. But that's an album I'm particularly in love with. What we tried to do…I thought other people would maybe start doing albums like that. Then, concept albums became like the kiss of death. And in *Berlin*'s case, that was savaged when it came out. It came out after *Transformer* and was perceived by many as a real bomb.

Now, of course, it's perceived as one of rock's seminal albums.

Is that true? I mean, you know, you couldn't even buy *Berlin* in the States. So that's a very painful thing, you know what I mean?

I did so love *Berlin*. And certainly, if it were a book, no one would have thought twice about it. I guess it comes down to thinking what a record should be about, could be about, and, you know, there's lots of arguments, and the argument breaks down essentially to, you know, it's pop music and it should make you really feel good and you dance and you play it at a party and that's the end of it.

With things like the *Between Thought and Expression* box set and the rerelease of *Berlin* and the *American Masters* documentary, does that help you step out of the shadow of Andy Warhol and the Velvets? You've had such a vast solo career, but it seems, sometimes, that the legacy of the Velvets is overshadowing.

Uh, it does seem to be overshadowing [laughs]. It's two enormous footprints.

Do these things help put Lou Reed as an artist in his own light, rather than, say, the Velvet Underground founder, or the product of Warhol's Factory?

[Laughs.] Those have been things I've heard for years and years. Whether I can have my own spot... I don't know.

Having followed your solo career, there are these moments like *The Blue Mask* album that have had such a tremendous influence on artists and now, maybe, through the course of

these box sets and the documentary, they're starting to go beyond the artists they influence and out to an audience.

I don't know. I was walking through the Village in New York with a friend and there was this guy selling albums on the street corner and there was *The Blue Mask* for five bucks.

Hey, that's a good price fourteen years later.

Yeah. I mean, it was also, you know, out of print.

Is that one of your favorite albums?

Yeah, that's another one. You know, all of them have something I like, or they certainly did at the time. I think they've stood up over time.

I always say that if you have to box Mike Tyson or something, turn down all the lights and throw on the song "The Blue Mask" and turn it up to eleven and that would probably have him shaking in his boots before you even get in the ring.

[Deadpan.] Oh, thank, you, gee. You know, we worked on a live version of "The Blue Mask," but I think we've only done it once or twice. You know, it's like, do people even know the song? For me, there's a lot of lyrics, and that's a real turn it up to eleven and aim for the heart. [Singing.] *Tied his arms behind his back to teach him how to swim...blaaaaahhh, prrrrrrchhhhh* [Reed mimicks the song's squalling feedback and laughs]. Well, to me, that's a stupendous song. Those kinds of lyrics make me crazy.

The imagery is unbelievable. How does that happen? Do you just strip yourself naked emotionally and that's where it ends up?

I just hear it in my head and write it down. I know that doesn't sound like much of an answer. If I understood it, then maybe I could do it twenty-four hours a day. You know, you amplify a certain portion of your head. It's not necessarily the way all of you is…*all of you is*? You know what I mean? You could take an isolated spot at an isolated time, and you make a song out of that. But it doesn't mean that there aren't more parts to you than that. I don't know…this is starting to sound pretentious again… It's writing.

Right. It's the same process, whether you are writing fiction or songs.

I think so. There are different painters that are doing things that are very intense when you look at it, you know? Certain things people are doing and it really gets a reaction out of you and it's really very intense and "The Blue Mask" is very intense. You know, you do something like that and, um, it is what it is…but, there's something very exciting about doing that. Do you know what I mean? There's another level kicking in…to records, to the music, to the lyrics, to what things are about, to what they can be about.

That sort of progression is very felt today. Arguably, the whole "alternative" category started with the Velvet Underground. Do you ever feel like the Granddaddy of the Alternaverse?

Oh, no [laughing]. I remember all the way back to "Godfather of Punk." You, it's like, is that really true? What does it mean? You know, it's funny. I've been trying to write a long thing, that's, you know, it's fiction, and what's funny is that the title of it was *Critical Mass.*

And it feels like we're at the critical mass of some cycle that, for all intents and purposes, your work was the catalyst for.

Is that really true?

Well, that's the way the history books will be written, whether it's true or not. As they, say, "history belongs to the victors" and you're still standing.

[Laughing.] That's a good one, who said that?

I don't know, William Churchill, or someone of that stature… someone with gout. How did you like working with Timothy Greenfield-Sanders on the documentary?

I liked working with Timothy. I wasn't sure about the idea, you know? *American Master*. I mean, Jesus Christ. I don't know how to get it across to you, I supposed, the ambivalence about it.

Of being perceived that way, especially when you're alive?

And…actively promulgating it.

I felt like it did a good job of going through your history without getting into idle myth making.

Oh, yeah, for sure. No, we're trying to stick to the work and the facts.

Is it hard for you to accept that you deserve this type of appreciation?

It's, umm. [Reed chuckles self-consciously]

Is that the Jewish guilt talking, or do we need another tape for that?

[Laughing.] Well, you know, that one deserves another tape, a couple of hours and probably a good Cabernet to go over that. In the Jewish tradition, there's a thing called the *Kinnahhura*. Have you heard of it? It's not a prayer, but it's more along the lines of these really good things happen and you've got to watch out for the evil eye because something bad happens to even it out. Do you know what I'm talking about?

Oh, yeah.

There's a wonderful moment with the documentary. It was showing at the Museum of Modern Art. That was quite a moment. You'd really have to search around to find a negative associated with that.

Right. Well…keep looking.

[Laughing.] I think it's great. I think being able to play with the band is really great. Being able to write, to still write, is really great. I didn't want this [documentary] to be perceived as a wrap up and that's it, and that puts you in that category on the shelf over there as opposed to an ongoing thing…an ongoing person.

You're not about to hang it up.

No. I was hoping I had just hit my stride.

The Birth of the Now

Originally published as "The Ghosts of Dogtown,"
LA Weekly, *August 22, 2001*

Author's note: G. Beato's "The Lords of Dogtown," written for Spin *in 1999, had turned me on to the only-in-LA exploits of Skip Engblom, Jay Adams, Tony Alva, Craig Stecyk, and the other characters who comprised the subversive, mid-seventies, Z-Boys skateboard team. Beato's account brimmed with high-stakes teen rebelliousness and the buzz of discovery. As the former editor of a couple magazines that had loosely adhered to an action-sports ethos, I was well aware of the ever-increasing influence skate culture was having in the world, particularly in music and art. And with Stacy Peralta's Dogtown and Z-Boys documentary looming, it felt like a zeitgeist moment that I wanted in on. Laurie Ochoa, the visionary editor who guided the* LA Weekly *to its mid-Oughts pinnacle, bit on the pitch.*

I did a ton of research for this piece. The walls of my tiny office in a derelict Hollywood Boulevard motel were plastered with notes as I tried to conjure a story while being under the Z-boy spell. The result is a sometimes-overheated (and somewhat dated) account of the ragtag, skateboarding rascals who, it turns out, were among the most influential disruptors of our days.

W HEN SKIP ENGBLOM WAS a boy, he lived near a roller rink on Sunset Boulevard where roller-derby matches were still held. He claims he was making crude skateboards out of old roller skates back in 1956, when he was eight. It was a Los Angeles that is hard to imagine today. His mom worked at the Farmers Market on Fairfax, which also hosted class-AAA professional baseball. The Dodgers, straight out of Brooklyn, were playing daytime games at the Coliseum. Back then, you could ride a trolley to the Catalina terminal, and the only freeway in town, the Hollywood, was considered a blessing, not a blight.

"It was a completely golden time in Los Angeles," says Engblom. "There were still Red Cars running."

Although he spends mornings scouting waves, he looks and carries himself like a retired pro wrestler. Come to find out his dad actually was a pro who, according to Engblom, went on to become one of wrestling's original carnival barkers, using now-familiar characters and storylines to promote the sport. Their house was a way station for midget wrestlers and guys like Haystack Calhoun, the giant who wore a chain around his neck with a horseshoe dangling from it. "I didn't see anything strange about it," Engblom says. "These were just the people who would show up."

Young Skipper, as he was known, used to ride his bike down to see his mother at work. One day he kept going, all the way down Santa Monica Boulevard to where the road meets the sand. There was a little stand there renting inflatable rafts and Skipper took one out into the water, where he saw a guy get up on a surfboard and ride a wave. "I completely flipped. It was probably the defining moment of my existence. I knew it was all I ever wanted to do," says Engblom. "I needed to do that more than anything." On weekends he'd ride his bike from Hollywood to the beach at 5:00 a.m., just to see the ocean.

In 1958, the year Engblom's mom finally gave in to her son's beach imperative and moved the family to Ennis Place, behind Venice Circle, the ghost of Abbot Kinney was once again rising from the sand. After making his fortune in the tobacco business back east, New Jersey-born Kinney literally sailed the seven seas.

The asthmatic insomniac settled in Southern California in 1880 after discovering that he could both breathe and sleep here. It wasn't long before he started turning a marshy backwater south of Santa Monica into a seaside approximation of his beloved Venice, Italy.

Kinney hoped his Ocean Park Pier, a grand amusement park thrusting hundreds of feet into the surf, would be the main attraction of his resort, and for decades it was a smashing success. Following a devastating fire in 1924, it was rebuilt bigger and better with fireproof concrete and steel. But the Great Depression, World War II, and television eventually dimmed the luster of Kinney's dream. By the time the Engbloms moved to the beach, the pier was all but closing down. CBS tried to revive it with ten million dollars and visions of a nautical theme park to rival Disneyland, and for a brief stretch, the new Pacific Ocean Park, or POP, would outperform the Magic Kingdom.

It didn't last. One of the problems with POP that nobody could solve was that visitors had to negotiate its environs to gain access to its pleasures. Those environs were falling on increasingly hard times as the money along the beach gravitated north and south, and Santa Monica began an urban-renewal project that turned buildings to rubble. After a while, braving the winos and broken glass proved more than the park's clientele could stomach.

POP closed down for good on October 6, 1967. For six more years, it would crumble into the waves, a fitting symbol of the no-man's-land between Venice and Santa Monica that generations of skate rats would come to revere as Dogtown.

Strolling the well-heeled wonderland that is Santa Monica's Main Street today, it's hard to imagine how neglected the area was back then. Main Street itself was a wasteland of vacant storefronts. Enterprises that were open for business included the Vixen Theater, a gentlemen's club not known for upscale talent, and the Pink Elephant, a transvestite bar. There was Synanon, a drug rehab place up toward Pico whose patients were dubbed "the eggplant people" because they were made to shave their heads and wear dark clothes. Across the street from the venerable Star Liquor, popular in the day because it sold Thunderbird wine, was Sunrise Mission—what was called an insane asylum back then. Go down the wrong street and you were in gang territory marked by vato graffiti.

Until it was torn down in 1973, Pacific Ocean Park's monolithic failure loomed over everything. It was picked over by Hollywood vultures, who used it as the set for *They Shoot Horses, Don't They?* and *The Fugitive* and just about every cop show from *Dragnet* to *The Mod Squad*. Underneath the pier, hippies, homos, drug addicts, surfers, and hustlers sought sanctuary. Cops from either side, Santa Monica to the north and Venice to the south, were loath to claim jurisdiction.

In some ways, the neglect was benign.

"Back then we were like a depressed ghetto," says Skip Engblom. "Main Street had all these junk shops, Sunrise Mission, winos, hookers, junkies. I enjoyed it immensely because you weren't bothered much. You could roam freely, pursue your own interests, and that was a great thing."

Others felt the same way, and in the mid-sixties, the area had become a bohemian hotbed that could have shamed Greenwich Village. Setting up shop on the side streets were the Chambers Brothers, Tim Buckley, the Doors, Canned Heat, and Spirit, to name just a few of the musicians. Photographers William Wegman and John Baldessari had studios off Bay Street, behind what would become the Zephyr surf shop, future birthplace of the Z-Boys skate team.

The lowbrow art of the booming modified-car scene competed with the lingering legacy of former resident artists David Alfaro Siqueiros and Stanton MacDonald-Wright, a founder of the synchronism movement in the early 1900s who went on to administer the WPA in the thirties. Muralists Dana Woolfe and Wayne Holwick, whose portrait of Anna on the wall of a house at Neilson and Hart still stubbornly defies urban renewal and acid rain, were igniting a public-art movement. "We were exposed to art and culture continuously," says Engblom.

Another local surfer named Craig R. Stecyk III was as attuned to these variant cultural influences as anybody. His father had been in the Army Signal Corps (he was one of the first to document the aftermath of Hiroshima), and Stecyk had access to photo equipment not readily available to most young people then. Early on, he became enthralled with legendary beach-life photographers like Peter Gowland and Joe Quigg.

Like many rooted in the urban beach culture of that area, Stecyk's father was into custom cars. For a while, he was in business with George Barris, who customized some of the most celebrated lowriders of the forties and fifties. Through his father, Stecyk met and became friends with outlaw car artists Ed "Big Daddy" Roth and Von Dutch, and later with Roth's art director and eventual founder of Zap Comix, Robert Williams.

When Stecyk wasn't surfing himself or shooting the locals braving the POP breaks, he was honing his spray paint and airbrushing skills. Having grown up between rival Chicano gangs, he quickly learned to decipher graffiti and appreciate what could be done with spray paint. He started tagging the walls around Dogtown with his own iconography, perhaps most famously his POP cross and "rat bones" figure. Later Stecyk would be recognized as a seminal graffiti artist. Back then, though, he was a prototypical tagger, an urban art guerrilla whose pranks confused outsiders and delighted peers. In one infamous antiwar stunt, he "rescued" the Independence Day beach crowd from a dummy bomb he had painted to look Soviet and then buried in the sand at low tide the night before.

Meanwhile, local boy Larry Stevenson started Makaha, one of the first dedicated skateboard companies, on Colorado Avenue and Twenty-Sixth Street, and also launched *Surf Guide* magazine. Stecyk became one of his sponsored skateboarders. Famous surfboard shaper Bob Simmons had a factory on Olympic. Vans would start a seedling shoe company in the neighborhood. Garage-shop surfboard shaping was a thriving cottage industry. You'd take your latest innovation out to the Cove, on the south side of the POP pier. If you looked good, you might have a sale. "It was kind of like stock-car racing," says Engblom. "Win on Sundays, sell on Mondays."

In those days, Stecyk's girlfriend back then lived in Stanton MacDonald Wright's studio. "You can imagine how crossed my metaphors were," says Stecyk. "I sort of had the high-culture and low-culture influences, although I didn't know what it meant. I just knew what I liked."

He had something else, too: an innate sense of the churn of history and culture. "A tremendous sense of propriety, or maybe even stewardship, came with having grown up with all this," he says.

Skip Engblom was eighteen when he met sixteen-year-old Craig Stecyk at the 1966 Pismo Beach Clam Festival.

"He came crawling out of this Volkswagen van that eight other people had crawled out of before him. They had all slept overnight there," recalls Engblom. "We started talking and walked up the street to get breakfast. I thought I'd lead him in there and do a dine and dash. Next thing you know, he and I are both on the street. We both dined and dashed simultaneously. We looked at each other and laughed and we became friends."

Around the same time, a Culver City kid named Jeff Ho was apprenticing at Roberts Surfboards in Playa del Rey under the tutelage of Bob Milner. Milner was a bit of a local legend himself.

"He was a crazy motherfucker. He used to ride his motorcycle up the hill outside the shop. In those days, dirt-bike riding was hill climbing. He had a crazy-ass view on life," says Ho. "He taught me how to build boards, to shape, glass, sand, repair, resin. The whole enchilada."

Pretty soon, the shortboard revolution was under way, and Ho was on the front lines, as both a shaper and a surfer. The surfing establishment, though, was late in catching on. Ho would take his boards—prototypes of today's bullet boards—to sanctioned contests and meet with either puzzlement or prejudice.

"These guys couldn't comprehend it, whacking the lips and doing S-turns," says Ho, talking from Hawaii, where he lives on the North Shore of Oahu. Once, in frustration, he entered the Santa Monica Open and almost won riding a shortboard plank fresh out of the mold. "I'm laughing the whole time. I shaped the board with a claw hammer on the beach. That's when I decided contests were a joke."

Ho found a more receptive audience at the pier, where his high-performance boards proved useful for dodging the pilings and other Pacific Ocean Park wreckage. He earned a reputation as an iconoclast both in and out of the water. "I was into doing my own things and making my own boards and selling them to people on the beach and to some shops. I was a kid. I was like eighteen years old," says Ho. "To me, making a couple hundred bucks was a big thing."

While Ho had heard of Stecyk and Engblom, they had yet to meet, at least in person. They did, however, share the pages of *Surfer* magazine in 1968. Ho was captured in the center spread slashing a Hawaiian fatty, while Stecyk and Engblom published photos and a story about local surfers such as Mickey Dora and Johnny Fain titled, in typically cryptic Stecyk fashion, "The Crackerjack Conspiracy."

In some ways, that story was a swan song for the postwar generation's optimism and good cheer, the last innocent days of the sixties, the days before Robert Kennedy was shot in front of Los Angeles and the Doors replaced the Beach Boys as the soundtrack to the California Dream.

"Nero fiddled while Rome burned. We surfed while America went down the tubes," says Engblom. "Robert Kennedy, before he got assassinated that day, I walked out of my apartment on Venice Boulevard, and he waved at me and my mom, and he was dead a couple hours later… Any sense that good things were going to follow pretty much died at that moment."

The draft hung over Engblom, Stecyk, and Ho like an onshore fog.

"All three of us were in the same boat because of the Vietnam War. I was 1-A from fucking day one. Any day, I'm thinking, I'm fucking gone," recalls Ho. "That whole thing you saw in *Big Wednesday*, I went through that. I was part of that. I had friends that went to Canada."

"I grew up in Venice around black people, Mexicans, and Asians," says Engblom. "The idea that I was going to go over and shoot Asians was totally repugnant to me. I didn't see these guys storming the beaches of Santa Monica."

Stecyk tried for student deferments. Ho fudged his physicals. Engblom hopped a ship in the merchant marines, staying out at sea as much as possible between 1968 and 1970. "I spent the war riding luxury liners," he says. When his ship finally docked, he came back to the beach with some money, but was "essentially unemployable."

The artist and the impresario finally met the shaper on a weird winter day in 1970. It had been raining constantly for about a week, and the whole area was practically underwater.

Eventually the storm gave way to a blustery, ornery sunshine. Stecyk and Engblom went down to the beach to check on the surf. They parked in a flooded lot while the tail end of the storm blew through. When they could finally see out of Engblom's old Cadillac, they realized they had parked next to the 1948 Chevy truck, the classic surfer's get-around, in which Jeff Ho lived. Stecyk told Engblom he should talk to Ho about going into business for real.

"These two guys walk up to me and say, 'Hey you, you're Jeff Ho.' And I'm like, 'Yeah, what the fuck do you want?'" says Ho.

They proposed starting up a factory to manufacture surfboards. It sounded good to Ho, who was in love with a white girl from high school whose parents didn't like his Chinese-American ethnicity or his surfing lifestyle.

"Her parents hated me. They thought I was a lowlife. My motivation was to make some money to buy some land on the big island and marry this chick."

They took advantage of their contacts and Ho's clients and started pumping out boards. Ho shaped new designs. Stecyk experimented with airbrushing techniques. They had imagination and a do-it-yourself attitude. Sometimes stunning progress was made.

"[Stecyk] invented the airbrushed surfboard. That was his invention," says Engblom. "I don't care what anybody is telling you, he was making airbrushed surfboards a year or two before anybody was putting them on the market."

They worked hard and played hard. They took surf trips. Stecyk sent pictures of them and their boards to *Surfer* magazine.

"It was a fucking really good time," says Ho. "The outlook was that everything could blow up tomorrow, so everything we did, we just did. The goal was to make money to do more projects."

Soon their production spilled over into another factory. It became clear they needed their own shop to keep up. Meanwhile, the girl for whom Ho was hording money in order to, "buy her a left-point break on the big island," left him for a more family-approved paramour. "She started dating some other guy who was actually going to college or something," says Ho. "Instead of buying the land, I bought the shop."

Jeff Ho's Surfboards and Zephyr Productions would occupy the southeast corner of Bay and Main streets in Santa Monica, across the street from Sunrise Mission and next to Star Liquor. It was the heart of what they would dub Dogtown.

◆◆◆

SEVERAL YEARS BEFORE HO's shop opened, a seven-year-old, blond-haired little grom paddled up to an older dude who was ripping the POP pier and said, "Oh man, that was a really good ride. Who are you?"

"I'm Jeff Ho," the guy answered.

"You make surfboards, don't you?"

"I do."

"I wish I could have one of your boards."

"Maybe you will. Maybe you will."

In time, Jay Adams was riding one of Ho's boards as part of the Zephyr shop's junior surf team. In a prescient move, by the early seventies Ho and Engblom were sponsoring not only a men's surf team but also a junior division that would keep the next wave of top talent in the pipeline. Adams was one of the youngest members of a team that also included Tony Alva, Stacy Peralta, Nathan Pratt, Bob Biniak, Wentzle Ruml, Shogo Kubo, Jim Muir, and others.

To get on the team, the kids had to prove their mettle in the water at the Cove—where guys like Engblom and Ho and Zephyr men's team members Ronnie Jay and Wayne Saunders ruled the waves. Before you could even get in the water, though, you might be required to do time on rat patrol. Rat patrol involved bombing interlopers off the beach with stones, bottles, wet sand, or whatever else was at hand. This intense localism, which became a part of the Dogtown/Z-Boys ethos, was born in part from the need to keep kooks away from the dangerous breaks of the Cove, where local knowledge could mean the difference between catching a wave and becoming a casualty. But it wasn't just a safety concern. As surf spots go, theirs was small, gritty, and barrio-like, and what little they had—a block of shoreline and one good wave—they had to protect fiercely.

"We were aware of it because we'd go surfing in Leucadia or Santa Barbara, where everything was beautiful and the trees went down to the beach and there was no smog on the horizon and you didn't have to worry about getting your tires popped," says Stacy Peralta. "We went to the beach here, and there were certain streets you just didn't go down because of the gangs and stuff like that. It wasn't like that in San Diego or in the South Bay."

Most of the Z-Boys came from financially stressed, broken homes, but the team "gave us a sense of family and empowerment," says Engblom. "We had an us-against-them mentality. It was so much more than just the business." The team was like a secret society, whose headquarters was the Zephyr shop. It was the kind of clubhouse a teenager could only dream of, chaperoned as it was by three barely adults.

"Parents would just drop their kids off with lunches and tell them they'd pick them up at five. We're trying to run a business, and I've got this group of kids who are just hanging out continuously," says Engblom. "The thing is, with me being so young and Jeff being so young and Craig being so young, it's hard to drop-kick somebody to the curb."

Given their lifestyles at the time—workdays were no reason not to make a trip to Star Liquor for beer or to the backroom for a toke—the shop owners weren't exactly in a position to preach about what not to do. Even so, they provided things that were hard to find at home or on the streets for the kids who were hanging around. Sometimes it was something as simple as shoes—Ho says he was in a constant losing battle to keep good shoes on their feet. Other times it was something more complex.

"All of us knew we weren't going to get respect playing football. We weren't good enough. Or academically," says Peralta. But earning a Zephyr team shirt was a way they could make their mark. "So we all wanted to do that."

As Alva puts it, "Skip gave me that kind of attitude where it was like, 'Hey, you got the skills, you got the talent, you got the drive, get out there and kick ass.'"

That attitude would germinate among the kids as they pushed themselves in the surf and on the concrete, waiting for a chance to show the world what they had going on.

"I knew it was something, I just didn't know what it was," says Engblom. "I could feel it was something special. I mean, these guys used to go out and practice every day on Bicknell Hill, and these were guys that had no sense of discipline or sense of order. But they all showed up every day because they knew that we had to go do this to excel, because somehow, in the back of everybody's mind, we knew this thing down there was going to be something."

"Down there" was the 1975 Del Mar Ocean Festival, where Bahne and Cadillac wheels sponsored the Del Mar Nationals as a showcase for skateboarding's resurgence. Del Mar, a well-behaved community just north of San Diego, appeared to be all that was right about the California Dream—sunshine, safe communities, and soft rock. It was a different world from Dogtown, and the Z-Boys were intent on going down there to let everybody know it.

"We had to work these people over," says Engblom. "We had to validate our existence."

◆◆◆

SKATEBOARDING HAD GONE BACK underground after its brief fling with mainstream popularity in the early sixties. It was perceived to be too dangerous, and the equipment—with slippery clay wheels—wasn't really accommodating to the dilettantes. But it had never let up in Dogtown. Most of the surfers skated around town when the waves weren't up. Particularly the ones who would make up the core of the Z-Boys. Skateboarding, however, started booming again in the early seventies, when Cadillac introduced the first urethane wheels. Technology was finally catching up to the imaginations of Tony Alva, Jay Adams, and the others who had long been outperforming their equipment.

Several other factors—a "disharmonic convergence," in Stacy Peralta's words—would come together to set the stage for the Z-Boys' assault on the Del Mar Nationals.

One was geography. Los Angeles is full of slopes, canyons, drainage gullies, and all sorts of natural assets civic leaders have historically paved over. Santa Monica and vicinity was particularly rich in playgrounds with high banks. There was Mar Vista Middle School, Paul Revere Junior High in Pacific Palisades, Kenter Canyon, and Bellagio. At these spots the waves were always up, and the Z-Boys found them just right for fashioning a new style of skateboarding that emulated their favorite Hawaiian surfer, Larry Bertleman.

Los Angeles also has one of the greatest concentrations of backyard pools in the universe. In the mid-seventies, the worst drought in the city's history drained them in unprecedented numbers. For Alva, Adams, Muir, Biniak, and the rest, the empty pools were the jewels of their delinquent empire. Steep and smooth, the bowls provided ample opportunities for aggressive skateboarding.

The Z-Boys would congregate at these playgrounds and pools and drive one another to new levels, refining a low-center-of-gravity, surf-influenced style that featured hard slash-backs at the tops of the concrete waves. They called these turns "Berts" in honor of Bertleman. In the pools, the coping on the lips was the line in the sand they were already starting to cross. Their pool prowess made an in-joke of the 1975 *Skateboarder* relaunch issue that featured a guy on the cover carving a turn barely four feet up a pool wall.

Jimi Hendrix, Ted Nugent, Black Sabbath, and Led Zeppelin provided the soundtrack to the boys' pool parties and street sessions. The outings were charged with teenage aggression and the adrenaline of dodging the cops as they violated public ordinances or trespassed on private property and indulged in the occasional breaking and entering. They had a "fuck you" attitude, and if you messed with the Z-Boys you would likely get your head knocked.

The world outside Dogtown would have to wait until the Del Mar competition to get a taste of what the Z-Boys were cooking, but to get an understanding of how radical it was, you have to understand a bit about the accepted standards of skateboarding in the mid-seventies. By and large, it was done on flat surfaces in an upright position. Things like handstands and 360s, tick-tack turns and nose wheelies were de rigueur. It looked like synchronized swimming on wheels. It had far less drama than figure skating. It only seems so ridiculous now because of what the Z-Boys did to it.

Which was to take it from whitebread, well-to-do Del Mar and the beach strands and competition platforms where it had died numerous deaths before and bring it back to the streets. They shifted the paradigm. It went from kook to cool.

Peralta's *Dogtown and Z-Boys* documentary is a barrage of indelible moments and images that communicate this energy. One of the raddest scenes is of Jay Adams debuting for the Zephyr team at Del Mar.

Entering the competition square, he gets lower and pumps harder than anyone outside of Dogtown had ever imagined. Just when it looks like he's going off the end of the raised competition platform, he slashes a Bert at the square edge of the skateboarding world. Then, as if to emphasize the point, he bunny-hops back across the platform in front of the judges, in a gesture of contempt of their rules and limitations. Before his two minutes are up, he skates off the platform and carves a violent turn, proving again that the world isn't flat. The other teams shake their heads and complain. The judges don't know what to do. The crowd goes crazy.

"The Dogtown guys came down to that competition and just terrorized everybody," remembers Warren Bolster, who would be the editor of *Skateboarder* when it relaunched a couple of months later. "These guys were so different and unique. They made quite an impression."

Two years later the world would hear Johnny Rotten proclaim himself an anarchist, but that was arguably the birth of punk.

◆◆◆

As with skateboarding itself, interest in the Z-Boys and Dogtown never really went away. It just went underground or entered the mythology of the culture's inner circle. The current Z-Boy fever, though, can be traced back most directly to a story by Greg Beato, in the March 1999 issue of *Spin*, titled "The Lords of Dogtown." Beato, a freelance writer, had been given the assignment after an editor saw an advance of Michael Brooke's *The Concrete Wave: The History of Skateboarding*. The Dogtown sections of the book jumped out at him. Following *Spin*, Hollywood came knocking. Rights to the life stories of various Z-Boys were purchased, and the machine started its slow, usually futile grind.

At the same time, Stacy Peralta's life and career were at a crossroads. It had been years since he left Powell-Peralta, started in 1979 and at one time the most influential skateboarding company in the world. His own foray into television as a director and producer had not been terribly fulfilling. Then there was an emotionally draining divorce. At some point in the middle of all this, he happened upon some old photographs of the Z-Boys in action. The pictures had the same effect on him as they seem to have on everybody.

Peralta went for a hike, thought about the prospects of Hollywood deciding who would play Alva and Adams and the rest, and called Craig Stecyk when he came back down. Work on the documentary, funded by Vans (the same company Jeff Ho tried to coerce into giving the kids shoes thirty years ago), began in earnest.

The documentary premiered at the Sundance Film Festival in January 2001. In skateboarding parlance, it killed. Most of the gang assembled for the premiere. Skip Engblom says it was obvious from the moment he touched down that the Z-Boys, many of whom hadn't seen each other in twenty-five years, were in full effect.

"I got off a plane. I got on this shuttle. I showed up at this house, and here are Wentzle [Ruml] and [Bob] Biniak sitting at a table. We looked at each other. Stacy walked in. We started laughing. We didn't say anything for the first five minutes. We just cracked up laughing," says Engblom. "We decided to walk into town to get some coffee and something to eat, right? We're walking, and this is a huge event and people don't know who we are or anything, but we're walking down the street and people are responding to us, and what they're responding to is that collectively we have this energy level that is so amazing. It's so intense that people, for whatever reason, they don't even understand it, but they get sucked into it. They get sucked into this black hole of Z-Boydom."

It didn't take long after Del Mar for Z-Boydom to suck the rest of the world in. Then, like a black hole does when the gravity becomes too much, it started collapsing in on itself.

It wasn't just the skateboarding that created this pull, although looking at the overall cultural impact of the Dogtown movement, it's sometimes easy to forget how good these guys were. Tony "Mad Dog" Alva was becoming the archetypal all-around skater in pools, on the banked playgrounds, or going for speed. He had a style and charisma that couldn't be matched. "Bullet" Bob Biniak was considered the fastest skater in the world and the one many say had the biggest balls. He'd try anything and often be the first to do so. Shogo Kubo was known for strength and flair. Jim Muir was earning a reputation as one of the hottest pool riders around. Stacy Peralta was smooth and precise, able to beat the "down Southers" at their own game while subverting it with the Dogtown style. And then there was Jay Adams. Peralta likens Adams to Mozart on wheels.

"The movie *Amadeus*, when Amadeus comes to the court where Salieri is, and Salieri plays a piece and then Mozart sits down and says, 'I think I can do this,' and he plays the piece so much better than Salieri could have ever conceived—he starts playing it, and he adds all this stuff to it without really knowing what he's doing, it just starts coming through him—that was Jay Adams," says Peralta. "Most people have a twenty-amp plug in them. This guy had one hundred amps. All the time."

Every time the boys skated together—especially in the pools they were so fond of crashing—it seemed like there was a new breakthrough. During these sessions, they started laying down the basic language of modern skateboarding. Pushed by Peralta, Biniak finally nailed a frontside kick turn at vert. Not long after, Peralta started stringing them together from tile to tile and a frontside forever was invented. Today, kids take this stuff for granted. It's part of the lexicon. Back then, it was almost unimaginable.

Not everybody saw what the Z-Boys were doing as progress. In a now-celebrated remark, Skateboarding Association executive director Sally Anne Miller told *People* magazine that Tony Alva represented "everything that was vile in the sport." This was after

Alva had appeared as Leif Garrett's thug rival, Tony Bluetile, in the 1977 movie *Skateboard*.

The assault on polite society didn't stop with Del Mar. In a series of stories and images that appeared in *Skateboarder* and then other magazines like *Thrasher*, Craig Stecyk and his young protégé, photographer Glen E. Friedman, began building the legend of Dogtown and the Z-Boys. In stark black and white that fit the mood of their beachside dystopia, Friedman introduced teenagers to Tony Alva flipping them off as his kicktail perched impossibly on the lip of a pool. There were shots of bombed-out buildings and graffiti-splattered walls. Then there was Jay Adams grinding the coping of some fat cat's pool with such disdain it looked like class warfare. Stecyk and Friedman created a raw, unapologetic style of documentation that put the boys' skating in the context of their hardcore, uncompromising lifestyle. It became the aesthetic template for skateboarding, snowboarding, BMX, and everything cool.

The Z-Boys' style and attitude resonated across the country. Kids in Michigan spray painted their own versions of Stecyk's Dogtown graffiti on their homemade halfpipes. San Francisco artist Barry McGee, a.k.a. Twist, is said to have tagged his first wall with the Dogtown cross. In D.C., Ian MacKaye of Fugazi fame was dressing like he was from Venice. (MacKaye, Henry Rollins, Jeff Ament, and Sean Penn were eager contributors to Peralta's documentary.)

Today, hip contemporary galleries like LA's New Image and New York's Alleged are dominated by skateboarder artists such as Ed Templeton, Mark Gonzales, and Thomas Campbell. Rich Jacobs, who curated a show of his peers' work at New Image this summer, explains the impact the Dogtown aesthetic had on him and friends like MacKaye. "I remember going to the skateboard shop in Long Beach and getting *Skateboarder* and being amazed at what they were doing. Stecyk was really good at documenting what was going on with his friends," he says. "In my personal opinion, it was the spirit and the energy as much as anything, going a little beyond being a rebellious teenager. They were attacking life with a vengeance that seems rawer than just the average teenager."

"Everything else seemed so mellow and laid-back in the seventies. They weren't that way. They seemed crazy to me."

If Sally Anne Miller was trying to protect the sanctity of organized skateboarding, she was fighting a losing battle. Posters of Alva and Adams were being pinned up on teenagers' walls almost as fast as those of Farrah Fawcett-Majors. To not understand why is to not understand the heart of male adolescence. As a young boy in 1976, you may have dreamed of being with Farrah Fawcett, but you dreamed of *being* Tony Alva or Jay Adams.

The business end of skateboarding wasn't as slow on the uptake as was Ms. Miller.

"After we made the scene in Del Mar, there were skate companies coming after us and offering us things. People started turning them down at first, but then, after a while, the team started to unravel," recalls Bob Biniak over coffee at the type of shop that wouldn't have been seen within miles of Main Street back in the day. Compact and still athletic-looking, Biniak is one of a handful of original Z-Boys who never left the area. "We all came from nothing. We wanted the BMWs, and we wanted the stuff, and that was partly how we got those things, and it was kind of a sad story."

Jeff Ho did his best to keep things together, but the Zephyr shop just couldn't compete with big companies like Gordon & Smith and Logan Earth Ski. Adding to the uncertainty, there were production problems with a signature line of fiberglass-deck skateboards the shop was trying to roll out with Jay Adams's stepfather, Kent Sherwood. That partnership dissolved, and

Sherwood started his own Z-Flex label. Adams and others went with him. The shop closed down soon after the team split up.

"The sponsorship money, all the corporate crap, guys wanting to make money and shit. Intellectually, I could understand it, because everybody had to move on and do their own thing, but it ripped everything up," says Ho. "It was just over."

Big sponsors picked the team members off one by one and started trotting out the Dogtown dog-and-pony show. For Biniak there would be a halftime demonstration in front of 85,000 people at a Rams-Raiders game at the Coliseum. For Nathan Pratt it would be a jump stunt in a movie for a fee negotiated by Engblom at $300 per foot (he'd warned that Pratt never jumped less than fifteen feet). Alva and Peralta would appear in movies and TV shows. Peralta even guested on *Charlie's Angels*.

It was high times, and the Z-Boys were quick to embrace the fame, fortune, and party. Biniak's apartment was the headquarters.

"Every one of the boys would come over. I'd be in there banging chicks, and they'd be going, 'Give me a couple of Thai sticks,' and I'd say, 'Go ahead, take a few,' and they'd go in my laundry basket. I had a wicker laundry basket full of them," Biniak says with a chuckle. "I was on my own from the age of fourteen. I had no parental guidance. I was running wild. We wanted to skate, party, and chase all the richest chicks up in the Palisades and see what we could catch."

Now the boys were running wild with money and license. Rich hangers-on appeared on the scene, wanting to be down with Dogtown. They gravitated to the Hollywood nights. Sponsors sometimes indulged their ever-increasing recreational drug use with freebies.

By 1977, to the outside world, the Dogtown scene was exploding. Jim Muir and Wes Humpston, another local who used to embellish skateboards with his hand-drawn art, trademarked the Dogtown name and went into business with some guys from New York. Peralta left Gordon & Smith and hooked up with George Powell to form what would become Powell-Peralta. An investor backed Tony Alva to start up his own line of skates. Skateboarding was booming. Shot out of the double barrel of urethane wheels and an attitude adjustment courtesy of the Z-Boys' punk-rock personas, it had turned into a $400 million business. For a while, *Skateboarder* was the hottest title on the newsstand.

It was a dizzy, headfirst time, but the inevitable passing of the Zephyr team coincided with the inevitable passing of their youth. Most of the team had graduated or dropped out of high school by 1978, and it was clear that the big world outside Dogtown had different plans for each of them. Before that would happen, though, they had one last brief and brilliant moment together. It was at a place they called Dino's Dogbowl.

◆◆◆

DINO WAS A KID with terminal cancer who looked up to the Z-Boys. In the summer and fall of 1978, he fulfilled a personal "make a wish" and got his dad to drain their pool in wealthy north Santa Monica. It was open only to Z-Boys and their guests, and it became the place where they rekindled the old Dogtown spirit. "It was like back to the old times because it was just us," remembers Peralta. "There weren't any officials, and it wasn't sanctioned. It was pure again for a while."

The Dogbowl sessions are still legendary. The friendly competitive fire was back, and the boys pushed each other further and further above the coping. Then, during one of the sessions, nobody's too sure on which day, Tony Alva barreled up the wall to vert. He blasted past the coping and shot out into open air. He grabbed his board, turned his nose and reentered. Alva had landed the first aerial. The line in the sand had been crossed, and the Z-Boys had changed skateboarding forever, again.

"It just felt like the ultimate adrenaline rush. We thought hitting the lip was the limit," Alva says of that day. "I realized I had more control over gravity. There was a whole new level to get to now."

The Dogbowl sessions lasted until Marina del Rey built a skatepark that became the place to go. The Z-Boys dispersed, and though they would ride together from time to time, ruling wherever they went, it was never *on* again like it was at the Dogbowl.

By the end of 1980, skateboarding had faded from view, too, going down in a sea of insurance issues, recession, and mothers who didn't want their sons to grow up to be Z-Boys. Wentzle Ruml fled to the East Coast to escape the hard-partying lifestyle. Biniak went to college. Even Alva was out of circulation for a while as he tested the waters of higher education before deciding the mainstream world was not for him.

Punk rock, since its West Coast inception, had been the sonic soul mate of the Dogtown scene. Jim Muir's younger brother, Mike, was the lead singer for seminal hardcore band Suicidal Tendencies. In punk, Jay Adams discovered another outlet for the hundred watts of aggression he had brought to skating. Although the Z-Boys had the reputation of never taking any shit, they didn't go looking for fights. With everyone gunning for them, they didn't have to. In the punk-rock scene, however, Adams admits he found an arena for what appeared to be sanctioned violence.

"During that time, I was into LA punk rock," Adams writes from jail in Hawaii, where he's serving time on a drug bust. "Life was filled with violence. In order for me to have a good night, somebody else had to have a very bad night. Now that I'm older, I know that shit ain't right, but at the time, it was fun and games."

It stopped being fun and games after a typically chaotic Suicidal show in the Valley. On the way home a tequila-soaked Adams and his crew made their usual stop at Oki Dog in Hollywood. A gay couple, one guy white and the other black, strolled by and met with typical catcalls. Happens all the time, right? Only this time the couple decided to shout back— something along the lines of "Fuck you, punk-rock assholes."

To Adams, those were fighting words. He and a friend put the guys on the ground and bolted. Unfortunately, the rest of the crowd moved in with steel boots and didn't stop until one of the guys was dead. Initially arrested for murder, Adams ended up serving a six-month sentence for felony assault.

If you wanted to look for a sad epitaph for this story, that would be it. But the Z-Boys' legacy endured. Stacy Peralta and Tony Alva, through their skate companies, introduced the world to the likes of Christian Hosoi, Tommy Guerrero, Mark Gonzales, Steve Alba, and, eventually, Tony Hawk. One of the most famous and recognizable athletes in the world, Hawk's first years as a professional skateboarder were spent as an original member of Powell-Peralta's famed Bones Brigade.

With Powell-Peralta, Craig Stecyk and Stacy Peralta would also pioneer the use of video to document not just the most progressive skating, but the irreverent, self-aware, and barely legal exploits of the Bones Brigade in equal measure. Powell-Peralta's postmodern marketing stunts, many of them imagined by Stecyk, would influence Spike Jonze, Shepard Fairey, and everything from *Vice* to *Jackass*. Wes Humpston and Jim Muir would formalize Stecyk's initial artistic impulse and make production-level graphics on skateboards the industry standard.

In effect, the Z-Boys remade skateboarding in their own image, an image that is still haunted by Pacific Ocean Park and the ghosts of Dogtown, and now skateboarding has remade youth culture in its image. It's the three billion-dollar cornerstone of an extreme-sports franchise that rises from ESPN to Capital Cities/ABC up to Disney. Skateparks are again flourishing, this time in partnership with mega-mall developers. All of which helps explain why Stecyk and Peralta's documentary is so aptly subtitled *A Film About the Birth of the Now*. It also helps explain why New Line has a feature film in the works, once again hoping to capitalize on the Z-Boys effect out there in the prized demographic of the teenage wasteland. One wonders if all the renewed interest in the Zephyr Competition Skate Team, once the fiery soul of skateboarding, can save it from this corporate takeover. At least Peralta won't have to worry about how the story comes out. He's been hired to write the script.

Understanding Craig Stecyk

Originally published as "Father of the Now"
New Times Los Angeles, *September 12, 2002*

Author's note: This is sort of the second part of an accidental ontology I began when I was researching and reporting the Dogtown story for the LA Weekly. *While putting that story together, the enigmatic C. R. Stecyk III made quite an impression on me. The more I learned about Stecyk, the more I wanted to know and the more I knew, the more I came to understand how much he had shaped the West Coast aesthetic while remaining an underground figure. Stecyk spoke in riddles, wrote under a pseudonym, and left his art unsigned by the roadside or tacked to trees. He had hard-earned trust issues and skirted along the edges of reclusion and asceticism, keeping company with a small inner circle. I thought he was a foundational figure, a confounding and unheralded genius, and I wanted to get his story out from the shadows.*

DECADES AGO, CRAIG R. Stecyk III tagged the walls near his seedy surf spot at Pacific Ocean Park, then a crumbling pier of abandoned rides and amusement parlors straddling the Venice and Santa Monica border. Among the graffiti were the terms POP and DOGTOWN running horizontally and vertically in a cross, a rat's head in the skull's position over crossbones, with the warning, "death to invaders." At first, these markings were little more than youthful insolence, meant to stake territorial claim for his band of surfers and skateboarders, many of whom were recently glorified in the documentary *Dogtown and Z-Boys*. In the seventies and eighties, though, through enterprises like Jeff Ho's Zephyr Surf Shop, Dogtown Skates, and Powell Peralta skateboarding company, these images would become among the first widely disseminated skateboarder graphic art: the first icons of a radical, street-savvy youth culture that reflected the attitudes of Stecyk and his Dogtown peers. Meanwhile, in magazines like *Skateboarder* and *Thrasher*, Stecyk's photos and essays about the scofflaw Z-Boys skateboarding team created and spread the Dogtown myth to eager adolescents across the country.

For this, many people credit Stecyk with all but inventing, and at the very least codifying, the modern skateboard ethos. For this, also, he has been called an outlaw and a reprobate. But to those in the surf and skate communities, he's more often viewed as a groundbreaker, the original skateboard artist—even a god. Yet in person, Craig Stecyk doesn't look any of those parts. In person, he looks like a walking joke about the contrast between the physical and the metaphysical.

Metaphysically, it could be argued that he's a big-bang theory incarnate, a major player in the decisive events of the past twenty-five years that have characterized the surf and skate cultures and, as a result, set the stage for how much of the world looks and feels to a large segment of the under-thirty crowd.

Physically, Stecyk's more demure. He's rangy and bald, with a bearing that might be imposing if he didn't droop like a shirt hung on a hook instead of a hanger. The droopiness may come from the time tumors were removed from his spine or from when his knee had to be rebuilt or his shoulder reconstructed. Then there's that face, which suggests Clint Eastwood's sidekick in those movies with the orangutan.

Instead of god or outlaw artist, he looks more like your average Joe. Except, maybe, for the smile. It's a Mona Lisa one, inscrutable, slightly bemused. There's something in that smile that says he's a step ahead of you. It's the smile of a guy who can read the ocean. A guy who knows days in advance when a swell is going to break at the old Malibu Pit, where the spirit of Miklos Sandor "Da Cat" Dora III still hums in his ear like the sea breeze blowing across the Pacific Coast Highway. It's the smile of a cat that didn't get any milk, but instead drank your beer and smoked your cigarettes and left behind a quick sketch on a napkin for payment. The smile, like the man, confounds friends and strangers alike.

Robert Williams, the famed "lowbrow" artist who's known Stecyk through many of his embodiments, had a typical reaction when he first met him. "I didn't like the guy," recalls Williams. "It took me a long time to understand him because he talks in abstract parables. Then, once he's in the background of your life for long enough, you begin to understand him, and even like him."

Understanding Stecyk is the difficult part, largely because he's so elusive. He likes to stay in the background, a Wizard of Oz behind the curtain. He rarely comes forward to take credit or even cash the check for what he's done. Some say he fears acclaim, and others say he's scared of responsibility. Maybe he just likes it that way. Whatever it is, thanks to the popularity of the *Dogtown and Z-Boys* documentary, the mainstream is getting its first fleeting glimpses of Stecyk as the man who (under the alias John Smythe) first photographed and wrote about Dogtown and the Z-Boys in a hyper-intense style that is still being copied in skateboarding magazines today.

Known as the "Dogtown Chronicles," his photos, articles, and essays appeared in *Skateboarder* magazine from 1975 to 1980 and are often regarded as a print-journalism branch of the punk movement. Long a cult phenomenon and gospel within the skateboarding community, the series eventually caught the eye of *Spin* writer Greg Beato, who published a nostalgic article about the feats of Tony Alva, Stacy Peralta, Jay Adams, and company—the Z-Boys—called "The Lords of Dogtown" in 1999. Always eager for fresh fodder to feed the kids, Hollywood got interested based on the article, which led to this spring's well-regarded *Dogtown and Z-Boys* documentary (which Stecyk cowrote with director Stacy Peralta).

The Dogtown phenomenon, billed in the doc as "the birth of the now," has since become a cottage industry. Recently, Stecyk protégé and renowned punk and rap photographer Glen E. Friedman published *Dogtown—The Legend of the Z-Boys*, a photo history of the era that includes a compilation of Stecyk's Dogtown-era articles. There is also a big Hollywood feature film in the works that will put Stecyk and the Dogtown myth on parade for an even larger commercial audience. Vans shoes, an original Z-Boys sponsor, has reintroduced an entire line of Dogtown shoes, shirts, and hats. Everyone from Peralta to Tony Alva to Glen Friedman will tell you none of this would have happened if Stecyk hadn't been there at the beginning to portray the breakthrough energy and attitude of the Z-Boys in his own myth-making way.

Beyond all that, skateboarding, and its spiritual forebear, surfing, has become the language of youth—shaping stylistic approaches to television, sports programming, movies, music and music video, fashion, marketing, and, most profoundly, the current art scene. In the art world, skate and surf artists fill hip galleries like Los Angeles's New Image Art and have found their way into venerable institutions such as the Whitney, which recently featured surf and skate artists Margaret Kilgallen and Chris Johanson at its biennial.

From the Dogtown hype, to the X-Games, to MTV's *Jackass* (a direct descendant of Stecyk's early skateboarding videos for Powell Peralta) to even the Red Hot Chili Peppers name-checking Dogtown in "By The Way," the signs that we've been indelibly marked by the hand of Craig Stecyk are everywhere.

"His interests became society's interests," says Skip Engblom, a partner in the Zephyr Surf Shop that spawned the Z-Boys in the mid-seventies and the skate team's manager. "It's just that he had the ability to articulate what he was feeling through his artwork, painting, photography, and words. He was able to articulate things and create an entire universe."

Some people would jump at the sort of recognition Stecyk seems primed for, but when the spotlight shines on his corner of the stage, he recedes into the shadows. He renounces his role in the making of the Z-Boys documentary and claims to want nothing to do with the Hollywood feature. He's in no hurry to explain how this universe came to be, even though he's the likely answer. In fact, he seems pained when asked to comment on his role in the current culture.

"There's nothing worse than someone talking about himself," Stecyk bemoans. "It's absolutely the most boring fucking bunch of shit. Just talk to someone else and whatever they say about me is fine."

OK. Here's someone:

"I was twenty-one, and it was like God walked in the door," says Aaron Rose.

Rose, an artist and curator, is referring to the time back in 1992 when he put together one of the first exhibits to focus on the skateboarder art explosion at his catalytic Alleged Gallery in New York. The show, a precocious demonstration of the talents of a whole generation of visual and conceptual artists, featured artists like Ed Templeton, Barry "Twist" McGee, Chris Johanson, and Mike Mills—who grew up in a street, surf, and skate culture shaped by Craig Stecyk.

"I think that Craig and the movement he was a part of—the whole Dogtown phenomenon—had an incredible effect on this whole generation of artists that I'm a part of. I took art classes my whole life, but the first time a piece of art moved me was seeing the Dogtown cross painted on a wall in Venice," says Rose, currently curating a three-year-long billboard display that will feature some of these same skate artists. "It was like, 'Oh, art can be cool, it doesn't have to be boring or unreachable.'"

This sort of homage turns Stecyk's enigmatic smile into a grimace.

"I mean, you know, uhhhhhh," he groans, "let's talk about the triangulation of the back of fucking coupes or something."

The what? Chicken coops?

"No, power transfer and coupes versus, like, open vehicles where there's no struts across the top. Trigonometry or something...three-dimensional models."

This is typical Stecyk. He twists talk about his past into debates about Fords versus Chevys. He turns retrospect questions about his life into historical lectures about his hometown and era. Even as the curtain slowly peels back to reveal the wizard as a man, Stecyk defies easy understanding or critical categorization. He's as broke as ever, bearing a painful divorce, suffering the deaths of many who matter to him, has no permanent address, pays bills with certified checks, and stubbornly refuses to cash in on the current acclaim.

The only explanation he offers: "I didn't choose this life. It chose me."

Forget about the mainline and the fast lane; the edge of the glide is all that is of value. The true skater surveys all that is offered, takes all that is given, goes after the rest, and leaves nothing to chance. In a society on hold and a planet on self-destruct, the only safe recourse is an insane approach.

We're talking attitude: the ability to deal with a given set of predetermined circumstances and to extract what you want and discard the rest. Skaters by their very nature are urban guerillas: the future foragers of the present working out in a society dictated by principles of the past. The skater makes everyday use of the useless artifacts of the technological burden. The skating urban anarchist employs the handiwork of the government/corporate structure in a thousand ways the original architects never dreamed of; sidewalks for walking, curbs for parking, streets for driving, pipes for liquids, sewers for refuse, etcetera, have all been reworked into a new social order.

—John Smythe, a.k.a. Craig Stecyk, from the "Dogtown Chronicles," *Skateboarder* magazine, 1980.

◆◆◆

THE WORDS ARE NOW accepted as fact, but when Stecyk wrote the "Dogtown Chronicles" and manifestos like "Skate and Destroy" for *Thrasher* magazine in 1980, they offered put-upon kids the oldest new way of looking at things in the book, which was basically, "Fuck you! You suck! We're going do things our way!"

In the hands of the Z-Boys and the next-generation skaters like Mark Gonzales and Christian Hosoi whom they inspired, that attitude rapidly morphed skateboarding from a tame distraction for surfers caught on a day without waves into a subversive and rebellious lifestyle for kids everywhere. It was the official sport of punks. In retrospect, it's not surprising that Craig Stecyk would be the one to sound the rebel yell. He was in the right place at the right time and had the right tools. If he will admit to anything, it's that he's a product of his environment, having come of age in a place and time when the extraordinary was everyday. Consider that he grew up next to a bust of Will Rogers and an attendant plaque that read: "The Main Street of America ends here."

"Just another victim of Manifest Destiny" is how he puts it.

He's not kidding about that. Both sides of his family have colorful histories that Stecyk doles out in small, cryptic parcels. Grandparents with whispered IRA links, frontier homesteading, scandalous interracial miscegenation with Native Americans on the western plains, a grandmother who went to the grave thinking the government would eventually give back the land she lent to Teddy Roosevelt for Yellowstone Park—these oral histories spun his own family's mythology. It's no wonder Stecyk would eventually turn his ear and narrative sense to the landscape of surfer heroes, skateboarding rebels, and outlaw artists outside his door.

The Ocean Park neighborhood in south Santa Monica was a lucky place to be born, and 1950 was a good year to be born there. While the East Coast was retiring into a post WWII stratification, a good 300 years of practice under its belt, Southern California was still an unruly adolescent. There was money to be made in defense, aerospace, Hollywood, and a thousand offshoots of those industries. On the Santa Monica/Venice border, life was boho and beat in the purest sense: you didn't have to sweat the rent, and cops and city ordinances were few and far between.

Stecyk didn't have to look far to find transgressive lifestyles. His father was a photo documentarian in the Army Signal Corps during the war. "He was one of the first guys to photograph Hiroshima; the ground was still warm," says Stecyk. Both his parents were artists, too, setting up a ceramic shop in their courtyard. They encouraged young Craig to experiment with the materials at hand, be they cameras or clay.

For work, his father painted cars at an auto assembly plant and became both a friend and business associate of legendary car chopper George Barris. Stecyk talks about when his dad drove one of the very first 1955 Thunderbirds from the assembly line.

"His first impulse was to drive the thing over to George's, which was a couple blocks [from the plant] in Lynwood, and they customized it before day one," says Stecyk. "The attitude was, 'You can't drive this stock thing.' It had a continental kit, different trim, fender extensions."

Before long, Craig was a regular in Barris's shop, apprenticing under the likes of Kenny "Von Dutch" Howard and Ed "Big

Daddy" Roth, both of whom fathered the custom car culture craze in the fifties and sixties by reviving the pin-striping tradition long after manufacturers had ceased putting such fanciful touches on stock cars. The work of Von Dutch and Big Daddy in turn bled into the lowbrow art phenomenon of R. Crumb, Robert Williams, and *Zap Comix*, a style of art that has recently been brought back to prominence in part by *Juxtapoz* magazine.

"I had access to all of them. I remember the paint, the technique, the materials. I had all that stuff around me. I was aware of it all. I mean later, obviously, I used a lot of it," says Stecyk, who still spends much of his time prowling the desert junkyards of Riverside and San Bernardino counties for parts to use in art projects. "Somewhere in there, there might be the whole idea of maybe deconstruction, or assemblage or something. The whole concept that you could take different elements and put them however you wanted to do and then change it around any time you wanted to. That was just how the people I knew did things."

Stecyk is quick to point out that this accumulation of influences wasn't in the least bit self-conscious. Given his environment, it was merely inevitable.

"It was what you thought America was supposed to be," he says. "Isadora Duncan danced nude down the streets of Santa Monica. C'mon, there was a lot of stuff going on. Robert Benchley [the humorist and one of Dorothy Parker's circle; the guy who, most importantly, said, 'There are two kinds of people in the world, those who believe there are two kinds of people in the world and those who don't'] was drinking at the pier with Stan Laurel. Mae West was down the street. There were honky-tonks, full-on carnival red light districts. It was a fun neighborhood. Then you'd have these women in bat costumes."

The women in bat costumes were the nuns who taught him at grade school. They were suspicious of Craig from the start because he came from a mixed Catholic/ Protestant household.

Their fears were confirmed when, in art class, the young boy painted a purple barn with a black sky. "All the bells went off. It was a Catholic school," says Stecyk. "There were tests and stuff."

Before long, he was sent for a series of psychiatric evaluations. Fortunately, the psychiatrist was a progressive thinker and thought it was fine that Craig's favorite color was black. He was recommended to a high school program for kindred eccentrics.

"At that point, I think Craig understood art had implications," says Skip Engblom, Stecyk's accomplice in more than a few guerilla art stunts, such as planting a fake bomb on Santa Monica Beach on Independence Day to protest patriotic celebrations at the height of the Vietnam War. "I think he saw that, through art, you could create impact. I think that might be one of the things that sent him on the path."

His environment also determined the type of artist he would become. It was not to be an effete, establishment sort, molded by painting fruit bowls in a Swiss finishing school, even though Stecyk did take a side trip into the formal art world, earning a master's degree in fine arts from Cal State Northridge by 1974.

Although his stint in Vietnam is clouded in mystery because of his refusal to discuss it, Walter Gabrielson, Stecyk's professor at Northridge, believes Craig was trying to find "some truth" in formal art after his disillusioning experience in Vietnam—a war that his father's decorated service in WWII may have compelled the young Stecyk to sign up for. Gabrielson, who counts Stecyk as among the handful of "original" students he met during more than two decades of teaching art, says the academic bureaucracy "failed" Stecyk. The budding artist quickly returned to the streets where he had grown up sidestepping clashes between two rival Latino gangs vying for turf in a ghetto section of beach between the jurisdictions of the Santa Monica and LA police departments.

Meanwhile, Pacific Ocean Park developer Abbot Kinney's unlucky dream of a Mediterranean-style resort at the Venice and

Santa Monica border, sat crumbling into the sea. North of there, the 10 Freeway was under construction, cutting a swath between north and south, leaving a wake of abandoned buildings and juvenile mischief. The local boys called this area of benign neglect Dogtown.

"For me, it was an endless source of material. You'd go in and rearrange furniture [in abandoned houses] so it looked better. Take out the windows so the air moved better, cut holes in the roofs to change the light. Paint up the walls. There were clubhouses, wardrobes. Pictures were still on the wall," recalls Stecyk. "I would venture about gathering up detritus from block after empty block and add it together, making these walk-in assemblages. I suppose, in that sense, it was empowerment."

It also offered a lesson about progress and its little-publicized side effect. "When they were building the freeway, it went through the heart of the neighborhood and created a barrier, and people who lived together went to different schools. [We witnessed] the continuity and the social structure torn apart, people moving, houses vacated. What emerged was a DMZ."

The theme of progress and dislocation would stick with Stecyk and pop up frequently in his more personal artwork. But, meanwhile, he and his friends threw block parties, because the cops rarely ventured into this area. The construction zone offered other possibilities, too. "I started riding skateboards on it," Stecyk recalls. "We'd ride down the off-ramps into the traffic on the 405. The first time, it was accidental. After that you'd do it on purpose. All the interesting girls would hang out there because all the interesting guys were there."

In the water around the rubble of Pacific Ocean Park, the scene was equally amplified. A testament to both inspiration and indifference, the pier, jutting as it did for hundreds of yards into the ocean, formed a dangerous but enticing surf break where the local surfers went through their rites of passage. The break became the proving ground for the Zephyr Shop surf team and famous skaters like Peralta, Alva, and Adams who became the Z-Boys. They'll tell you being a Z-Boy was great, but you had to cut it at POP first.

Taking cues from the local gangs, Stecyk began tagging his own tribe's turf with graffiti, creating icons and images that would find their way onto the Zephyr Shop surfboards and skateboards and later across the country and eventually into skate culture's lore. The Dogtown cross, the "vato" rat-bones icon, the ominous warning of death to invaders sprayed in a familiar hand on the concrete walls of their local break—all became marks of a movement that would wait years to be given its name.

◆◆◆

CRAIG STECYK WAS PROFOUNDLY influenced by his friend and mentor Mickey Dora. This could account for some of his idiosyncrasies, or what friends might call his "obstinacy." Those who know Stecyk have said you have to understand Miklos Sandor Dora III to understand Craig. As a person and as a persona, Dora loomed large along the waterfront and in Stecyk's life. Though fifteen years his junior, Stecyk had an almost spiritual connection to Dora, right down to the III at the end of their names. Dora, along with Johnny Fain and Lance Carlson, ruled Malibu Point and were known as the three kings. Dora may or may not have been the best surfer, but he was the most charismatic character. Whether he was mooning judges at the peak moment in a contest (he disdained the idea that surfing grace could be quantified with points) or whether he was hanging out with Hollywood celebrities, dark, mysterious Dora defied the conventional Beach Boys stereotype of the blond surfing bimbo. Frequently called the surfer of the century, Dora was the James Dean antihero of surfing, the type of guy whose magic everyone wanted to rub up against.

Together, Stecyk and Dora set about shooting holes in the Gidget-glossed surfing image of the early sixties that drove kids in Ohio to cruise around with surfboards strapped to their cars and that also unleashed a flood of kooks on Dora's hallowed Malibu surf breaks. By the late sixties, the friendly surfing fad all but forced Dora from the scene at the height of his powers—only to see him resurface in stunts and hoaxes put on with Stecyk. For example, after long absences from the public eye, Dora would show up in photo shoots for *Surfer* magazine that set him against a desert background in a wig and fur coat, flashing diamonds or standing in front of Camarillo mental hospital holding a surfboard adorned with swastikas. Dora's refusal to take part in the commercial surfing craze prompted graffiti and bumper stickers around Malibu that said, "Where's Mickey?" or "Free Mickey Dora."

The point is, Dora did his best to perpetuate the image of the surfer as a rebel living outside convention. Stecyk pitched in with a series of articles for *Surfer* magazine in the late sixties that resharpened the radical edge of "the sport of kings" and separated the poseurs from the real deals. The works are now viewed in the surfing culture as important exercises in contrariness and iconoclasm. They drew lines that needed to be drawn: there were kooks, and there were surfers who understood the culture of surfing and the antiestablishment statement it made. The difference had always been known at the Malibu Pit. Articles like Stecyk's satirical "The Cracker Jack Conspiracy" in 1968 would tell the rest of the world.

Perhaps Stecyk's most formidable dissent from the newly scrubbed-clean surfing image was "Malibu: Curse of the Chumash," which appeared in *Surfer* in 1976 under the nom de guerre Carlos Izan.

Done in vignettes, "Chumash" is a dense 450-year history of the development of Malibu and its surf scene using the area's long-gone original inhabitants as a metaphor. It became an instant classic and inspired many surfer artists, Chris Wilder among them, to reflect their surfing subculture back to the world in a less-sanitized manner than Gidget or Beach Blanket Bingo. Most notable of these artists, perhaps, was legendary psychedelic-era poster artist Rick Griffin, best known for his work with the Grateful Dead and Jimi Hendrix. Griffin based a painting on "Chumash" that has become a staple of surf-culture exhibits.

"By the mid-seventies, surfing had gotten kind of groovy, and there was much less subversive stuff. That's what made 'Curse of the Chumash' so significant...because in that Jackson Browne world, we got a dose of Lou Reed. It was a really self-critical, subversive look at what had become, at least to the world, a cliché—and that is Malibu," says Sam George, editor in chief of *Surfer*. "[Craig's] point of view didn't jibe with the direction of 'surfer as product spokesperson' that the sport was going."

Though Stecyk continues to write for *Surfer's Journal*, these early contributions helped establish much of the cultural history with which today's surfers paddle out into the water, just as his "Dogtown Chronicles" and his later contributions to *Thrasher* were among the earliest articulations of a new, aggressive lifestyle oriented around skateboarding. It was all uniquely Los Angeles.

"He helped define the way people here lived and our identity. How [people saw] themselves regardless of whether they skateboarded or not," Aaron Rose says. "Stecyk helped shape a modern understanding of the California dream. It's grittier than the Beach Boys, but it still has that idea of self-determination and freedom and all the things we Americans believe in."

Influential as these early writings were, it was Stecyk's work with the Powell Peralta skateboarding company that truly turned skateboarding into a populist counterculture movement. If the Z-Boys heralded a radical change in skateboarding's action and attitude, Powell Peralta ensured that the change would become a popular phenomenon. For better or for worse, it was during the Bones Brigade era at Powell Peralta that the revolution was sold. Photographer Glen E. Friedman, whose *Fuck You Heroes* tomes are the textbooks of this movement's genesis, calls the Powell Peralta era "Stecyk's great rock 'n' roll swindle."

By 1980, original Z-Boy and world-champion skater Stacy Peralta had teamed with enigmatic Santa Barbara businessman George Powell to create what became the biggest commercial skateboarding company in history. Peralta wisely brought Stecyk onboard as the creative director. Together, Peralta and Stecyk drew a blueprint for reaching the prized demographic that is still being imitated today. The trick, they realized, was that you didn't try to sell a line of bullshit that young people were far too cynical to buy. In fact, you made fun of the traditional marketing approaches that did just that.

Many firsts stemmed from the philosophy. For instance, when Powell Peralta assembled its skate team in 1981, standard procedure had been to print a T-shirt with the team's name on it—like Zephyr Skateboarding Team—and then send the boys off to competition. Hopefully, they'd win and attract allegiance. To that end, Powell Peralta corralled a veritable hall of fame of skaters: Tommy Guerrero, Steve Caballero, Lance Mountain, and a gangly kid named Tony Hawk, among others. From the outset, however, Peralta and Stecyk were determined to be as innovative at presenting the team as its skaters were on their boards. It began with the name.

"I wanted to call it a different thing," recalls Peralta over breakfast on Main Street in Santa Monica, today a tidy and safe version of their old stamping grounds. "Stecyk said, 'Bones Brigade,' and I said, that's perfect." Peralta explains that the idea was to storm contests and the world without calling their team a team because it was more than that.

"It was a lifestyle, that's what it was all about," says Peralta.

Some of the industry standards Powell Peralta established seem obvious only in hindsight. One was adorning the full skateboard deck with edgy graphics, many of which were evolutions of Stecyk's early street art, such as the signature Rat Bones icon.

"Everyone said you couldn't do that because there's a kicktail and you can't bend the silkscreen. We said, 'We think you can,'" Peralta says. "It completely started that graphic trend. Now, [full-length graphics are] standard issue."

Then, there were the T-shirts, adorned with B-17 bombers with "Bones Brigade" printed in military lettering, bombs lining the sleeve. "That shirt was such a hit and so disturbing to so many people," recalls Peralta. "Right now it sounds tame. But back then, whenever you put something on a shirt, it was a 'literal read.' [Our imagery] had no reference to skateboarding whatsoever."

At action-sports trade shows, the Powell Peralta booth was a mini-forerunner of Lollapalooza (an event at which Stecyk would later be a guest artist). One year Powell Peralta's booth was a detailed reproduction of a 1950s gas station. The next year it had a full bar with operational slot machines, later it was a vintage pinball arcade, later a tattoo parlor.

Greg Escalante is a partner in Juxtapoz, Culver City's Copro/ Nason Gallery, and a sometimes consultant to Laguna Arts Gallery, venues that are striving to put grassroots subcultures like skating and surfing into a larger cultural context. Over time, he has befriended Stecyk. First, though, as an art major at Cal State Long Beach, he studied him.

"Stecyk went beyond the museums and got it out there with the surfers and the skaters, against their will at first," he says, speaking of the trade shows. "But it was different. It was a stunning, bold thing to me. He took what he had in museums and brought it to the trade shows."

Like many who got sucked into this world, Escalante's biggest charge came from the visceral thrills of the Bones Brigade videos that Stecyk directed and which bore titles such as *The Bones Brigade* and *In Search of Animal Chin.* The best was *Future Primitive.*

"It was a skateboarding movie. At that time, the worst movie I'd ever seen was some skateboard movie by a guy named Hal Jepson, a surf video guy who was making a skating video. It was playing at the Surf Theater in Huntington," recalls Escalante. "So this video is called *Future Primitive.* I know it's going to be bad, but I just want to know how bad it's going to be. I watch it and right from the beginning, it's good. It's so good it blows my mind. It had high production values, good music, good story, and good visuals. It was super-intelligent. I thought, whoever made this movie made an art movie disguised as a skate movie. I ended up watching the video over thirty-five times."

It's easy to dismiss a piece of trivia like a skateboarding video, but, for many, Bones Brigade videos were like punk rock. They were subversive, irreverent, and full of manic energy, like the skate movement itself. With the Bones Brigade and Powell Peralta in general, the evolution that began with the Z-Boys and that took skateboarding from a distraction to a lifestyle to an influential, multimedia creative field became complete. The career arc of former skate punk Spike Jonze demonstrates how it resonates today.

Picking up where Powell Peralta left off, Jonze did his first filming for the Blind skateboarding company, including *Video Days* with skateboarding hero and future artist Mark Gonzales. His videos took the high jinks of the Bones Brigade videos to even more deviant levels, including driving a Buick off a cliff in one scene. Like Stecyk and Peralta, Jonze went on to establish his own skate company, Girl, in which he's still active, before becoming a music-video director. He's famous for Beastie Boys videos, including "Sabotage," "Root Down," and "Sure Shot," which incorporate skateboarding in the footage. These days, of course, Jonze is best known as the coproducer of *Jackass*, the MTV series about the crazy stuff skateboarders do, and as the director of *Being John Malkovich*.

Other artists, like Mike Mills, followed similar paths. Mills went from semi-professional skateboarder to skateboard graphic artist (X-Girl) to director of music videos featuring skateboarding (Air's "All I Need") to television commercials (Gap, Miller Genuine Draft, and, along with Jonze, Levis) that frequently retain the grainy, jump-cut, high-speed, street-level feel of the Bones Brigade movies.

For Larry Reid, a Seattle-based punk impresario and the city's Center for Contemporary Art curator, the Bones Brigade videos were the shots heard 'round the world in a budding counterculture that has only recently become mainstream,

"What Craig was doing was almost transcendent. [He spoke] to America's youth in a language he was inventing in a way, but everyone understood. [It was] just this collective unconscious response to the words, images, and attitude in those videos. These people were telling a story, and that story was defining a movement. We're all used to it now from MTV, but this was before," says Reid, who claims Stecyk's work inspired him to open the Craven Image Gallery in Seattle—an influential underground nightclub, punk rock clubhouse, and art gallery. "Craig wasn't just the poet laureate, he was the artistic savant. He was the apostle of the birth of this youth-culture movement that pretty much permeates our [American] culture. It's even finally infiltrating fine art."

Given the importance of emblems in the skateboarding and surfing worlds, it's perhaps not surprising that skateboarding has launched an art movement of major significance. Artist Shepard Fairey, known for pasting his Obey Giant stickers in public places, a stunt that later evolved into billboards and a cult phenomenon, found inspiration as a kid in *Skateboarder* magazine's early "Dogtown Chronicles," in *Thrasher*'s "Skate and Destroy," and in Stecyk's work with Powell Peralta.

"Whether it was accurate to [Stecyk's] intention or not, the vato rat was the skateboarding version of Kilroy was here. The endurance of this skateboarding iconography is pretty amazing, too, in that it beckons you to look back into the history of it because the context doesn't give away what it's about, necessarily, which is what I love about street art," says Fairey. "I think it goes back to a very primitive urge to not necessarily mark your turf in an aggressive way, but in a way to signify what you're about and also to reach out to other people who are similar. That's what I always loved about skateboarders; they always seem to leave evidence of their existence behind in ways that are sometimes destructive, sometimes creative, and sometimes a combination of the two."

The pop-culture magazine *Tokion* recently dedicated an issue to tracing the growth of this art movement, dubbing it "The Disobedients." Although it profiles a diverse lot, there is a clear unifying theme.

"Looking at the issue, they are all skateboarders, except about three out of a group of about thirty, and *Tokion* is not a skateboarding magazine," says Fairey, who's among a mix of artists including Ed Templeton, Margaret Kilgallen, Thomas Campbell, Barry "Twist" McGee, Geoff McFetridge, Mike Mills, Mark Gonzales, and Jonze who're making waves in the art world.

"It's not an intentional thing," says Fairey, "it's just who the people are who're affecting popular culture, [who're] starting to be embraced by the fine art world—but who, before they were being embraced, were doing skateboard graphics, album covers, clothing lines, whatever. The stuff every seventeen-year-old lives by. This thing is a document of our time."

Tokion's "Disobedients" issue comes with a pullout poster charting the history and family tree of "The Disobedients" with an East-to-West map. Craig Stecyk's name is at the top of the map, on the West side, right above Dogtown.

"The thing that's ironic and the thing that sometimes annoys me with the culture is that it's taken thirty years for people to appreciate Craig," Rose says. "Stecyk should get a ten percent cut on every ad that's made in America these days, anything by Mike Mills, Spike Jonze, or Levis or Adidas. They all go back to him."

◆◆◆

FOR A GUY WHO in his younger days spent a lot of time sneaking into empty pools with scofflaw skateboarders, Stecyk has little tolerance for nonsense. Almost everyone familiar with him describes him as intellectually intimidating. In person, though, there's a melancholy about him. Some friends trace this mood to his recent parting with his longtime partner and wife, artist Lynn Coleman. It's been an unpleasant separation, and, as a result, a good deal of Stecyk's work is tied up in legal proceedings. The break happened a few years ago, after Stecyk had traveled to the Maldives. At sea, he had a bad reaction to medicine for an ear infection. It made him delirious. He passed out and banged his head on the deck.

"I was laying in the sun on the equator for hours, and that's not a good idea," says Stecyk, who suffered severe dehydration. Though he was in rough shape when he got back, he immediately went to San Francisco to work on a show—Surf Trip—with Barry McGee. He was exhausted, manic, and obsessive. Working didn't help.

"I'm not known for my user-friendliness when I'm focused on doing a show anyway," Stecyk admits.

Though Stecyk's difficult demeanor had long been a joke among friends, this time they were worried about his sanity. Something happened after the Maldives, and a breakup of his marriage followed. It's obvious that the split has taken a toll on him. A friend said he's never seen anyone as sad as Stecyk not kill himself. The friend says it was the death of faith for Craig.

Stecyk resists the conclusion, as he does most attempts to characterize him. "I hear all kinds of rumors about what I'm supposedly about. Let's see... I never made it back from 'Nam. I made a killing off a movie, and I live on Malibu Point. I play horses for profit. I am currently committed to a mental hospital. How would anyone know what's true? One man's mania is another man's modus operandi."

Could be. Stecyk's sadness, though, is the kind that evokes empathy, for sure, but can also evoke humor and art. It may have been there for a long time before the Maldives, or the divorce. It could also be fallout from people close to him—Don James, Ed Roth, Mickey Dora, and Margaret Kilgallen, among others—dying lately.

The sadness comes through when he's asked about his life and career, which he claims not to think about at all. Then he's asked what he does think about, and he says, "Well, today I'm thinking that eighteen people who I've been connected with have died in the last year, and this morning they called me and told me that a friend of mine has gone into pneumonia and he's unconscious and it's a matter of seconds, a matter of hours, a matter of days. I mean that's nineteen that I know about."

"I try to see good in it," he says. "There's something good in it somewhere. That's what I try to find."

The reason Stecyk has trouble talking about himself and his legacy could be that such conversation seems arrogant in the face of all this encroaching mortality. "I don't know if you have any control over what you do," he says. "It's pretty egocentric to assume that...you are responsible for anything. There are a lot of circumstances, varying forces that are brought to bear for anything to come to pass."

Stecyk drives an old Chevy El Camino that was given to him by a friend. He claims to have practically no money. When he's in town, he crashes at either his family's house in Ocean Park or his girlfriend's pad in Venice. Otherwise, he goes wherever his artistic pursuits take him, living out of motels in the desert where he scours junkyards for inspiration, staying down at Laguna Beach where he curates the current Surf Culture exhibit at Laguna Art Museum (more on that below). When asked how he makes a living, he jokes, "Not very well." He steadfastly clings to a gypsy life, and opportunities to cash in on his commodity, like the current fascination with all things Dogtown, do not appeal to him. In fact, Stecyk has distanced himself from most of the hoopla surrounding Dogtown and Z-Boys. So much so that he claims not to have seen the documentary since its award-winning debut at the 2001 Sundance Film Festival. He's also said no thanks to participating in the forthcoming Hollywood feature, for which Stacy Peralta is writing the screenplay. Stecyk's involvement has been limited to signing away his life's rights. He says doing so bars him from discussing his past in detail, particularly the Dogtown era, something he's glad not to do.

"In that sense it was the best deal I ever made," he says. "So all of it never happened. It was a life I never led."

His disdain for Dogtown nostalgia is based on his insistence that his contributions to the skate culture were coincidental. "I was sort of an incidental documentarian. The skateboarding thing I got involved in because Tony Alva asked me," he says, perhaps apocryphally. "I had shot pictures of them all, and I was kind of doing it, but I didn't have any interest in the magazines or any of that stuff because it didn't have anything to do with my life."

It's as if Stecyk were leading two lives: one under the aliases of John Smythe and Carlos Izan, who documented and popularized the lifestyles of radical skaters and surfers, and another as Craig Stecyk, conceptual artist, a man focused on creating a thematic body of work that is as far removed from the current, highly commercialized skate culture as graffiti is from Monet.

For example, in the early seventies, long before the Z-Boys surf or skate teams, Stecyk went about the desultory streets of his neighborhood dressing them up with large aluminum poles he planted in the ground that were marked with fluorescent icons. They were called Streetrods. At the same time, he bolted cast-bronze plaques bearing his trademark Calavera mask on walls across the city. Both projects were anonymous public offerings that hinted at secret worlds beyond the radar of mainstream society. They were symbolic of the dissident nature of his crew, whose members were executing guerrilla art protests like Bomb Plant, in which he and Engblom buried that surplus bomb painted with Russian insignia on the beach. When high tide revealed it to the July 4, 1968, beach crowd, people fleeing the sand saw a man dressed in bomb-squad gear rushing to carry the shell safely away. That was Stecyk.

His interest in using public spaces to make loaded statements with art grew more pointed with *Road Rash*. For this early-eighties project, he drove across the country with a casting furnace in the back of his truck gutting every dead animal he found, casting them, and then sewing their hides back over a bronze caste. He then bolted the animals to the ground where they had been killed—symbols, in his mind, of man's rapacious drive for a better life somewhere over the next horizon, or with the next invention.

Perhaps those themes were no better illustrated than in 1989's Northwest Passage and 1990's *La Frontera*. The former was an installation Stecyk did at Ruth Bloom's much-missed gallery in Santa Monica, a thriving venue for underground artists before Hugh Hefner took it over in the early nineties for Playboy Studios West. The intention of *Northwest Passage* was to illustrate the penalty exacted on life and the environment by sheer wantonness. The story was told through a painstaking assemblage of Day-Go cast ducks, a shotgun rotating in a turret, a decaying marsh, and pictures of famous duck hunters through the years: Harry Truman, Ivan the Terrible, Hitler. Typically, it was a critical success and a commercial bust.

"I thought there was something so unique about what he was doing, and we ended up doing two or three large installation exhibitions. His work was never easy work to sell," Bloom says, laughing. "He's definitely one of those people who could use a MacArthur genius grant for his work."

La Frontera also appeared in Bloom's gallery. For it, Stecyk went to a spot on the US/Mexico border and built a shack made from effluvia such as license plates discarded in the crossings. The artist inhabited the shack on and off for eighteen months, documenting things with the trash left behind in the desert outside the doors of his art-piece/living space. Later, he assembled this experience into a montage that told the desperate stories of illegal immigrants.

"It was absolutely amazing," recalls Judy Spence, a renowned art collector and local psychiatrist. "There were four different border stories and each one broke your heart more than the one before."

An experiment is under way at the Laguna Art Museum that attempts to resolve the conflict between the lowbrow identity that cultural institutions typically assign to the beach culture—which Stecyk represents (whether he wants to or not)—and Stecyk's own conceptual art projects/ambitious journalistic endeavors. It's called *Surf Culture: The Art History of Surfing*, and it's a summation of the decade that Stecyk, museum director Bolton Colburn and others have spent discussing how beach culture has come to symbolize the California dream. With Stecyk's *Papa Moana* exhibit in 1989, *Kustom Kulture* in 1993, and now *Surf Culture*, the collaborators' point is that this beach culture-inspired California dream is now an integral part of the youth-and-freedom-loving American psyche.

"*Surf Culture* is about getting a sense of what this culture really is," says Colburn. "The idea that surfing has been...an icon that represents the idea that somehow you have pleasure in your life now. You know, you don't have to work your entire life and die and go to heaven to have pleasure—you can have pleasure in your lifestyle and at work. That's what surfing has come to represent."

"Papa moana" is a Hawaiian phrase that means "ocean board." The *Papa Moana* show used surfing to explore the impact of the mainland's cultural imperialism. For instance, the exhibit's corrugated steel facade employed the primary building material in the Pacific Rim during the 1940s and 1950s, an era that saw the rise of primarily US military and colonial intervention in the Hawaiian Islands. The Stecyk-made surfboards propped against the exhibit's facade were shaped in the tradition of the kahunas (Hawaiian kings) and were adorned with symbols conveying mana, or spirit.

The symbolism got more intense once you entered the installation. The "Aloha Ha" montage featured artifacts from the mixing of Anglo and Hawaiian culture, among them a broken-down Philco floor radio (popular during the territorial period) that served as a table for snuffed cigarette butts, beer, sunglasses, and a postcard of a bare-breasted Hawaiian girl submissively offering a lei. A Japanese ceramic cup and fan symbolized that the islands were long ago overrun by haoles (whites) and the Japanese, Filipino, Portuguese, Koreans, and Chinese they brought in to work the plantations. A neon sign on the blink flashed "Aloha" and then "ha."

Four years later, *Kustom Kulture* was one of the first major institutional attempts to put the lowbrow art of the likes of Ed "Big Daddy" Roth, Robert Williams, R. Crumb, and Raymond Pettibon into context with the custom car movement of the fifties and sixties, which had begun in the South Bay.

Kustom Kulture opened not long after the death of the movement's spiritual godfather, Kenny "Von Dutch" Howard.

Stecyk cocurated the exhibit and wrote the catalogue's historical essay. It was a major undertaking that furthered the role of cultural historian that Stecyk had been playing in surf and skate magazines for years. The show brought together a seminal group, including Greg Escalante, Robert Williams, *Thrasher's* Kevin Thatcher, and, of course, Stecyk. The group followed *Kustom Kulture's* success by starting *Juxtapoz* magazine in 1994. Today, it's the fastest-growing art magazine in the country, mostly because it's the first in a long time to trade in the language and culture of the young.

Surf Culture is on display at Laguna Arts through October 6, after which it goes on tour to Australia and other international destinations. Stecyk is again the curator and author of the companion catalogue's main essay. The exhibit contains thematic elements and artifacts in keeping with both *Papa Moana* and *Kustom Kulture* as well as contributions from a vast array of artists, such as Kevin Ancell, Chris Wilder, and even Stecyk's ex, Lynn Coleman. The exhibit is a history of surf art, featuring everything from posters for movies like *Endless Summer*, to the surfboard used by Colonel Kilgore (played by Robert Duvall) in *Apocalypse Now*, to the political art of Raymond Pettibon's giant-wave murals (coded with messages like "the next president should be a surfer"), to the "surfer-crossing" road signs that Cris Hicks got permission to post in the town of Encinitas, and, especially, Ancell's painting of battered Hawaiian "hula" girls fighting back against haoles with M-16s and grenades. The exhibit also presents an impressive lineup of surfboards, from the earliest planks to today's tricked-out short boards, that documents the long progression of surfing from a small, insider coterie of "soul" riders to the global granddaddy of "extreme" sports it is now. In the end, the show is perhaps the most comprehensive look to date at surfing's enduring power as a lifestyle and a metaphor.

"It really goes back to the kernel of what it is to be an American, the idea that you can do things without traditional impediments," Colburn says. "You're not going into a caste system. There's a possibility that you can be something great. What you're seeing ties into that, because, in the extreme, that gets manifested in subcultures like surf culture and car culture, where literally you are on the outskirts of the social norm and you're really pushing the envelope. You can say it's rebellious, and it is, but on the other hand, it's so American. I don't know if we would have arrived at this, or if this dialogue would have gone the direction it's gone without Craig's influence."

In his less-guarded moments, Stecyk forgets that he's a man who has given up claims to his past. He accedes to the undeniable evidence that he was and still is a part of something that matters. He just contends it should be understood that it isn't he who matters.

"[It's about] the theory that you were part of a related group of people and you were interacting," he says. "The nuances and relationships had value, and it wasn't about what any one person accomplished." Stecyk says the beach culture has, at its heart, an ancient sense of community. "In Polynesia that's more of an attitude because it's more clan-related, more village-related, more archipelago-related. In surfing, that's kind of the thing."

The Malloy Brothers' Conspiracy

Originally published in the LA Weekly, *December 9, 2004*

Author's note: I had no idea when I went back to school in the early nineties with ambitions of wielding the journalist's pen in the fight for justice that I'd end up writing so much about surfing. But once you start surfing, it can take over your brain, and it was certainly on my mind a lot by the time I became aware of the brothers Malloy. As at home on a cattle ranch as they are paddling into twenty-foot surf, the Malloys were at the forefront of a back-to-basics movement that harkened to the days when surfers were watermen first and wave riders second. Tall, handsome, able to start a fire with sticks and stones, not to mention tie the right knot for the right occasion, they'd be annoying if they weren't such gentlemen.

THE HILLS ARE THERE in front of us, the sun behind, and he's getting smaller and smaller, framed by the burnishing light, the water, the sand, the hills. I remember for a moment how much beauty is still left in this world. And now here's my wave, lifting me gently and sending me off in the direction of where he's glided down the line, disappearing into the reflected light.

I'll never catch him. He's a Malloy. He goes first.

It's a Friday afternoon, and I'm at the place that Chris Malloy and his brothers come back to when they're done with the adventures that send them off to the rugged shores of western

Ireland or the malarial jungles of Indonesia or the jagged reefs of Tahiti. They go to these places in search of things out of the reach of most of civilization: moments of purity, grace, and thrills—a type of simplicity bounded by nature and determined by the sea. Spend time with these guys, and you too will start to believe that civilization has its drawbacks.

The place Chris Malloy has taken me will always be the best place in the world to him. Etiquette forbids me from telling you exactly where this place is, but it's not far from where he and his younger brothers, Keith and Dan, grew up on a ranch near Ojai. It's close to where they live now. It's near his family and his sister, the one sibling who doesn't surf and never will. It's where their story began. It's where their story continues to grow and where it's likely to become part of the rich local lore, before they're done. For all their traveling, these part-Irish, part-Mexican young men are still homeboys, after all.

◆◆◆

In late September, I drove to Laguna Beach for my first in-person encounter with the Malloys. Laguna is about a hundred miles and many light-years from where they come, yet there was Chris, the oldest of the three at thirty-two years old, nervously addressing the packed amphitheater at the Laguna Beach Festival of Arts. More than three thousand tickets—up from three hundred last year—had been sold on Saturday alone for that day's installment of the weekend-long Moonshine Festival, a surf-spawned art, music, and film event named for the Malloy-led Moonshine Conspiracy—a collective of surfers and artists who share a certain retro sensibility. Jack Johnson, Will Oldham, the Shins, and others like surfer-musician Donovan Frankenreiter would perform. Among the photographers and artists showing were John Severson, Scott Soens, Barry McGee, and Alex Knost. The event's proceeds would benefit the Surfing

Heritage Foundation, dedicated to gathering, documenting, and making available to the public the artifacts and history of surfing, something to which the Malloys are precociously attuned.

I'm not sure the parade of *The O.C.*–minted, hyper-sexy girls—and the boys who dogged after them—cared so much about surfing heritage as they did about just seeing and being seen at what has become the Woodstock of surfing, a pursuit that is now officially the primary cultural signifier of the young and/ or the tragically hip (like fifty-something *Blue Crush* producer Brian Grazer), but that didn't stop Chris from trying.

"Welcome to two years of home movies," he said, by way of introducing the main attraction, the premiere of the Moonshine Conspiracy's *A Brokedown Melody*. Malloy, who directed the film, was as inconspicuous in khakis and a flannel shirt as a man on a large stage with a spotlight on him could be.

About a month later, fans would be turned away from the film's premiere at the two-thousand-seat Arlington Theater in Santa Barbara. Something, it's clear, is happening, because this film, even more than the rest of the Moonshine Conspiracy's catalog, isn't a typical surf film. The Malloys don't pimp their rides, and their films are leagues apart from typical punk-adjacent contemporary surf videos. Without losing its relevance (how could it when it features Kelly Slater, Rob Machado, Tom Curren, and CJ Hobgood?), *Melody* is thematically and aesthetically reverent to an older, more classic idea of what it means to be a surfer. It draws a direct line from pioneers like Duke Kahanamoku—the Hawaiian 1912-Olympics gold-medal swimmer who traveled the world spreading the concept of surfing—to Slater, who is the greatest surfer who ever lived, and who, like the Malloys, believes in a broader definition of surfer as waterman and steward. Those waiting throngs might not have known it going in, but when *A Brokedown Melody* is playing, surf church is in session, and the Malloy brothers are leading a revival.

I've got all three Malloy brothers in one place, which should qualify me for permanent membership at the Magic Castle considering the difficulty of herding these guys. Keith, the middle brother at thirty years old, has just returned from an excursion to Indonesia's Mentawai Islands on behalf of Surf Aid. The mission involved traveling upriver to visit an indigenous tribe that still file their teeth into fine points and fashion loincloths from tree bark. The group brought doctors and dentists with them and tried to promote malaria awareness, still the biggest killer in places like the islands. Prior to that trip, Keith had spent most of the summer training for an epic, coed paddleboard contest in Hawaii called the Molokai. He and his partner finished second. Meanwhile, Dan, who is twenty-six, spent the better part of the last month traveling the country to promote artist and fellow Moonshine conspirator Thomas Campbell's art-damaged surf film *Sprout*, in which he's a featured player. He also managed to work in a couple of weeks of surfing in France. Chris, for his part, is just coming off an editing schedule for *A Brokedown Melody* that would have given a speed freak pause.

We're at Keith's house, where Dan also lives, sitting in the bright living room that overlooks the break north of Ventura where Chris and I surfed. A tree in the front yields edible bananas. The place is half home, half warehouse for a collection of gear that can outfit the boys for every kind of water adventure from towing into big waves to paddling sixty miles up the central coast—something Dan and Keith recently accomplished.

Individually, these boys are impressive—each one seemingly taller, more rugged, and more handsome than the other (Dan was recently paid to model for Ralph Lauren). Together, they are formidable. As Scott Hulet, the editor of the great *Surfer's Journal*, told me, "If Hollywood, in its unquenchable hunt for schlock rereleases, ever spanks a *Bonanza* redo, these three would be a good place to start for the Cartwright brothers. They're all too smart to bite on that, though."

Chris Malloy peppers any discussion of surfing with references to legends, like their neighbor, big-wave pioneer Pat Curren, and others like champion swimmer, surfboard innovator, photographer, and philosopher Tom Blake. Or John Severson, the man who started *Surfer* magazine and was the original surfer-artist. These were men who knew their history, made their own boards, dove for their food, and approached their lives with a poet's heart and a beatnik's wanderlust.

"Those guys did everything. They did film, photography, writing, and Pat was just a legend. They were the kind of people I aspired to be like and to experience some of the things they did," Malloy says. "You know, when my time finally came, and I got to surf these places that I had always dreamt of, and then came home and looked at this depiction of my experience [in articles and video], it wasn't representative of anything I had experienced. I got sick to my stomach. They were product-driven and missing the experience. Surfing was becoming a commodity so fast. What was a cottage industry has become a billions-of-dollars business. It just wasn't what I dreamed of being a part of."

Earlier, at the Moonshine Conspiracy's headquarters in a renovated Victorian in downtown Ventura, where much of the staff (mostly family) lives and works, Chris drew up a schematic of the gladiator pit that is the North Shore's famed Pipeline lineup. Pipeline is the serious surfers' proving ground, and the pecking order goes from Pipe Rulers, right at the wave's peak, and descends down the shoulder to the Mob, the Brazilians, the body boarders, and, finally, the Japanese body boarders. Lately, there has been an influx of jujitsu enthusiasts among the Brazilians, and the local Hawaiians, who have long seen outsiders crowd their turf in hopes of catching some sponsor's eye, are always ready to fight. The Malloys have all scrapped their way, literally, past the Mob and into the Rulers.

When they are surfing, they approach the level of daunting—fearless and fearsome, not flashy but powerful, fast and seemingly in total command of their environment.

"There are a lot of guys out there who are fast, and a lot of guys out there who are powerful—they have to be—but we surf every day. If it's twenty-feet, we surf. If it's two-feet, we surf," says Chris Malloy. "By far, if there's anything that's significant about us, it's that we surf every board in every condition, and there isn't so much of that anymore, which is something they prided themselves on in the olden days. You use the ocean for what it is. It isn't something we tried to develop on purpose; it's just that, at age thirty-two, I still surf every day."

Adds Dan: "If they're trying to figure out whether it's big waves or small waves or cold water and they're trying to figure out who would go, they'd be, like, 'Get one of those kids. If it's big or small or rocks, they'll go do it.'"

"We love it. We'll go do it," says Keith.

Usually, they'll do it together. There is one entry for all three Malloy brothers in Matt Warshaw's indispensable *TheEncyclopedia of Surfing*. Whether they like it or not, they are indelibly linked in people's minds. They seem okay with it, the linking part, but they do want people to understand that they are three individuals as well.

"I always tease them that they're the guys you don't want to sit next to on an airplane, because they're going to talk your ears off the whole way," says Keith, who fashions himself to be the quiet one, more like his father. "We usually get along real good, but we're normal people. We'll scrap it out. Usually not in a fistfight, but you know. We never get to the end of the day without figuring it out and making amends, you know?"

You can see that in person, all three shooting the bull in Keith's living room. Despite their prowess and their *über* competence—they are the kind of guys who can do what men are supposed to do: fix things, work things, lift things—they're just too damn gentle to be intimidating. We're talking story, as they say, and the brothers are regaling me with some of the gnarlier sides of being a modern-day adventurer. Like the time a few years ago when Keith was in the Spice Islands coming into a break on his boat and the water got lit up with Uzi gunfire. It was just days after Muslims had massacred 500 Christians.

"We pulled up, and these guys started firing off rounds. They jumped on their motorized canoes and were coming out and firing shots. I was thinking, I'm fucking dead in a couple of minutes." He tells of walking around Indonesia and natives wearing Osama bin Laden T-shirts with the Twin Towers blowing up on them.

On a recent trip to get footage for *A Brokedown Melody*, Dan found himself delirious and alone at a rat-infested hospital in Jamaica, suffering from Dengue fever. "I was so tweaked and dehydrated, and I'd be asleep and awake and asleep and awake," he recalls, smiling with gallows humor. "They call it break-bone fever. Every joint in your body and your eyes and everything hurts. Never have I sweated so much in my life."

These, though, are the risks they take in search of the golden moments, like the one Chris had with surfer, musician, and Moonshine Conspiracy cofounder Jack Johnson. They were on a mission to find a never-before-surfed break in the Bay of Bengal that was just a wild rumor at that point.

"I had been talking to this guy, this crazy guy named John Callahan, who had been doing his homework on that area for years and mapping out the weather systems and timing when he thought there'd be a swell. So we said, 'If we get to Thailand on this day, we can drive through the jungle for nine hours and get to Burma, where there's a boat we can catch that goes across the river, and from that island, we've got a charter company that will take us across,'" Chris tells. "We're sitting there with maps, and it's real old-school, and for the final boat trip we got this funny English guy and his sailboat to take us out and go do it. He'd done dive charters and fishing charters before. He said, 'Yeah, I'll take you out there, sure. There's nothing there, no waves.' We said, 'Well, we think there are.'"

They found a wave, all right.

"I remember sitting out there on the bow of the boat, and the sun came up and just watching it and thinking: This is the last time this wave will ever be a virgin wave. It's surreal, taking off on a wave that's never been ridden before, and people come out of the jungle to watch you and they're cheering. I'll never forget it." That session became the inspiration for the Moonshine Conspiracy's *Thicker Than Water*, the first of the four films the independent-minded collective has put out in the past five years, *Melody* being the fourth.

◆◆◆

THESE STORIES AREN'T TOLD with any dick-swinging swagger, but rather with an appreciation that the world is a sad and beautiful place—a place where people like them surf virgin waves while the locals die of malaria. They spend more time than most of their contemporaries trying to close those gaps. It's a rare quality to find in young men, especially those who can glean the tube of a triple-overhead closeout. But once you know who they are and where they come from, it's not surprising that the Malloy brothers should possess it.

Who they are is inexorably tied to where they came from. "Let me put it like this," says Chris. "My brothers and I literally came out of the sticks. We grew up with pigs and horses and chickens and goats. It was a few acres up in Ojai at the base of Los Padres National Forest."

Back then, Ojai wasn't the New Age spa getaway for well-heeled Westsiders that it has since become. The Malloy lineage goes back five generations in these parts. Their great-great-grandfather was a muleskinner and worked the oil fields. Throughout the fiftiess and sixties, their father, Mike, was a fixture on a longboard at Topanga Beach's right-breaking point. Topanga Beach was different then, too. It wasn't a state beach, but an eclectic beachside community, home to colorful characters, dropouts, derelicts, and Miki Dora when the break was working. Mike Malloy felt comfortable there.

But change came quickly in the early seventies. Los Angeles was getting more and more crowded, the Topanga community was razed, a state beach was put in its place, and Mike Malloy, a construction worker with a little cowboy in him, moved his fledgling family up to Ojai, where they had roots and the land was cheap.

Although the father was turned off by the shortboard revolution that came with the late sixties, he encouraged his boys to surf. They'd get dropped off or hitchhike the fifteen miles over the mountain to the beaches where they still surf today.

"When he wanted us to start surfing, he gave us this equipment that was like 1965 equipment," says Chris. "I remember the first contest we ever went to. Keith made the finals, and he was on a single fin and all the other kids were on these little thrusters. I remember Keith was waiting for the semifinals and was almost crying because all the kids were making fun of his big, single-fin board."

"He didn't know what he was doing," says Dan.

I suggest that it was so old-school it was new-school.

"Yeah, but it was so long ago, it wasn't cool at all," says Keith. The brothers laugh at the memory. But Keith made the finals and finished second.

"I made all these enemies," says Keith. "They were like, 'I can't believe you beat us on that piece of shit.'"

"When we were kids, we only had one wetsuit," recalls Dan. "So, two of us would be in trunks and the other one would get the wetsuit. I remember the first suit I got was a short john, and I remember I was out there in the winter thinking how warm it was."

"The first day he got his wetsuit, he slept in it," adds Keith.

During the summer months, after their father put them through a couple weeks of working on the ranch and on construction sites, he would drop them off at the beach. "We'd have a tepee set up, and my dad would come once a day and drop food off and we'd stay there the whole summer. I was probably in eighth grade," says Chris. "People would come and take pictures. We thought they were taking picture of the waves. We'd always be like, 'It's shitty out there; why are they taking pictures?' And they'd be taking pictures of these kids staying in a tepee on the beach."

"It was really unconventional growing up," he adds.

The boys were so out of the culture of the competitive-surfing world—a cutthroat culture that would make Little League dads blush—that there'd be competitions right around the point from their tepee, and they wouldn't even know about it.

Still, they managed to do well enough with their hand-me-down gear that the surfing Malloy brothers started to get talked about around Ventura. Soon they caught the eye of local board-shaping legend and surf guru Al Merrick, whose Channel Islands Surfboards was the industry standard at the time. Merrick was among the first to recognize the talents of such revolutionary modern surfers as local boy Tom Curren and, later, Kelly Slater. Merrick anointed the Malloys all at once, together.

"Al Merrick was the first person who ever had faith in us as far as sponsoring us, and at that time he had the best surfing team in the world," Chris says. "We were these kids from Ojai, and he saw that same hunger to surf in all of us."

For the Malloy brothers, family became a brand, not a word. "It made sense, and it was easier going that way than not. It was rare that anybody would say, 'We want Keith or we want Dan or we want Chris,'" says Keith. "It was always like, 'Hey, we want to talk to you guys about working together.'"

"I think the sponsors knew how tight we were," Chris adds. "It would seem inorganic to do it any other way."

The Malloys' careers skyrocketed throughout the nineties. Chris's fearless big-wave charging began earning him invitations to the Eddie Aikau big-wave contests. Keith was one of the most photographed and filmed surfers of the nineties. Dan was poised for perhaps the most glory of the three after winning the Ocean Pacific Pro Junior in 1996 and placing second in the 2000 U.S. Open. A couple of years ago, his peers selected him in *Surfer* magazine's poll as one of the ten best surfers in the world.

Then, in 2002, Dan quit the competitive circuit, having decided, like his brothers, that the circus was in the way of the surfing.

The feeling that something was getting away from them had been building in all three Malloys even as their dreams were being realized beyond their wildest expectations.

"Even since the time we signed those first contracts, the face of surfing has changed so much. At first, it's 'Hey, I can pay my rent and get to do what I love.' It goes from having enough money to pay rent and barbecue to having your face on billboards and MTV and people in the Midwest wearing the stuff you're hawking, and you realize maybe you've gotten into more than you thought you were," says Chris. "After a while, about five years, it's become apparent you're a trained seal. It's wear the trunks, wear the shirts, smile. Don't say too much when you're interviewed and everything will be fine. You're helping surfing grow exponentially; surfing is growing like mad, but you're helping create a bunch of loose cannons because of people who think surfing is fashionable or they are drawn to these idols that they see in surfing magazines and you step back and you start to feel like you've betrayed something that's dear to you."

The first step in finding their way back was sort of a joint internal affirmation. "We wanted to surf for the reasons we started to surf; over the last four or five years, that's how we've felt. We didn't want to compete. We weren't going out there trying to create attention with these hideously bright colors that they were using in surfing for so long," says Keith. "It wasn't something we talked about or anything, we just moved in the same direction together. We do spend so much time together, it just rubs off. We feed off each other."

Once they had reclaimed surfing for themselves by dropping out of the competitive grind, they slowly started a process that would be dedicated to reclaiming it for those who had gone before and those who would come after.

This is where the Moonshine Conspiracy comes in. It's a loose affiliation of like-minded surfers, musicians, artists, and filmmakers, but it's really a code name for Chris Malloy, his brothers, former pro surfer and now-famous musician Jack Johnson, cousins Emmett and Coley, wife Carla, other family members, and anyone else they can inspire. Lately that's come to include even full-time surfer and part-time rock icon Eddie Vedder, who contributed a ukulele song to *A Brokedown Melody*.

They released their first film, *Thicker Than Water*, in 1999. It was a definitive step away from the prevailing mode, which was to make corporate-funded, quick-cut, heavy-action, and heavier-music affairs that were little more than adverts for the surfers and their sponsors. Aside from featuring the biggest waves ever ridden in Tahiti and debuting Jack Johnson's music for most people, it is one of the few surf films ever to be shot entirely on sixteen mm film. The same year, the Conspiracy released Thomas Campbell's incongruously longboard-centric *The Seedling*, also shot on sixteen mm. Then came *September Sessions* and *Shelter*.

The films were so out of context with the mainstream that they were subversive. They didn't identify riders or locations, had little of the standard (and annoying) voice-overs, and were infused with subtle messages and inside jokes. The idea was for viewers to be inspired to figure things out for themselves: who it is surfing, what they're doing, what the references are. They depicted the Malloys and their friends as a band of adventurers, using the water in a variety of ways, living off the land, and gathering around the campfire to play music and tell stories of their predecessors. The films were independently made and distributed out of the Conspiracy's headquarters in that renovated Victorian in Ventura. They were as much art projects as surf films, throwbacks to a bygone era that showed surfers living out an older definition of what it means to be a surfer.

"I feel like where we come from, our heritage, is better than anything I do," says Dan. "I have a whole lifetime of learning about the ocean, about what that lifestyle is. We're trying to learn what it means to be a waterman." That sentiment has resonated, and each film has become a cult classic in the surfing community.

The recently completed *A Brokedown Melody* is the most fully realized of them all—a perfect balance of state-of-the-art surfing and high aesthetics. Shot in saturated, deep hues of blue, violet, and amber—which serve to close the distance between the viewer and the action—the film seamlessly moves from moments of aching beauty to seat-grabbing adrenaline. But it's never over-the-top, always neatly calibrated to the overriding message, which is that to be a surfer is to understand one's responsibility to both surfing's past and its future.

Among the film's many poignant moments is a jam session with Tom Curren and Kelly Slater. Curren is like the Steve McQueen of surfing, an almost mythical searcher and the heaviest influence on the Malloys' and Slater's generation of neo-romantic surfers, which includes other stars like Rob Machado. The sequence intercuts between them out in the surf in Indonesia, which includes some of Curren's best moments on a board in ten years, and on the sand, where they try to out-insinuate each other.

"You kind of have to be a surfer to get the humor in this," says Chris. But you don't have to be a surfer to get the meaning of these two icons surfing together.

Later in the film, Slater, Machado, and others are joined in the surf by local kids who are flat going for it on broken boards. You can feel the kids spurring on the elders and the elders inspiring the kids. The segment is a hosanna to the ability of surfing to induce joy and exorcise cynicism. If your skin doesn't get goosy watching this, you may be dead.

"Without being preachy or trying to tell people what to do, I wanted to, in a fun way, or in a simple way, just remind people a little bit about where we come from and what is there for everybody as surfers, and that this carrot that people are trying to chase now, and the Hollywood depiction of surfing and the glory that comes with it, that there's something more than that," says Chris. "But in a fun way."

It's not a new thing, someone reclaiming something that has a pure heart from the maw of commodity and commerce. It happens in music, it happens in art, and it happens in surfing. But it's a good thing, nonetheless.

"What you see on film and in magazines represents about one percent of the surfing population. What the Malloys represent is the rest of surfing: the way the rest of people experience surfing—going on trips, camping with friends, playing music, and enjoying a beautiful setting. That's the feeling you get when you watch their movies," says Machado. "I definitely want to be a part of it."

◆◆◆

BEFORE I KNEW ALL this stuff about the Malloys, before I knew about their work with Surf Aid, or teaching autistic children to surf, or that they had taken a big pay cut to leave surfing giant Hurley to develop an environmentally sensitive ocean division with unfashionable Patagonia, or that they had turned down big bucks to do a Sunkist commercial because they don't think soda is good for kids—before any of that, I knew there was something different about these guys.

I had seen them in *Step Into Liquid*, Dana Brown's mega-surf flick from last year, in a segment that took place in Northern Ireland. They were teaching kids on both sides of the schism there to surf and maybe find some common ground in the bargain. That was cool and one of the movie's touching moments, but also impressive was how the brothers turned the burly surf on the northwest coast of Ireland into a playground. People from the village came down to gawk as if they were watching aliens land. But the brothers came across as humble and grounded. There was something different about them, and I wanted to know what it was.

I thought I found my answer more than a year later when I finally watched photographer and artist Alix Lambert's *Box of Birds* documentary, which aired on PBS and which followed the Malloys from a surf trip in New Zealand to their family's ranch in Ojai. Her film introduced me to Mary Malloy, the youngest of the Malloy siblings, the one who doesn't surf.

By the time I get around to asking about Mary, the brothers and I are sitting at an authentic Mexican cafeteria, one of the few remaining traces of old Ventura, a place that's in the middle of a franchise takeover they say has caught the town all but unawares.

"I heard the Gap and all these places are just circling, looking to try and kick out the antique stores, the old ladies who have had antique stores here for fifty years, and putting in the Gap," says Chris. "There's a real tug of war in this town right now."

The brothers say Ventura was the kind of place where cowboys, Hell's Angels, and farm hands all mixed comfortably.

As if to punctuate the statement, a roar of motorcycles announces a couple of guys on Harleys cruising down the street. Chris says they're probably weekend warriors, not the real thing, because he doesn't recognize them. The windshield on the front of one of the bikes would seem to confirm that. To illustrate the changes taking place, Dan tells me about last Halloween. "Some kids came up to trick or treat, and my dad opened the door and they were like, 'No way! He's a *worker* for Halloween.'" They all laugh.

I ask if their dad would have been happy if they'd all stayed on the ranch. "Yes," they answer in unison.

"I was thinking about that the other day, how when I go out to work with my dad, he has to show me what to do," says Dan. "He calls us city boys and says we have hands like girls because they aren't all fucked up like his are."

I wonder if there is any tension.

"I was just going to say, he has a tremendous amount of respect for what we do now," Keith says. "He enjoys the big-wave surfing stuff. Although we don't have the working hands he does, we have plenty of battle scars."

They hear it from their mom, mostly, about how proud their dad is of them. "We come from a family that if you sit there and talk about it, it degrades the whole thing," says Chris. "He admires people whose actions speak for it. He'd rather show us his approval over the course of six months in a subtle way than say, 'Gee, son, I'm so happy with you and I love you so much.'"

The brothers, though, will be the first to say that they aren't the real heroes in the family. The lessons of courage, resilience, and generosity were taught to them by their sister, Mary, who was born with cerebral palsy, a bad heart, and no hearing or sight. She's fought harder for her moments of joy than they ever will, and they all know it. Mary is twenty years old, and that's twenty-one more than anyone said she'd be. When the Malloy kids were growing up, the fire station was between the school and their house. "So for, like, ten years, every time I'd hear a fire engine, it'd be awful," says Keith.

There's a scene in *Box of Birds* where Chris is lying next to Mary, who even now is not much bigger than a toddler, and he's remarking that the doctors told them she isn't sentient—that she doesn't know what's going on. Just as Chris says it, she reaches up and lovingly rubs his face. And then she does it again, a wide smile on her face. It's more beautiful than any wave the boys have ever ridden.

"Her being there gave us a perspective that I think a lot of people don't get, you know? I think that just shaped us to be just a little bit unique in what is important to us just because we got that perspective from having our little sister, Mary, who has all these problems," says Keith.

"With her, the biggest lesson was no matter who you think you've become, no matter what a magazine has written about how good you are or what you've done, coming home to her and our family always made you realize that you were that same kid that you started out as, and that life's not perfect. In fact, it's way off center," Chris says. "And the other thing is…"

"She's probably happier than all of us put together," Dan cuts in, laughing.

"You'd come home from school and there'd be an ambulance or something, and it was a really strange way to grow up," Chris continues. "Here we had this wonderful place we lived and these great parents and we had each other, but it just gave you an appreciation for every day and what was in front of you, and to be optimistic, too. It gave you confidence. You're told that things are going to be so wrong; she's not going to make it past two weeks old, they said at first…it gave us optimism."

Chris can see where this is going, though, and doesn't want me getting all soft on them. He has a warning for people who think they're some kind of saints just because they've taken advantage of some of their time and privilege.

"I just want to call bullshit on it," he says, almost pleading. "We get wasted, and we get in bar fights and do stupid shit."

"If I read the stories about us, I'd be like, 'Jeez, dude, what are you trying to prove?'" adds Dan.

In the end, they say, they're not out to save the world, or even surfing, for that matter. Their goals are much more modest. "My new goal is no more goals. That's what I told my wife," Chris laughs. But then he gets a little serious again and says, "All those guys who came before us, they've passed on a really precious thing, and we want to take off all the bullshit and leave it just how we found it. We don't want to be seen as anything other than that." Well, there's one other thing, Chris sheepishly admits: if they ever write the story of this odd place called Ventura and the characters who lived and surfed here, maybe, just maybe, there will be a page in the book on them.

Who's That Girl?

Lauren Weedman's Search for Home

Originally published in LA Weekly, *April 25, 2007.*

Author's note: I saw Weedman's one-woman show, Bust, *and came away from the performance feeling as buzzed at forty-three as I'd felt after seeing* The Who *when I was seventeen. I went into work the next day and all-but demanded we put the relatively unknown Weedman on the cover of the* LA Weekly. *Laurie Ochoa heard me out and said that would be fine so long as I did the story. I was embarrassingly nervous at the prospect of meeting Weedman, and when we got together for lunch, I overcompensated by eating too much and trying too hard. She indulged me nonetheless.*

D<small>ID YOU EAT MY</small> napkin?" asks Lauren Weedman when I return from dousing myself with cold water in the bathroom.

No, but it's a fair question seeing as how I have eaten all of our bread, plus the calamari-in-marinara-sauce appetizer, my chicken ravioli, some of the better bits of her scraggly chicken marsala, coughed up two gumball-sized pieces of garlic, and nearly passed out.

We find the napkin on the floor.

"How come you don't eat those?" I ask, pointing at her plate.

"What do you mean?"

"The broccoli."

"Because I secretly know you want them. I think I may have a piece of chicken in my teeth you can have."

Damn. Who is this girl? I haven't felt this awkward since I took Sue Cistello to the Steak and Ale when I got my driver's license.

You may not know about Lauren Weedman. She's not a big star. She may be someday, or she may not, but when she's onstage I'd advise that you duck—painful truths go whizzing by like bullets, send-ups rain down like bombs, an uncensored IED explodes like shrapnel out of some internal minefield. It kills me like art. Killer art. I'm not sure we've seen anyone like Lauren Weedman before.

In her latest one-woman journey to the center of her psyche, *Bust*, which ran for three mostly sold-out dates in March at REDCAT, Weedman details the descent of a naive, self-absorbed creature/victim of Hollywood into the bowels of the prison system, where she has volunteered as a kind of inmate pal in a program called Behind Bars. Along the way, Weedman, acting about fifteen different roles, mercilessly, lovingly, and hilariously skewers her vapid network of friends and colleagues (unforgettable is her pillorying of a women's mag editor and a dog-rescuing friend), the inane prison bureaucracy, the self-defeating prisoners, the earnest volunteers, and mostly herself. And while I'm watching it, I'm shitting my pants at how funny and poignant, ferocious, and *precise* the whole thing is, and all I can think is: Who is she? Why isn't she a huge star? And *I've got to meet this woman.*

Seriously, you want to meet her. You want to know her. You want to be friends with her in that way you always dreamed of being friends with, well, Lou Reed is the other one. I know being starstruck isn't very professional, but there it is. And on the way out of the show, I realize I've had this feeling before, of wanting to meet her. It was the time years ago when my

wife dragged me to some fringe theater festival in which
Weedman had a cameo monologue in one of choreographer
Hassan Christopher's dance and performance-art pieces. Time
stopped then just as it did during *Bust*. You got the sense you
were seeing something rare and great and that surely she'd be
everywhere soon. And she may be.

Or she may not. Who knows? I'm not sure we know what
to do with her, or that she knows what to do with *us*. But she's
here now. And the fact that I'm getting my chance to meet her
just a few days after her *Bust* run must be making me nervous.
I'm fidgety, distracted, and can't think straight. Weedman,
on the other hand, despite coming straight from volunteering
at a women's prison in Torrance is, rather incongruous to her
stage persona, completely together. She's dressed casually cool,
with slightly curly blond locks doing a nice cascade around
her pretty face. She's friendly and gracious and funny without
even saying anything as she sits across from me at a small table
in what's described online as a local's-favorite Italian joint in a
nondescript (what else?) strip mall on Venice Boulevard. The
only thing missing is the locals. We're practically alone, which
might have something to do with why I'm sweating profusely,
though I blame it on the nuclear-powered candle on our table.
Weedman moves the candle over to her side and says, "If one
more weird thing happens in here, I'm fucking leaving. There's
a lot going on."

◆◆◆

LAUREN WEEDMAN GREW UP in a loving, buttoned-down
Midwestern family from Indianapolis. Her dad was a
businessman, and her mom was kind of a socialite. She was
adopted. She didn't escape the attendant issues. Like when she
was nine and her friend, who was a foster child, was returned to
sender. "I thought we were the same thing," she says.

Being funny started early. "It's the adopted thing—you don't want to be sent back."

I ask her how her mom came to adopt her. "She did a lot of volunteering, and I'm sure she was like [in a stuffy English accent], *I'll take one.* She had an English accent... No, she didn't."

Weedman wasn't as buttoned-down as the rest of her family. Not to get too psychobabble about it, but she struggled and still seems to struggle if you want to read into her work (and you do) to find a comfortable sense of self.

"I know, it sounds so dumb, but I was in trouble a lot. I got in trouble for stealing, for drinking, for that kind of stuff. It was a pretty strict family."

And there were always boy issues, it seems. "I was, uh, fat, about fifty or sixty pounds heavier, all through high school," she says. "And when you grow up fat, you definitely do not see the best side of boys."

"Did you badly want approval from boys?" I ask.

"*I'm not a lesbian,*" Weedman jokes. The gay thing is a running gag with her—she is constantly being pegged as the jolly dyke by Hollywood casting.

"What I'm getting at is, were you a slut?"

"Yeah, um, not good boundaries. Growing up, I wasn't very smart, *so flattered* if anybody liked me. My mom would be like, *You don't have to kiss the guy at 7-Eleven.* And I'd be like, *But he asked me.*"

"How old were you when you had your first gangbang?"

"Seven. But that's different, that's like family stuff. That's more reunions and that kind of thing. It wasn't anything, you know, painful."

◆◆◆

TRULY PAINFUL IS WHAT probably amounts to the first major turning point in her life, when she was in her first year of college at

DePaul University in Chicago. After a rough night during which she'd been ditched by everyone at a party, she went back to her dorm room feeling lost and lonely and called her ex-boyfriend, who, it turns out, was gay, and told him a little lie: that she'd been raped. It worked. Suddenly she was the center of attention. Unfortunately, her roommate overheard the conversation, and by the time Weedman woke up the next morning, she was in the proverbial system, as a rape victim.

The fallout from that incident provides much of the impetus for *Wreckage*, perhaps her best-known show locally, one that played at Highways Performance Space in Santa Monica in 2004 and at REDCAT in 2005. Watching *Wreckage* and watching Weedman get entangled in her own web of deceit, and, more to the point, the traps sprung from her need for attention and approval of any kind, is like watching a self-immolation, only it's hilarious. Though, Weedman cautions, "I wouldn't recommend it to the youth."

Not surprisingly, she left school. Almost as not surprising is that she took up with a thirty-two-year-old "waiter–spiritual seeker–meditation guy" who drove them out to Colorado on his motorcycle to live in the Rockies. She was nineteen.

"Then he found Jesus and asked me to sleep on the couch until he could figure out if sex was 'right' or not," says Weedman. "We broke up."

Eventually, she went back to school, this time at Indiana University, where she met a six-foot-seven-inch Dutch guy who was getting his master's in film directing. She moved to Amsterdam with him in 1991, when she was twenty-one.

"I wanted to get Indiana out of my system. I wanted to have a break from who they thought I was when I left. I did not want to be that person anymore," she tells me. "It was kind of heavy, but for one, I was known as a rape victim, and I wasn't raped."

Weedman and her Dutchman broke up soon after they got to Amsterdam.

"Dutch people in Indiana are *very* exciting," she says, "but among their own people? Not as thrilling."

"Are they still tall?"

"Super tall, still holding on to that. Still blond and very stoic," she says.

Weedman spent the next four years having what she describes as a very fine ex-pat experience. "I was just sort of… a heroin prostitute," she says, gamely sawing away at her too-gamey chicken. "I was more fit then, it was different."

She didn't really sell herself on the streets, but she did start studying experimental theater. I ask if that meant miming, because experimental theater in Europe must mean miming. "No," she says. "I was always like, well, one of the roles I had was 'Crazy Lady Under the Bridge.' I was always in sort of odd roles where it was, like, 'Okay, you're a piece of paper, you're representing a piece of paper in this play, *but you're torn…* You know, it was always this weird kind of stuff. But I also did straight American plays."

◆◆◆

THERE ARE A COUPLE of themes that run through Weedman's life and, by extension, her work. There is her transparent ambition, something she has a love-hate relationship with and is able to observe as acutely and cuttingly as an outsider might, and there is her constant desire to start over and find a place that feels like home. These impulses are often in conflict with each other. In 1995, she chose to start over in Seattle, a place that seemed like it might accommodate both. "I wanted a liberal, coastal, culturally vibrant city," she says. "And I wanted it to be a place with a vibrant gay culture, even though [in a deep voice] *I am not gay.*"

Also, a small theater there responded the most enthusiastically to the raft of letters she sent out seeking internships, which may have had something to do with the inclinations of the company's director. She tells a story of the time she was housesitting for the married director and noticed a desk drawer bound shut with electrical tape. After some deliberation, she said, "Fuck it," and took off the tape. "The entire drawer was filled with threesome pornos," she tells me. "Everything was like *You, Me, and Her*, or *She, She, and Me*, and this big bag of Cheetos."

"Was that bag open?"

"Yeah, and just covered with cum. I ate the whole bag."

From that inauspicious beginning, Weedman's career as a solo performer and comedic anthropologist of her own life was born. It's a career we're playing catch-up to in Los Angeles. By contrast, they "been knowing" about her, as the kids say, up in Seattle for a long time. George Lugg, who is the associate director at REDCAT, and who was instrumental in bringing *Bust* there, held a similar position back in those days at On the Boards, a contemporary performance center in Seattle. He remembers the first time he saw Weedman.

"She auditioned for On the Boards and did a twelve-minute piece that was in the vein of these very funny, fairly autobiographical, but clearly ramped-up versions of her experience," says Lugg. "It was just completely memorable, and there was this sense that, ah, here's someone who's going to take this work to a really interesting place."

The vignette Weedman auditioned evolved into a full-length show called *Homecoming*, which chronicled her search for her biological parents. The show toured for a year with the Seattle Repertory Theatre and eventually made it to off-Broadway. (*The New York Times* compared her performance in *Homecoming* to "Bob Newhart in his early stand-up routines.")

Weedman has since debuted most of her major theatrical works, including *Amsterdam* (about her time in Amsterdam); the twisted holiday fable *If Ornaments Had Lips*; *Rash* (about, among other things, her ill-fated experiences as a correspondent on *The Daily Show*); and her divorce-reckoning show, *Wreckage*, in Seattle.

◆◆◆

IN SEATTLE, SHE IS loved. Reviewing *Rash*, a writer for *The Stranger* penned a letter to God thanking him or her or it for Weedman. The letter begins, "Dear Lord, I know bombs are about to drop" and goes on to thank the almighty for "the richness of the human creatures Weedman manifests," and most of all "that there is a reason to be alive, Lord, and that is to see the brilliance of Lauren Weedman, the funniest woman alive."

Keep in mind this writer seemed to be in the grips of some, as history has clearly shown, completely uncalled for despair regarding the pending war in Iraq, but still, I understand. Weedman does things to you that only true artists can, among them making you feel life is worth living. Another follower of Weedman's career, former *Seattle Weekly* and current *Seattle Metropolitan* magazine arts editor Steve Wiecking, was equally taken aback.

"The solo-show thing seems so tired until you see her, and you realize this must be how people felt when they saw Lily Tomlin for the first time," Wiecking told me. "She's just one of those [performers] who people would take someone to go see, and you'd be talking about the stuff for the rest of the week. Some stuff hits you as funny at the time and some stuff you remember a week later on the bus and you're like, 'Oh, my god.' It's the little things that get you as much as the big things."

Of course, the little things are often the personal things, and in Weedman's hands, the personal things, like a self-defeating desire for reassurance and a self-fulfilling prophecy of unworthiness, often have a horrifying resonance.

For example, in Seattle Weedman landed what everyone seems to acknowledge was a prize catch—a rugged, sexy, sensitive boyfriend. She got married, and the tumult of that relationship, lots of which she'll ascribe to her own insecurities, forms another of *Wreckage*'s narrative themes. There's a scene in the play—and I think it is unjust to call her solo shows anything but plays—in which Weedman stops by the bar where her husband is bartending and stares in through the window to observe him in action. On the other side of the window, she sees a man, confident, smiling, surrounded by adoring women— younger? hotter?—hanging on his every word. He's king in this court and she doesn't recognize him as her own. She ventures insecurely inside, and a change comes over him. He seems less alive than he did just a minute ago. But yes, he's so glad she came by. Only there's that devil inside her that refuses to believe it. She sits down and has a few too many drinks and sets upon him with a form of verbal Chinese water torture that's excruciating for him, her, and the audience. She doesn't let up until she forces him to confess that he would indeed prefer it if she, who is by now killing everybody's buzz, left. The scene is funny, painful, and all too familiar—who among us hasn't engaged in this sort of dark-hearted self-betrayal?

"She recreated that moment so perfectly; you can take from it what you want. She gives you a full moment, where you can see everything," says Wiecking. "She can't help herself."

He's right, she can't. And it's not just recreating moments, which she does so well, both because she understands the often hideous nature of those moments and because she's such a good actor, a true actor who inhabits every moment, but because she isn't afraid to cop to them in the very realest sense. We see ourselves in those moments, and as hideous as they are, she lets us laugh. It's kind of healing, in a way. "She has an ability to get down to the base nature of each person, each character that she tackles," says Jeff Weatherford, who was an actor in the Seattle theater scene back in those days and who would later direct Weedman in *Wreckage* and serve as dramaturge for *Bust*. "And there's an equality to her characters, and that comes down to the humanness of them all."

◆◆◆

WEEDMAN SOON BRANCHED OUT beyond the local stages in Seattle, landing a stint as a writer/performer on the highly popular local show *Almost Live*, a sometimes topical sketch comedy and news program (think *Saturday Night Live* meets *The Daily Show*) that had, among its many charms, a bit where Soundgarden's Kim Thayil yelled "Lame!" at whatever topics the announcer brought up. It all sounds so great: a hottie hubbie who can mix a drink, a supportive artistic community, cool TV gig. Not to mention, I hear you can get great tech support for your PC up there and you pay in whole-bean French roast. What more could anyone ask for?

Oh, yeah, there's that ambition thing she does, and after five years in Seattle, Weedman got hot feet. "She was seeking to be amongst people where she wasn't always the most talented person in the room," says Weatherford. "She really is probably the most talented person I've ever worked with." Maybe he should be taken with a grain of salt, since he currently cohabitates with Weedman, and that's just good politics, but then again maybe not, since he told me not to take what he says with a grain of salt because he's worked with Juilliard people and all sorts of fancy theater folks, and he means what he says about her talent.

So at the turn of the century—what better time?—she packed up her bartending hubby, her latest show, *Homecoming*, and tried New York. It almost worked. Weedman remembers one morning dawning particularly brightly. It was the morning after *Homecoming* opened at The Duplex to a great audience response and reviews; it was the morning that marked her first month as a *Daily Show* correspondent. It was another sort of morning, too.

"That morning, I was riding my bike up Sixth Avenue to go to this, like, Wrigley gum commercial, and I'm riding my bike *up* Sixth Avenue and it was one of the most self-absorbed mornings of my life," she recalls, "because I was like [in Valley-girl voice], *I can't believe it, I'm on* The Daily Show, *I'm off-Broadway*, and it looks like everybody's looking at me in some weird way, because they're all looking that way [toward downtown] and I'm like, *This is so bizarre*—it does sort of look like everybody's noticing me today—*There's something about me...* And I mean...obviously they're watching the Twin Towers, and it was like the, I'd say *the* most self-absorbed day of my life. And I was very humbled afterward because it turns out there was a terrorist attack... I don't know if you heard about that."

As it turns out things didn't go great on *The Daily Show* either, an experience Weedman used for fodder in *Rash*, her fourth full-length theater piece. Well, maybe it wasn't *The Daily Show* exactly, just something that looked a lot like *The Daily Show*. Anyway, apparently a nervous Weedman forgot to shake Jon Stewart's hand after one of her first bits and apparently Stewart isn't Gandhi, and well, they never quite clicked. Or maybe it wasn't Stewart, just someone who could be mistaken for him.

"I didn't feel like I had enough to do. I wanted to do more of my own thing. I had one character, and I had to wait to be told when my thing was coming up. There was a lot of waiting around," says Weedman of her time with Jon and company. "Everyone was just like, *Shut up and don't say anything, he's glad you're here. Just shut up, here he comes.*

"I'm still on freelance contract. I might still have to go back."

Before long, her marriage also started disintegrating. "Once we stopped drinking together, once I was like, *I have to go to work*, he was like [slurring], *it's not working*," says Weedman. "That's not true, actually, it was deeper than that. It was more fucked up." In the end, she admits, both 9/11 and *The Daily Show* proved too much for the couple to handle. "Our marriage survived neither, and I wanted to keep on striving 'upward and onward' and he told me he could no longer be married to 'Lauren Weedman,'" she says. "He used the first and last name."

Time to start over again.

Soon, Weedman found herself back in the comforting embrace of her gay ex-boyfriend from Indiana, who was living in Laurel Canyon with his partner. "I spent most of my early depression there, after the divorce, and then moved out so I could Internet date more freely without their judgment."

She moved into a place on Franklin and Argyle. "I hated it," she tells me. "Yeah, I know [doing caricature of vapid Angeleno], *It's a great strip—Birds!* My friend John was like, 'Lauren, that's your area, it's so arty, like you. You're gonna love it there. There's a place there, the Bourgeois Pig, *it's your place.* And you go in there and I've never seen so many people write like this—type, type [stretches out], *Oh, gosh.* Type, type, *Oooh, it's sooo hard.*'"

◆◆◆

In LA, where all the clichés hold true, but where the whole is much greater than the sum of its parts, she may have found her muse. If *Bust*, which is both a valentine and a scathing indictment, is any indication, Los Angeles and its legion of strivers (foremost among them Weedman herself) will provide a bottomless well of material.

"When I first moved here, people were like, let me tell you something, Lauren, *You and I are sooo alike.* You read the newspaper, I read the newspaper."

Then, there's auditioning. "When I'm just an actor, sitting out with the actors, and, literally, it's like [self-important voice], *Who took the pen from the sign-up sheet? Can I have that back, please? Thank you, pay attention.* Even that little thing, I'm like, oh boy, I'm not thirty-seven-years-old sitting here. I'm like, *This is not my adult life.* This is not where I'm supposed to be."

But still, she can't help herself. "I feel sometimes the fact that I'm even in LA, I'll feel as if I have some crack addiction, like I'm even trying to do this, something's up with me. It's like, what am I doing here?" she says. "I'm like auditioning for Fat Al, where it's like, *We don't know if he'll be a man, or fat, but just read the part.*"

Sure, there's that. But Los Angeles has provided other things she may not have expected. Like a home. She's in a great relationship with Weatherford, a friend who became a lover and a collaborator. He's a widower who has a nearly grown son. Of course, that too is a great source of material, stuff that hasn't found its way onstage yet, but has been the subject of several hilarious short stories—one of which, "I'm Hugging You With My Voice," appeared in the literary journal *Swivel* and recounts the difficulty of making love while staring at a picture of the man's ex.

"For the first time in my life, I could see how being blindfolded was hot," Weedman writes. "But pictures of Hannah were all over the house, which wrecked me. Obsessively staring at her photos and attempting to show how okay I was with the whole situation, I would chirp, 'This is a nice one. Oh, and this one, too! Look at her here! I see she's wearing a sweater, so I take it it was wintertime?'"

One of the things that is apparent from Weedman's stage shows, aside from her obvious acting and comedy chops, is how well they're written. Each has a fully realized narrative arc, which makes them so much more engaging than a lot of solo shows in which people just get up there and puke out their drama. So it's not surprising that she's developing a bit of a side career in the literary world. Her story "Diary of a Journal Reader," which also first appeared in *Swivel*, made the Dave Eggers–edited *Best American Nonrequired Reading, 2005*, and the collection

A Woman Trapped in a Woman's Body: Stories From a Life of Cringe comes out from Sasquatch Books in the fall. She's also recently received a fellowship to the prestigious MacDowell Colony ("Or, as my friends call it, fuck-fest 2007...not my good friends," jokes Weedman), where writers like Mary Gaitskill and Arthur Bradford (author of the quirky collection *Dogwalker*), and genius composers and playwrights and architects and visual artists go to plan world domination.

So the question remains, who is this girl? Is she the woman blowing minds onstage, where her precious, nuanced, scathing, brave, hilarious pieces have the room they need to breathe and grow and get under your skin? Is she a budding humorist, like an Amy Sedaris, only funny? Or is she the woman who keeps trying to find fame, fortune, and a place on the screen, currently toiling away in stuff like *Reno 911*, and VH1's *Best Week Ever* and other forums that just seem too small to capture the thing that is Lauren Weedman? The question hangs in the air as the restaurant empties of its other four patrons (local's-favorite?). It's a question that demands a cigarette, and we repair outside to smoke.

I ask her if she feels like she needs to be a star in some traditional way.

"No, I don't think so," she says. "I like how it's going. For instance...I'll get some hardcore compliments that are the best kind of compliments that are like—the one that I get that I love is, *I hate every fucking thing and I fucking loved that.* That's perfect."

Maybe the answer is the thing she keeps coming back to, despite the TV auditions and the striving. Maybe it's up on the stage where it's always been, where that intangible thing she does/she is makes all the sense in the world.

"I love being at REDCAT. REDCAT was perfect," says Weedman. "I felt so inspired after this weekend. I had this burst of integrity and confidence that it's okay to turn down things that don't feel right."

I light up another cigarette before she's halfway through hers. It's a good thing I never met Lou Reed. I'm not sure I'd have survived.

"Would you just keep doing what you're doing, even if you don't make a lot of money?" I ask, and I really hope the answer is yes.

"Well, I have," she says. "I'm thirty-eight. I'd love to have health insurance regularly, you know, just in case I have a one-hundred-fifty-pound cyst on my ovary or something. That would be nice."

"Hopefully you'd notice by the time it's fifty pounds."

"I think I have a five-pounder in there now. Or else I really have to go to the bathroom."

Christian Bale and the Art
of Extreme Acting

Originally published in the LA Weekly, *July 3, 2007*

Author's note: Scott Foundas, the LA Weekly's *film editor at the time, asked me to do this piece on Christian Bale, which would be tied to the release of Werner Herzog's* Rescue Dawn. *I tried to demur—the film wasn't very good and for whatever reason, I was indifferent about Bale, despite his obvious talent. Thankfully, a few of the ladies in my life insisted I take the assignment, and Bale turned out to be a great conversationalist, an interesting man, and just a cool guy.*

CHRISTIAN BALE IS AN actor who may be as well known for what he does to his body as he is for his body of work. He's done extreme things to that body in the name of art. Turning it as hard and sharp as an ice pick for *American Psycho*. Hollowing it out enough to nauseate in *The Machinist*. Making it lethal enough to become the first Batman we can really believe. Running it down to the bone again as a prisoner of war in Werner Herzog's new film, *Rescue Dawn*. But did you know he did a movie in 2002 called *Reign of Fire* in which he battles (sometimes on horseback) fire-breathing dragons in a post-apocalyptic Britain? And were you aware of *Equilibrium*, the *Matrix* junkies' *Matrix*, which also came out in 2002—a movie that, according to Bale, is a big hit with our servicemen overseas?

Let me tell you about *Equilibrium* and me. I first learned about it weeks ago when I went to Blockbuster video with a list of Bale movies to rent. The clerk told me I *had* to see *Equilibrium*. We spent the next fifteen minutes trying to find it. The clerk worried that someone had lifted it, something that apparently happens frequently with this film, because the studio gave it a limited pressing or something, and copies are hard to find. We came up empty.

Over Memorial Day weekend, a friend and I went on the quest again, this time to a video store in Silver Lake. When I announced that I was there for *Equilibrium*, a young Asian male straight out of a John Hughes movie who was sitting heretofore unnoticed on the floor digging into a carton of Chinese food with chopsticks, looked up and fairly screeched: "*Equilibrium*! That movie is awwwwesommme." But that store's lone copy had disappeared. So I went to the famed Video Hut on Vermont, where everything is possible. The clerk there registered an immediate look of comprehension when I told him what I was after—apparently there is a secret society of *Equilibrium* admirers that I was on the verge of joining. But, to his chagrin, the store's only disc had become corrupted. "I couldn't let you rent it in good conscience," he told me. So back to Blockbuster we went. Another search of endless racks, another heartbreak. Finally, a week later, I found it at my old reliable stop near the Mayfair Market off Franklin. I had earned my induction.

2002 was also the year Bale played the fussy son of a wild music producer (Frances McDormand) in *High Art*-director Lisa Cholodenko's wistful *Laurel Canyon*. Talk about range. Bale can fill the sensible shoes of a wallflower, like the one in *Laurel Canyon* or the charming *Metroland* (1997), as easily as he can don the cape of the *Dark Knight*.

In fact, such is the degree to which Bale disappears into a role that one could watch his entire filmography, as I have not quite done, and still not be able to peg him the way one could peg Brando as primal, McQueen as cool, Nicholson as uncanny, Clooney as classic, Depp as daring, and Pitt as, well, Pitt. At thirty-three, he may be the biggest movie actor on the planet who isn't a celebrity. When he walks into a room, as he does on a sunny, late-spring morning at Shutters by the Beach in Santa Monica, heads don't turn. There's something enigmatic about this Christian Bale, something indefinable that serves him in his craft, a craftiness that springs from not being crafty at all. He's done about three dozen movies, and he's utterly lacking a persona, other than the one that makes women—and by women I don't just mean my wife—swoon at the mere mention of his name. Despite his vast and varied career, Bale remains a bit of a cult figure. Those who know have known for a long, long time. Those who don't may never.

The great Werner Herzog—and whatever you may think of *Rescue Dawn*, let us not argue the greatness of the man who hauled a 340-ton steamship through the Peruvian jungle and over mountains to make *Fitzcarraldo* and who has made more than fifty films, some in the most remote and extreme conditions imaginable, and for the money that falls into the cushions of most Hollywood moguls' couches... Well, Herzog told me the decision to cast Christian Bale as a real-life fighter pilot shot down over Laos in the early days of Vietnam, in the film upon which this great iconoclast and outrider pins his hopes of Hollywood anointment, was a no-brainer.

"It was instantly clear that he was the guy," Herzog says by phone from Austria, sounding, with his thick accent, like a charming version of Arnold Schwarzenegger. "There's casting where there's absolutely no question. He was onboard long before he was chosen for *Batman*. I said to him, 'No matter what, you have to be Dieter, and if you're not going to be Dieter, I don't want to make the film.'"

So what attracted Herzog to the young actor in the first place?

"What drew me to Christian is that he is the best of his generation," he says.

Oh, yeah. There's that.

◆◆◆

WHEN THE BEST ACTOR of his generation pulls up in front of Shutters, a place famous for seeing and being seen that could only have been chosen by a publicist, it's in a black pickup truck. He's wearing a baseball cap and an unassuming getup of T-shirt and jeans. The look is trucker chic, though I'm pretty sure Bale has no idea what trucker chic is. He tells me the pickup is for hauling his motorized dirt bikes, which is what he's into these days, though he confesses he's not very Zen about the art of motorcycle maintenance.

"I know how to ride. When something goes wrong, I just look at it and want to kick it and bang it with a camera," he laughs.

As we sit down at a large table in the grand lobby, where it seems everyone has a severe case of cell-phone ear, the waves are breaking at Bay Street, and the wind is just starting to pick up. I've brought my surfboard, and I'm worried about getting to the surf before the wind craps it out. Bale's worried about, well, this uncomfortable part of the business. I eye the surf nervously; he looks like he could use a nap. A big question hangs stagnant between us, though it's unspoken, and it's a matter of degrees: How much does either of us want to be here? I'm breaking a long-ago pledge to never do another celebrity interview; he's on record as not giving a damn about the trappings of stardom. For a minute, there's a feeling that we're the two most bored people in the room. It's a dicey situation.

These situations, of course, are accidents—the kind of accidents that happen when the son of a circus-dancer mom and a Bunyanesque adventurer of a father, who was born in

Walesbut, who moved around a lot as a kid, gets picked to star in a Steven Spielberg film after auditioning on a dare from his sister and eventually ends up in Santa Monica talking to someone who, by his own conspiracy of accidents, has ended up sitting across the table from the greatest actor of his generation with a tape recorder in hand. Since there's always the chance this will turn out to be a happy accident, we gamely order coffee and water and settle in.

Why all the moving around? What was going on—was that just life with a circus-dancer mom?

It was more partly wanting to go to new places and partly wanting to get away from other places quickly.

What does that mean? Was there a little hustling going on with the family?

Ah, just that my dad was an interesting character, you know? He was somebody who pretty much lived on his own from the age of thirteen, and that never really left him, you know? Being a roamer. That was what he did.

And your mom was a circus dancer?

Yeah, I know. She hates it whenever I talk about that, but how can a kid forget? It was definitely the most memorable job she had, in my mind. She says, "That's not all I did." But, you know, when you're six or seven years old and your mom's dressed as a clown, or mucking about with tigers or elephants in a circus, it kind of sticks in your head.

So, there was a lot of starting over and reinvention, that sort of thing?

Yeah, and just the dissatisfaction with the rut that you can fall into very easily, anywhere, but that he felt very much so in England. He was just looking for something new.

Was your dad the one who moved you to America? Or were you already over here acting?

There was always an idea of the States being the place. I remember there were a few times, when I was like seven or eight, not really understanding how things worked, and hearing my dad talk [about moving here], and saying goodbye to my friends—*I was going to the States*—and then being back in school by Monday. Eventually, I got work over here and brought my family with me, which was a really good thing.

Bale was eighteen when he helped the family realize its long-dreamed-of escape from dreary England. Today, he's living proof that while you can take the boy out of the old country, you can't take the old country out of the boy. He still speaks with a distinct brogue, and his conversational manner is that of a guy sitting at a pub having a few pints next to a stranger—friendly but not overly familiar. He doesn't really look you in the eye, but he's game so long as it doesn't get wanky.

Does this feel like home now, or do you still have an emotional tie to British culture?

Well, talking about football or something... If I see England play, I can't help but get goose bumps, you know? There will always be that. But that's what half of America is anyway—people who come from somewhere else. This is definitely my home now. I've ended up being here for almost half my life.

Your uncle was an actor and your mom was in show biz; was that what brought you into the business?

It wasn't really in my face, growing up. But seeing my mom doing that, and I think also just realizing there was a chance for not having any kind of nine-to-five job and the chance for travel and for good, weird experiences, and, um, it just kind of grabbed me more than anything else. I didn't really have any notion of wanting to go to college or anything like that.

Were you conscious of all that as a kid? I'm asking because you started acting at a very young age, and you're expressing fairly mature ideas about why you wanted to do it.

Well, it was kind of a surprise to me, first of all, just how much I did enjoy it. I always hated doing any kind of school production, or anything like that, because, for me, what I liked was the complete insanity of everybody believing in what they were doing and taking it really seriously. So I didn't like it when you were doing a school production, where it was just a laugh for a few people.

I was serious about it, and I realized how much I enjoyed this going off and becoming someone else for a while and really obsessing about it. I didn't see a chance for that in much else that I was looking at, and I'd kind of stumbled into this in a very lucky fashion and thought it was something I didn't want to lose a grip on. That was very early on. It was unbelievable that I got a job [*Empire of the Sun*] out of nowhere that had me going to Shanghai and Spain... See, growing up with my dad, he had all these great stories from when he was a kid, because he ran away at thirteen and he ended up living in Egypt. He ended up living in the Caribbean for a while. He just didn't give a crap. He'd jump on [a ship] and get a job with somebody, and he'd jump off at some other port somewhere, see what happened, you know? Nobody looking after him, doing it on his own, and it sounded fantastic.

How come I was sitting in some fucking dingy little town in fucking England, just sitting under a freeway, smoking out and, you know, getting drunk with friends? And, hey, that's all good, but it's not quite the thing that I knew he was doing as a kid.

So, he told you all these epic tales of adventure?

Well, yeah, he wasn't actually very overblown about it. You had to drag it out of him… It was just that sense of there being a lot more out there, and you don't have to get a bunch of money for it, so long as you're prepared to end up sleeping on benches sometimes, or get taken in by people and stuff. That's what I kind of fantasized about, thinking, *That's the life, that's what I want to do.*

Do you know what your dad ran away from?

Um, boredom, basically. There were adventures out there. There were crazy places to visit; there were crazy people out there you should meet.

He sounds like an English beatnik.

Yeah, that's it. That's exactly what he was. Also, he was a tough bastard as well. I saw him in situations…it was hilarious.

You mean in bar fights?

Well, I never saw that. Just, when he wanted to be, he could be a very intimidating figure. He was a lot bigger than me.

Was that onerous in a way, or did you feel close to him?

Oh, no. Really close.

There's an interesting coda to the story of Bale's father. The world traveler eventually became an airline pilot. He and Bale's mother divorced. When I ask when, Bale's eyes wander to the middle distance and he says curtly, "That was a while back." Then, in 2000, Bale's dad ended up marrying Gloria Steinem, when he was fifty-nine and she was sixty-six. He died three years later, and she has said he was the love of her life.

When I ask what it was like being Gloria Steinem's stepson, Bale's discomfort becomes apparent. "You know, she's an extraordinary woman," he tells me, "but usually family are the last people to recognize any kind of brilliance, you know what I mean?

As it should be, because you're meant to just be another member of the family."

I wonder if he's talking about himself there too, but he leaves no doubt that it's the end of the subject. The message is clear: it's okay to talk about family mythology, but probably best to steer clear of the real thing. It's an honorable request, and it's time to get back to the business at hand before wankiness sets in.

Doing *Empire of the Sun* at such a young age must have changed your life pretty dramatically.

It was crap for a while. It was crap because, suddenly, you got the real experience of actually doing it, making the movie, traveling to these countries, working with these people...and then, suddenly, it was all about the other side of it, which is the fraudulent side of it. I've found, doing the whole press thing, and I sort of couldn't get my head around it. I couldn't quite work out why people were asking me to do things, what they expected of me. I just didn't quite get it. So that put me off everything for quite some time.

You know, I was still only fourteen. When I say I wanted to kind of take a step back from my career, I didn't even consider that I had a career. I just found myself doing this thing which I liked a great deal, and suddenly people were talking about it as though it were a career. It seemed to be taking the fun out of it for me.

Did you even know what it meant to be in a Steven Spielberg movie?

No, no, I couldn't have cared less. It didn't matter. Vaguely knew him, vaguely knew movies, but movies were never something that was very important to me—remain not that important to me, really.

So how did a kid who never spent much time in the movies end up getting tapped for a Steven Spielberg blockbuster? Bale tells me *of hearing about the casting auditions on the radio and something about that prompting his sister and others to push him to go for it, and suddenly a thought that had never occurred becomes a life. "It really came out of nowhere," he says. "Lucky beyond belief, since I'm still doing it, and I'm here and everything, 'cause if that never happened..."* He doesn't finish the thought, and one struggles to imagine other alternatives, how a life like Bale's father's could unfold in these coarser times. "There was certainly no intention, and we weren't a family that had any connections," he says. "It was nothing like that."*

I tell him that I understand that things can be accidental and chosen at the same time.

"Yes, yes, that's exactly what it was," he replies, "and it wasn't until a long time after that I realized, 'You know what? I think I will keep doing this.'"

On *Empire*, do you remember the process? Was it something innate? Do you remember how it happened?

I didn't really try, you know? It wasn't me thinking, "Oh, I'm an actor. I'm acting." I just sort of did it. It was just having a laugh and not giving a crap if you made a fool of yourself, if you looked like a tit doing it, and that was fun. I've always enjoyed making a total tit out of myself and the feeling of people going, "What did he do there? Why would somebody do that to themselves?"

That was before you *do* get self-conscious and embarrassed, and you start to think about other people's reactions to what you're doing instead of just doing it. That comes later, into the more advanced teenage years, where you get the awkward teenage feelings, and you're suddenly consumed with embarrassment permanently, and you're somebody getting a sense of yourself by comparing yourself with other people. But at that age, you don't have that, so you can do anything, and it's just a laugh, and it's all hilarious. It's the perfect age to be an actor because you don't care if you're misunderstood.

Do you try to find that place now, where you're totally ingenuous and guileless and not being self-conscious?

What a great life, if you could live that way completely, almost thinking about no consequences. When it concerns yourself, I mean. Obviously, you can't help as you get older—and you shouldn't—but recognize consequences on other people. But for yourself, yeah, it's more fun that way.

◆◆◆

RESCUE DAWN OPENS ON Fourth of July weekend. It wasn't intended that way. "It's a strange and wonderful coincidence that the film is going to be released on July fourth," says Werner Herzog, puckishly. "You see, we've had a couple delays, and the competition is murderous, but it doesn't matter. We're coming out on the right day now."

The film tells the tale of Dieter Dengler, a German-born American who was inspired by watching American pilots bomb his native country to become a pilot himself. Dengler, who died in 2001, got shot down over Laos on his first mission in the early days of Vietnam, before it was even called a war, and spent six months in horrific confinement in a jungle prison before plotting a harrowing, and disastrous, escape. In 1997, Herzog made an Emmy-nominated documentary about Dengler called *Little Dieter Needs to Fly*, and he calls *Rescue Dawn* unfinished business—a work that, for obvious reasons, has enabled him to go beyond the narrative confines of documentary. The director, known as a brilliant documentarian and the maker of a handful of brilliant, iconoclastic features, has high hopes for the film.

"I'm out for new horizons," he tells me. "Well, it's like before *Grizzly Man*. It's not foreign films anymore. This was my first feature film with English dialogue and American actors. I'm proud of it, and it fits very well into the line of movies I've made so far."

In some ways more than others, perhaps. Last year, a lengthy article in *The New Yorker*, written by Daniel Zalewski, titled "The Ecstatic Truth—Werner Herzog's Quest," described a shoot rife with chaos, rebellion among the crew, tense run-ins with machine gun–toting local authorities, and near catastrophes at every turn. In other words, if legend is to be believed, a typical Herzog set. Herzog takes issue with the article's characterization of the shoot.

"It wasn't a difficult film at all," he says. "I've made much more difficult ones. What the *New Yorker* article describes… you have to understand the journalist was there in the first week of shooting. We had an inexperienced producer and technical crews from Hollywood, Europe, and Thailand, and it took a few days to get it streamlined, which was witnessed by the *New Yorker* journalist. Three different philosophies about how to make a film had to come together. But do not worry about this: I have the authority to make a crew follow me, which came through a very clear vision of where we were going."

And there's no doubt that, despite this being Herzog's "Hollywood" moment, *Rescue Dawn* bears all the imprints of a signature Herzog film. It's meditative and oddly paced, and how it will play with mainstream audiences remains a very open question.

To Herzog, though, the film is a valentine to the best aspects of the American character. "Everything that I like about Americans was in Dieter Dengler," he says. "Courage, optimism, self-reliance, loyalty. It's what is, in essence, America. I'm not in the business of America bashing."

In the end, the film is also why Bale and I find ourselves staring across a wood table at each other on a burnished morning in a luxurious beach-side setting.

"*Rescue Dawn*, I guess we have to talk about that," I say.

"Oh, did you see the movie?" Bale asks.

"I did."

"You did, but you didn't like it."

"What makes you say that?"

"Because you said, 'I guess we gotta talk about that.' You're like, *we gotta get on with that.*"

"I gotta be honest, I didn't love it."

"Why was that?"

Bale is almost laughing as he prods me. It's reassuring to know this shit is funny to him too, and it betrays the quiet confidence that has been evident in him from the beginning. He doesn't really care whether I liked the film or not, but he isn't above provoking an interesting conversation about it. I tell him that, though the performances are great—and they are—I thought there was an odd flatness and distance to the film. Things stopped just short of where I felt they needed to go in order to fully pull in the viewer. I suggest—and this shouldn't surprise fans of Herzog's docs— that there was, despite the incredible attention to the physical geography of Dengler's imprisonment, almost too much room left between the audience and the internal landscapes of the characters as they go through their Job-like struggles. In other words, I know what Dieter endured—torture, deprivation, and hopeless jungle— but I'm not sure I came away knowing him.

Does that make sense?

Let me put something out there and see if this might be what it is. I can't speak for Werner, but I can say what my understanding is of some of his beliefs about moviemaking. He loathes quick-cut editing and the reliance on editing to manipulate an audience. He feels that it's a fraudulent way of approaching film. He will go for a very simple setup. He doesn't believe in creating a heightened tension, or comedy, or anything through editing. He believes something is either there or it's not there, and you should just sit back and watch what unfolds.

The article in *The New Yorker* raised a lot of questions about Herzog's methods, one of the more interesting ones being: Is he making a movie or is he on an adventure? Did you ever question that yourself?

You see, I like being on an adventure. I would say, yes, he's on an adventure, with the belief that that will become part of the movie as well. Certainly, with Werner, there's a whole lot more than what is going on the screen. Which is why you can get whole movies made about the making of a Werner Herzog movie... there's a whole world of, like you said, adventure and craziness going on outside the movie.

I want nothing more than heading off to strange places and having an adventure. I never felt with Werner that there's such a strong pull for that adventure that he forgot there was a movie being made. He's very, very passionate about that actual movie and what he's making. He's a very intense man, or he's the most gentle and laid-back you ever met. It's one or the other. There are no in-betweens. He's extreme in that degree.

As long as it's not just posturing or vanity, then I love that. I love seeing people who care very much about what they're doing, and the fights that ensue because of it, or the crazy ideas...you just try it, you know? Just give it a shot. And Werner still has a sense about him... Like you said, is it really fifty-odd movies? And yet there's still this sense about him, like he's trying it for the first time.

How deeply were you put to the test—physically, mentally, your patience?

Ah, I could have been pushed a lot more than I was. I mean, it's not like there aren't...I mean, when I see [costar Steve Zahn] again, there's always great stories to reminisce about—ludicrous situations we'd find ourselves in, sitting in rivers with snakes going down it, or squatting in a patty field for hours on end, or, you know, torrential rains coming down and flooding the whole set, or whatever.

I kind of love getting pushed like that, you know. I love it, and Werner's the man for doing that. He would just keep on pushing and pushing and pushing. There's no limit to how much he'll keep pushing somebody, but he'll do it with himself as well. He'll be in there, you know, head-to-toe covered in clay from crawling around in it one day. He'll be washed down the rapids with us. He'll be coming away with losing toenails. He loves doing that. He just absolutely loves it. He doesn't really want anybody else to have more of an experience than he does. There's definitely a kind of competition going on there. And I was very much up for that. I think there's a great, almost *Boy's Own* idea of struggling through the jungle and coming across snakes and diving into pools and not knowing what's in there and doing things that other people would look at you and think, *You're nuts, why would you ever do that?*

How many chances do you get to fly with a crazy Thai helicopter pilot who's flying a foot above the trees and who is doing this crazy shit you'd never get to do in a helicopter and—not only that—I'm standing outside the helicopter on the rails? Well, I don't want anyone else doing that. I want to be the one doing that.

It occurs to me that Bale, especially in his most memorable performances—whether it's in American Psycho; *or* The Prestige, *in which he plays a magician who goes to absurd lengths for his craft; or* The Machinist, *for which he lost sixty pounds to play a haunted insomniac; or* Harsh Times, *in which he's a violent Gulf War vet returning to the mean streets of LA; or even* Batman Begins, *as a superhero who's a borderline sociopath—is attracted to roles that explore the limits of both character and actor.*

What draws you to a role, especially to such extreme roles, where you have to do such extreme things?

I mean, doesn't everybody have that? It's kind of like being given a dare. Can you go through with it? Can you test yourself, push it, and how far will you go and how far can you go? It's a craving to know the answer to that, you know? I know that I get obsessed with what's right in front of me, and I'll just be thinking about that, and I may look back later on certain things I've done and think, *What was I thinking there?*, you know? I kind of lost the plot a little bit, didn't I? But I know nobody could have convinced me otherwise at the time.

You seem uninterested in attention or fame. You seem like one of the least movie-star-like movie stars that I've come across. How do you get to the level you're at and stay so removed from that part of it?

Maybe just by obsessing about your failings instead of focusing on your strengths. [*Laughs.*] To be honest, I don't know what else to do. What else would I do? You can start prancing around, but you're becoming just a model or something at that point, you know what I mean? I like being comfortable as much as anybody else, but you get too used to that, and you become a right little whining softie. I guess it's just not interesting. What's interesting about it? What is there to that, except for swanning around pretending you're not interested in what anybody else is doing? That sounds boring as hell to me.

With that, the accident is over, and I go off to ride waves, Bale to ride dirt bikes. We'll be seeing a lot of him in the near future, though—if not as one of many Bob Dylans in Todd Haynes's meta-biopic *I'm Not There*, then perhaps in the remake of the Western classic *3:10 to Yuma*, which promises to show off more of the actor's horsemanship. Both come out later this year. And if not there, then surely in *The Dark Knight*, director Christopher Nolan's sequel to *Batman Begins*, which is currently filming. If he isn't careful, the best actor of his generation will also soon be the biggest, but something tells me he'll be careful.

There's only one bit of unfinished business that I feel compelled to address. It's the question I get asked by every woman whom I tell that I've recently interviewed Christian Bale. The question comes accompanied by a raised eyebrow and a sly, carnal grin.

"Well???" they ask.

"Well, what?"

"Well, what was he *like?*"

And then they go on to tell me how they've loved him since *Empire of the Sun*, fell more in love with him in *Swing Kids*, the one about a group of prewar German kids who'd rather dance to the beat of swing music than march to the beat of war drums. And, oh god, they say, "that body in *American Psycho*." And what they mean by the question is: was he just as hot in person?

Well, ladies, here's what I remember:

He had more facial hair than Charlie Chaplin, but less than two out of three members of ZZ Top. His eyebrows were luxurious. His cheekbones were noticeable, but not quite as noticeable as they are in the pictures accompanying this article. His hair was thick, but bordered precariously on mullet-esque beneath the baseball cap. He was tall enough to be commanding, but not tall enough to tower or loom. He wasn't cut enough to chop ice, but I don't think anyone's gonna kick sand in his face. His style? More American Apparel than *American Psycho*.

Would I do him? Well, a good rule is to avoid sex with anyone—no matter how hot—that you wouldn't want to have a conversation with, and as I learned, Bale is someone you do want to have a conversation with. Or as Mr. Herzog says, "You see very handsome actors and they don't have depth. He has so much depth behind what you see on the surface."

"Sean Penn, With His Own Two Eyes"

*A version of this story was originally published
in the* LA Weekly, *September 19, 2007.*

*Author's note: For awhile there, it seemed like Sean Penn was
everywhere—kayaking to the rescue in New Orleans, railing
publically, unapologetically, and sometimes hilariously against the
Bush administration, and releasing* Into the Wild, *a beautiful film
he adapted, directed, and coproduced. I admired Penn's righteous
dissent and his willingness to take action in service of it. On a
September afternoon when we both seemed to need a timeout
from our lives, we cruised around in his battered Range Rover,
smoked cigarettes, shot pool, and discussed what it means to be an
American in opposition.*

> *Let fury have the hour, anger can be power*
> *D'you know that you can use it?*

> —The Clash, "Clampdown"

THE DRIVE FROM OAKLAND to Mill Valley sends you across
the Richmond/San Rafael Bridge. It's worth the four-dollar
toll for its breathtaking views of Mount Tamalpais, the sentinel
of Marin County, and the gilded burgs over which it watches.
Near the end of the bridge is another landmark: San Quentin
State Prison, a place that teases the hard cases locked in there
with a panorama of Mt. Tam that, from the prison yard, feels so

close you'd think you could reach out and touch it. I don't know if that's irony or cruelty, but I do know prisons sure are given prime real estate in these parts. One of Sean Penn's best friends is stuck there in San Quentin, maybe for good, and Penn cites this unfortunate fact as one of his main reasons for choosing to live in this corner of Marin County. He simply wanted to be closer to his friend.

I don't think Penn cared much about being closer to the Acqua Hotel in Mill Valley, where we are to meet, a place that looks like it was dreamed up by a set designer for the James Bond franchise. Even with its backside views of a San Francisco Bay inlet and its sun-splashed interior, the Acqua feels sterile, its elegance—all clean surfaces, unmolested bright walls, lots of light, and sharp lines—contrived. It's tragically hip, and it seems like an odd place to be meeting Sean Penn. It's more like a place one of his characters would inhabit, like the bright and soulless loft Jack Nicholson's bereft Freddy Gale retreats to for booze and bad sex in *The Crossing Guard*.

When Sammy Hagar, the man who achieved the impossible by killing Van Halen, pulls up in a black Maserati and emerges wearing extra-long shorts, bad footwear, and a T-shirt promoting some bunk product or event, and is urgently greeted by a severe blond publicist type straight out of central casting, the whole thing starts to feel absurd. I poke my cigarette into the air, thinking some dimension will surely burst. It doesn't.

Actually, it does. About fifteen minutes later, when… well, picture if you will a sleepless and forlorn journalist chain smoking in front of the all-glass doors of the David Lynchian Acqua Hotel. A plume of smoke fills the foreground just as a beater of a Land Rover rambles into the parking lot a little too fast and all but crashes into a tight parking space. As the smoke dissipates, Sean Penn tumbles out of the Land Rover in worn work boots, jeans, and a gray T-shirt. He approaches with the athletic grace of a cat, all body parts in motion at once. He's muscular like a construction worker. His hair is wild and magnificent, and there are deep crags around his cowboy eyes. The first words out of his mouth are:

"Can I bum one of your cigarettes? I'm sorry, I left mine back at the house."

"No problem," you say, and then, for no good reason, or because you have no impulse control: "I'm getting divorced."

"Shit," he says, exhaling and looking you in the eye. "I'm sorry about that. That's a bear."

Sammy Hagar should watch that entrance in slow motion, repeatedly.

I'm up here interviewing Penn because a film he wrote and directed is imminent. But instead of settling into a hotel couch for the standard grilling, we finish our cigarettes, and Penn suggests we take quick leave of the Acqua. He spent the previous day— beginning at 5:00 a.m. and ending at 6:00 p.m.—rafting the North Fork of the American River and is still hungry and a bit worn out. We head for a local sushi joint in a civilized Marin County commercial center that would be a strip mall anyplace else. On the way there, Penn drives in a manner I'd describe as intent but not overly aggressive. I study the ink on his arms, which I had noticed immediately upon greeting. It's authentic old-school work, almost of the prison variety, and a refreshing contrast to the rote tribal decorations that have become de rigueur for frat boys and young Hollywood alike. (Is there a difference?)

Penn's new movie, *Into the Wild*, based on the Jon Krakauer book of the same name, tracks the journey of a young man away from the conventions of his birthright and into a deep, deep wilderness that is both literal and ontological. It's an epic and ultimately fatal quest, one that Penn has rendered onto screen in ways that feel more relatable and intimate than Krakauer's account, which, as a mostly journalistic undertaking, couldn't help but keep its protagonist at a short arm's length. I read the book and saw the film, but it was the film that made me feel like I got to know Chris McCandless. It's touching and heartbreaking and infinitely more accessible than Penn's previous efforts as the writer and director of such dark and troubling ruminations as *The Indian Runner* and *The Crossing Guard* and as director of *The Pledge*.

Penn began pursing *Into the Wild* almost immediately after the book came out in 1996. Securing the rights was no easy task; a family and all the legacy they have left of their son were at stake. After reading the book, Penn found out a lot of Hollywood folks were trying to nail it down. He got in touch with Krakauer's agent, who got him in touch with the McCandless family—father Walt, mother Billie, and Chris's sister, Corine.

"Jon flew to Virginia, and I flew to Virginia, and we all met there," Penn says. "After two meetings they had mutually decided on me. I was going to do a third kind of close-the-deal session, and I was leaving [for the airport] at five in the morning, and I went to the shower. I got a call and Robin [Wright Penn, his wife] got me out of the shower, and it was Billie, the mother. She had a dream that Chris did not want the movie made. '*Do not get on the plane*.'"

"So, I didn't. And I remember repeating this, because it was the truth—I said to her that if I didn't believe in dreams, I would not make movies. So I left it at that."

Penn stayed in touch with the family over the years. When he was in New Orleans last year filming *All the King's Men*, he got a call from the family's representative asking if he was still interested in making the film.

"That was a decade later," Penn says.

This film, and the book before it, contains a subplot to the narrative of Chris McCandless' journey—one of family secrets and dysfunctions, many of which fueled the young man's uncompromising and, in the end, lethal ideology or idealism (you decide). That families have secrets and dysfunctions a young man or woman might struggle to come to terms with is no revelation. What is a revelation, though, is the courage the McCandless family shows in turning its dark underside toward the light so that we may learn whatever we will from Chris's tale. That exposure is particularly raw and unabashed in the film.

"It is tougher in the movie," Penn agrees. "It is something, you know—they struggled with it. I know. But I felt, it is my speculation, that there is a degree of penance involved in their decision, and I think it is a brave and selfless decision. But they struggle with it still. They go in and out, and I just got very good news that they are coming to the LA premiere, which really makes me happy. I'm just grateful to them for seeing it through…revisiting it in such a loud and public way."

This film means a lot to Penn. Not just because he wants to repay the trust given him by the McCandless family and by Jon Krakauer, which he does, but also because, well into a career as one of the most, if not the most respected actor of his generation—though one who can't guarantee box office—and after directing three well-regarded movies that never quite transcended cult status, Penn would like to know somebody's out there.

"I really want a lot of people to see it," he tells me. "I want it to mean something to people. I am going to feel that I have exercised my last piece of language in finding out if I am completely alone in this world or not if it is not responded to. So I've got some investment on that level."

Penn tells me this near the end of our time together, a time during which we will smoke a pack of cigarettes, shoot pool, and talk about everything from the role of language in civil society, to the importance of rites of passage, to what it means to be a citizen. Look, I know what you're thinking, because everyone is immediately thinking something about Sean Penn. But I want to tell you: I think you'll be surprised.

◆◆◆

I'M GOING TO BE honest with you about where I'm going with this: I like this guy already. A lot. He had me before we even met, when last spring he made a speech in which he called Dick Cheney and Condoleezza Rice "villainously and criminally obscene people, obscene human beings, incompetent to fulfill your own self-serving agenda, while tragically neglectful and destructive of ours and our country's."

Actually, he had me way before that (but I really like that one), back when the initial Iraq war drums were beating and anyone with an ounce of intelligence and insight could predict the looming disaster that has since unfolded beyond our worst imaginations. Penn was one of the first Hollywood voices to speak out. On October 19, 2002, he published an open letter to President Bush in *The Washington Post* lamenting his "simplistic and inflammatory view of good and evil." And he called out the lapdog media that has been complicit in this calamity: "Take a close look at your most vehement media supporter. See the fear in their eyes as their loud voices of support ring out with that historically disastrous undercurrent of rage and panic masked as 'straight, tough talk.'"

Penn's opposition to this regime has been uncensored and unrelentingly memorable ever since, whether it's fishing old people out of flooded New Orleans—something for which he earned wide criticism as a PR hound, despite the insistence of New Orleans historian and author Douglas Brinkley that his efforts were genuine and responsible for saving forty or so people— or writing (quite well) about his experiences in Iraq and Iran, visiting with Venezuelan President Hugo Chavez, or posting his frequent tirades against this administration's chronic criminality.

For me, his protests exist somewhere between metaphor and metaphysics. And I'm all for it. But it seems to make a lot of people uncomfortable, as if metaphors actually exist that are too strong for declaiming the calamities of the Bush era.

One of Penn's more priceless moments came during a speech he delivered at a town meeting held last March by Democratic Congresswoman Barbara Lee, who represents much of the East Bay. Addressing the president, Penn said, "We cower as you point your fingers telling us to support our troops. You and the smarmy pundits in your pocket—those who bathe in the moisture of your soiled and blood-soaked underwear—can take that noise and shove it."

Forget whether you agree with him or not (and how couldn't you?), how about a little appreciation for the sheer poetry of it? That speech, and those lines in particular, earned him a rare moment of comic relief on *The Colbert Report*, during which he and Stephen Colbert engaged in a Meta-Free-Phor-All judged by former poet laureate Robert Pinksy. Penn won the contest ten thousand points to one by working the soiled-and-blood-soaked imagery into every metaphor, whether the category was world leaders or love. ("Love is a fragile flower opening to the first warmth of spring whose crimson petals are not as red as George Bush's soiled and blood-soaked underwear.")

The bit was hilarious and has become an Internet favorite. But the line was actually a late addition to his speech. "I was on the freeway, kind of going over the speech in my head, and I just started thinking about those guys, and I got angrier and angrier. I pulled over on the side of the road and that was the last thing I added to it."

The Penn of *The Colbert Report*, the self-deprecating one, seems genuine. As I see him today, he appears to be a far cry from Jimmy Markum, the vengeful father he won an Oscar for playing in *Mystic River*, or the popular caricature of a thuggish celeb out to bash any hapless paparazzo who gets in his way. He's engaging, thoughtful, and, despite a physical presence that suggests a coiled cobra, gentle. We take a table in the back of the restaurant and order a modest amount of sushi and talk while chewing. The staff here seems to know him, and he treats everyone courteously.

In a way, *The Colbert Report* send-up was perfect because the show operates as a parody of the phony journalism we're fed from so many sources, including major networks. Penn himself is a sharp amateur journalist. He has traveled to Iraq twice since the war began and wrote about both experiences for the *San Francisco Chronicle*. His second account, from a January 2004 visit, contains this caveat about the challenges he faced selling the trip to his family: "My reputation within our own home is one of impulsiveness, hubris, and an overall bloated sense of my own survival instincts. Of course, this is entirely unfounded, but we'll leave that for another day."

The reports are well-observed and non-polemical, rich in detail. One observation proved particularly astute: "It is a compelling experience to have been in Baghdad just one year ago, where not a single Iraqi expressed to me opinions outside the Baathist party lines, and just one year later, when so many express their opinions and so many opinions compete for attention. Where the debate is similar to that in the United States is over the way in which the business of war will administer the opportunity for peace and freedom, and the reasonable expectation of Iraqi self-rule."

While reading his accounts, it occurred to me that Penn has an abiding respect for the practice of journalism.

"Yes, you know, if there is going to be a turn," he tells me, "it is going to come out of that."

I ask if he's disappointed in the level of journalism that's been practiced over the past several years.

"I'm disappointed in actors who become models and journalists who become contest-show hosts," he says. "I feel what disappoints me the most is somebody who can do something well and does not do it. The people kind of letting the culture lead them instead of leading the culture. I mean, freedom of speech exists in North Korea—if you trust your wife. But where it counts is with journalists... I mean, it's not the domain of journalists, is the problem. It's the domain of all of us, but where I worry about it the most is in journalism."

Penn, of course, received a ration of shit for his much-publicized recent visit to Venezuela as Hugo Chavez's guest. He won't talk about it now because he's writing a piece on it, except to say "it was a fascinating trip" and that things there, including the press clampdown, aren't quite what we're led to believe. Why, many have asked, would Penn play guest to Hugo Chavez and risk being seen as naïf? I believe the answer is that he is not a proponent of received knowledge. Take Chris McCandless's sojourn, for example. Even though it was well-documented in the Krakauer book, Penn took it upon himself in researching his screenplay to retrace much of McCandless's path. He spent time in the Anza-Borrego Desert, visited seminal characters in McCandless's life, and even made a somewhat harrowing trip to the Alaskan wilds, where he crossed, with Krakauer, the river that penned McCandless in when he'd finally had enough and wanted to return to civilization—a river that, as much as anything, played a fatal role in the young man's story. The through line, though, whether it be post-deluge New Orleans or post-invasion Iraq, is that Penn is going to see for himself.

He makes this clear to me when I suggest that his public tirades, and such indelible images as him rowing a boat through the streets of New Orleans, plucking people from the flood, are a form of political theater.

"I'm not that smart," he says. "I have noticed some things have happened that are working that way, or firing that way. But no,

I'm a guy who watches a little television, gets pissed off, and decides I am pissed off because I don't know enough about it to make a good argument. But my gut knows they are full of shit, and then I go out and force myself to learn by getting in the middle of it."

When did Penn the actor become Penn the political animal? It would be easy to blame George Bush, if blame is what you'd like to do. But Penn cautions against such an easy read. He tells me he'd been politically active for a while before the Bush presidency but felt it better to maintain some separation between politics and art. That changed when he had kids.

"I grew up in a politically engaged family. My father [actor and director Leo Penn] was blacklisted, and he was a very strong, patriotic guy nonetheless," he says. "I felt that in lieu of the silence of what was going on in my field at that time, particularly related to the Iraq war that was about to happen, that I was not going to go to bed proud just on the faith of what good work I do politically anymore, because I did not think we had time for that. And I am still not sure we have time."

There is, of course, silence, and then there's what Penn does. His public denouncements are saturated with a rage that frightens some, while others witness these performances and think, *Fuck yeah, I'll take another dish of that*. But there is something more than urgency feeding his swing-for-the-fences activism—something internal.

"I think you got to go with where your voice comes from," Penn tells me as softly as the breeze is coming off the Bay on this post-card day. He exhales a large plume of smoke (we've moved outside by now so we can take minutes off our lives unfettered) and adds, "I have largely been fueled on anger. There is no question about it."

I ask where that anger comes from.

"I am one of these people who went through a series of demon doors of my own creation. It was just like, I mean the only thing I can think of is that I have put much of it in *The Indian Runner*, you know, where there is a generation of us that grew up every day as my kids are today—but we had real coverage of the Vietnam War. It was real. It was my neighbors' older brothers and shit. I love that fucking Mustang, or maybe it was a Firebird, that is now up on the blocks in the garage of my buddy's house because his brother, whose car it was, had to drain all the oil before he went overseas and then he comes back dead, and I am seeing things that are related on television. I was growing up in the Valley at that time, and we had six or eight kids on our street that went off and were killed, and they were not kids to me at the time. They were adults to me, but they were the coolest adults on the planet because we were all about go-carts and motorcycles, and we were younger. They were just these cool guys, and they were all slaughtered."

So, are you suggesting that anger can be power?

"Yes, but you can't live alone," he says. "There has to be balance. I could see an idealistic movement, if it just had a lot of people agreeing to go with it. Dennis Kucinich *will* be president. All we have to do is vote for him.

"You know, I am shamefully Johnny-come-lately to it, in a way, but once you've stepped into the arena, my own experience is there's no going back."

◆◆◆

SEAN PENN'S FAMILY MOVED from the Valley to out near Point Dume when he was still a kid. It was the country part of Malibu back then, and he says he had a "Huck Finn kind of existence with surfing" growing up. Penn says he can handle an eight-to-ten-foot Pipeline on a good day if it isn't too crowded.

"I am comfortable in ten-foot surf in most places," he tells me. "After that, I watch from the beach."

I tell him that five-foot is about my cutoff.

"Well, that's the best, the most fun, three-to-five-foot perfect waves. My favorite place still today in the world is the Ranch."

The Ranch is the legendary surf spot north of Santa Barbara on untrammeled, privately held land. It's one of the most beautiful areas in the world. I have been fortunate enough to have surfed it with Dana Brown, son of Bruce Brown, the man responsible for *Endless Summer*. Dana himself directed the wonderful *Step Into Liquid* a few years back. It was at the Ranch where Penn made one of his most significant discoveries.

"I had my fourteenth birthday there in a tent for four days with a buddy of mine," he tells me. "There are two things that happened. I fell in love with the Ranch, but the other thing is, I fell in love with mustard. You know how you get a hunger like nothing else when you're surfing? Well, we had run out of our food supply pretty fast down there. One night, we were surfing Rights and Lefts [surf breaks]. We camped right in front of Utah's just down the beach, and some guys were camped down the beach and they're making hot dogs. I always hated mustard. So, they go, 'You want some hot dogs?' We came running up there and they had already put mustard on it, and I was like, 'No, no, no!' But I was so hungry I ate one anyway and then I was like, 'Aahhhh.' Ever since then, I ate a lot of mustard."

For some reason, though, it seems like there's always a dark side looming on the edge of Southern California paradise, and it soon began to envelop the beach culture Penn grew up around. By the seventies, Mike Hynson, the golden-boy star of *Endless Summer*, was battling with substance abuse, running afoul of the law, and even ending up on Nixon's enemies list. Miki Dora, the dark prince of Malibu, was off on his outlaw escapades. A lot of Penn's friends became casualties.

"They found a reason to get into so much trouble and kill themselves and kill others," Penn says. "It was the weirdest thing.

One of my best friends from that time, whenever we got drunk, that is all we'd talk about. It's all those guys that are gone."

I ask if it was just the times, or something else.

"Well, four out of five of the things were drug related, if not drug overdoses. It was criminality based on drugs, mostly," he says. "Yeah, it was the times."

Penn was lucky enough to have escaped to New York at age seventeen to pursue theater and get on the path he is still on.

"The other stuff happened as we were becoming adults. My life moved away, so that stuff happened later to those guys. It was not part of my life. But those years, certainly, that I had were mostly positive. It was a rite-of-passage period. It was colorful at the time."

Rites of passage are important to Penn, not in a facile, symbolic sense, but in the way that men and women test themselves and their boundaries to find a better sense of themselves and the truths and principles by which they are going to live their lives. It's a theme that runs through all the films he's written and/or directed, and it's what drew him to the plight of Chris McCandless, a young man who, if nothing else, was searching for a code by which to live.

"The sense of traditional rites of passage are gone in our male culture, and I think increasingly there's a hunger for it in our female culture as well," he tells me. "And so there is not a rite of passage unless you create one for yourself. You never make that next step."

And we become stuck in an infantile culture?

"Yes, exactly," Penn says. "So the child-man who is also an economic slave goes home exhausted. He has worked his second shift in a day. His wife is now doing her shift, or something. The kids are screaming in the other room and he would rather watch Bill O'Reilly criticize Paris Hilton than think about something. It's self-perpetuating. So I think with Chris McCandless, it was a young person taking advantage of his own wisdom, because young people still have that available."

It seems clear that we're going to have to make a move soon because I'm almost out of cigarettes, and these are the types of talks that cigarettes were made for.

"I am now returning to the philosophies I had when I was seventeen or eighteen years old," he continues. "That is when I *knew*, and I was militant about it. The militancy is what makes you leave them, because that is wrong—you're a fundamentalist-idealist, and you are bulletproof. When you are real and combine that philosophy with some humility, which comes with being forty-seven years old...I become a more mature version of [that seventeen- or eighteen-year-old], and here is how: The rite of passage is humility, one way or another. The biggest strengths in things that ever happened to me were humiliations, and humiliation is a term we always use as a bad thing. It is not a bad thing, and it contains the word, *humility*. You add humility to that kind of idealism. Then you put tolerance with idealism, and it makes you interested, and that is what leads to other things that are good things."

I ask Penn, a man who saw his father and brother die too soon and who has had his share of public struggles with the delicate art of growing up, what he considers to be his own rites of passage.

"Well, in my case, I'd say the closest thing to a catharsis was having children. My rites of passage when I was a young man were in the water. It is not the only way to do it, but it is the way that I found myself doing it that related to Chris McCandless, not in such a long-term sort of spiritual search, but definitely the most life-changing things were the times when I put my life on the edge. I don't think it's because of the life on the edge, literally. I think it's because of the humility that comes with dancing with something that shows itself to be clearly bigger than you are."

I tell him that I had that experience not long ago when I had to be pulled from the water by a seventeen-year-old girl.

"Hey, you know," he laughs, "salvation comes in small packages. Surprising packages."

♦♦♦

PENN'S MAIN MUSE IS language. And his love of language is evident in the journalism he's practiced—the attention to details, the facility with structure—but even more so in the films he's written and directed. *The Indian Runner*, *The Crossing Guard*, and *Into the Wild* (and also *The Pledge*, which he directed and which, like *Into the Wild*, was adapted from a book)—watching those films, the thing that struck me the most was that they were first and foremost *written* works, an element much of modern filmmaking lacks.

He cites movies like *His Girl Friday* and *A Streetcar Named Desire*, even with its atmosphere of working-class melodrama, as examples of an era when language reigned supreme in filmmaking, and our movie-watching experience was the richer for it. Penn tells me his literary heroes are Steinbeck, Saroyan, McCarthy, García Márquez, Dostoyevsky, Ford ("Oh, and Krakauer," he adds, laughing), and that it is in the tradition of language that we may find some measure of hope and salvation.

"With more access to language with television and now the Internet and everything else, the kind of lazy speech between friends is what people are now doing formally," Penn explains. "This is how we talk, and those abbreviations are part of the culture. There is no culture in the language of the culture."

He asks me if I have ever read George Washington's *Rules of Civility*, and it isn't a rhetorical question. No, I confess.

"He wrote that when he was about thirteen years old. It is shocking," says Penn. "Television, computers, radio, what else do you have? Name it—the industrial revolution, the technological revolution, and all this stuff, and a thirteen-year-old without any of that wrote *Rules of Civility*. Dostoyevsky wrote *Crime and Punishment* without any of that. You know, without any of that. That stuff is not the answer. I think tradition is part of the answer.

"But we do not even value language when we talk to each other anymore—this is where tradition matters. It is our best song that we can sing for each other. So if all we are going to sing is da, da, da, da, da, da...then there is no dancing in the culture, because there is no dancing in the language," he continues, and given the levels of nicotine that are coursing through our neuroreceptors, I'm not about to stop him. "And so, the thing that I miss in my life more than anything—and by the way, I feel markedly guilty of it myself—is that we do not walk out the door in the morning with a culture that has a traditionally steep value of language."

I ask Penn if he sees himself primarily as a writer, a hunch I'd come to while watching his films.

"Yeah, I think that's most of what it is," he says.

"Did you ever write a novel?" I ask, on another hunch.

"I played with one, got pretty far into it, and it burned up in this fire. At that time, I still wasn't able to use a computer and I was just typing on an old typewriter. I had all the pages stacked up on my desk and it burned right on down. It was very nuanced, and the language of it is not something I could try to repeat. I've played with a couple ideas that I think I will eventually try."

"You're a good writer," I say.

"Oh, thanks. I like doing it. I like when I catch a wave."

♦♦♦

WHEN WE'RE PERILOUSLY CLOSE to the end of my smokes, Penn takes me to his house later in the afternoon. It's up a few windy, tree-lined roads in a burg that is upscale in that tasteful mid–Marin County way. Think Brentwood sans the ostentation. On the way over, Penn fields a few calls and gives me some advice about my pending divorce. It is mostly of the try-to-be-a-gentleman-and-don't-succumb-to-the-temptation-to-blame-yourself sort. Oh, and get some Ambien. Nothing revelatory, but I appreciate the tone, heartfelt and free of empty platitudes. Standing out among the nondescript family trucksters in Penn's driveway are a Porsche and a Ford Shelby GT500, if I'm not mistaken.

"That's my baby," Penn grins mischievously, as we pass by the Shelby. A perfect quarter-pipe for skateboarding sits in the middle of what was once intended to be a basketball or tennis court.

His house is beautiful, of course, tastefully decorated in an elegant country style. When we enter, his teenage son walks by, a blur of blond hair and limbs, already bigger than anyone else in the house. From somewhere in the deep interior, I hear the disembodied voice of Penn's wife, Robin Wright Penn, shouting instructions as to where Penn might find the keys to one of his cars. It all seems so normal.

Penn is eager to show me the editing house where he cut *Into the Wild*, which is on the second level. It looks like a really elaborate home-entertainment center to me. Of more interest is the pool table in the back of the room.

"Wanna shoot a game?" I ask.

Thankfully, Penn has a pack of American Spirits nearby. We light up and I break, sinking a high ball. I make a couple more shots. Penn raises that one eyebrow in the way he's famous for and squints through his cigarette smoke. He misses. We talk about the beauty of Eddie Vedder, who did a gorgeous soundtrack for *Into the Wild* ("I love that guy," says Penn), and the decision to cast Emile Hirsch as Chris McCandless. Hirsch caught Penn's eye in *The Lords of Dogtown*, for which he played the seminal skate punk, Jay Adams.

"It was right in my era, and I knew those guys peripherally and everything at the time," says Penn. "It felt pretty genuine to me."

Despite the spiritual and intellectual quest that was at the core of McCandless's restlessness, playing him would require someone capable of such Herculean physical tests as running rapids in a canoe, hiking brutal desert climates, packing into the Alaskan wilderness, and basically shedding an amount of weight that would give as adept a weight-loser as Christian Bale pause.

"We met. I knew Emile could act the part, I got that feeling pretty fast, but I did not know if he could act it for eight months under the conditions that we were going to be facing," says Penn. "And he was amazing. He really had to live a monkey's life for the eight months."

I make a couple more shots, and Penn jokes about me being a pool sharp. He sinks a couple and then I finish off the table, save the eight ball, which is stuck near the corner pocket behind one of the many, many balls he has left on the table. I take a gamble and jump his ball, miss mine, and scratch the cue ball. Penn wins.

"That was great," he laughs. "Perfect."

Indeed, a lesson in humility.

Fucking With Drew Barrymore

Originally published in the LA Weekly, *April 22, 2009.*

Author's note: I was (and am) a big fan of the girl-power vibe in the Charlie's Angels *movies produced by Barrymore's production company, Flower Films. I kind of liked her style in general. She had a real up-with-life thing going on despite being raised by wolves. When I met her at her office, she was finishing up a phone call related to her directorial debut. Exhausted from some personal-life issues going on at the time, I took the liberty of lying down on her couch. If I recall correctly, her golden retriever joined me there, welcoming me to Barrymore's world with a few sloppy licks.*

DREW BARRYMORE LOVES *FUCKING*. Mostly it happens when she gets excited. And she gets excited about a lot of stuff—movies, music, historical icons, roller derby, challenging herself. She likes fucking so much, she starts up with it before the interview. Like when I present her with an ancient Lou Reed cassette I find in a crumb-infested corner of my car while searching desperately for a tape because I seem to have forgotten one for my recorder, and Barrymore insists that no human hand can keep up with how much and how fast she talks.

"No way," she says, when I hand her the Lou Reed. "This is the greatest gift ever. I *fucking* love cassettes."

Dylan Tichenor, the guy editing *Whip It*, Barrymore's directorial debut, and who also edited *There Will Be Blood*,

Brokeback Mountain, The Royal Tannenbaums, Magnolia, and *Boogie Nights,* to name a few, is "fucking dope."

At one point, she's so excited that she interrupts a discussion about *Donnie Darko*—the 2001 film, written and directed by a then-unknown kid named Richard Kelly, which Barrymore got made when nobody else could or would—just to start fucking with the *Weekly*.

"If I could say one periodical that is my favorite and most important, and I live or die and breathe from and can't *fucking* function without, it's the *LA Weekly*."

By my calculations, Barrymore drops an F-bomb every two minutes. "I'm a dirty girl," she confesses with a sly grin.

I have to admit, I'm a bit taken aback when I encounter Ms. Barrymore on a shimmering Friday afternoon at the postproduction house a stone's throw from the Arclight Theater, where she's overseeing the editing on *Whip It.* And it's not because of the ribald language she deliciously slathers on her speech like mustard on a hot dog. Even the dirty-girl joke isn't dirty. It's sweet, and the slyness is about inclusion, not about using sex as a weapon. Her F-bombs are about enthusiasm, not aggression.

What surprises me is how tiny she is. Greeting me in some sort of workout pants that look like she picked them up in the eighties and decided to remain loyal to, a concert T-shirt, and a surplus-store army jacket, with her hair undone and no makeup, Barrymore seems smaller and more vulnerable than I'd expected given her oversized personality. And she's very skinny, most likely a symptom of the stress she's been under while directing her first film and having recently tackled the enormous role of "Little" Edie Beale for HBO's dramatic rendering of *Grey Gardens.*

"I've never been so scared in my life," says Barrymore, of taking on "Little" Edie. "She's such an icon, and it's the scariest part. That and directing are the two scariest things I've ever done in my life. If I haven't given myself a cancer ulcer, I'll be shocked because I've never been more fucking freaked out than in the last two years of my life."

Grey Gardens is based on the famous Maysles brothers' 1975 documentary about "Big" Edith Bouvier Beale and her daughter, "Little" Edith. An appetite for the eccentric (some would say tragically so) mother and daughter and the East Hampton mansion where they went to seed, while clinging to their affectations like life preservers, has been fed over the years with numerous books, more documentaries, a Broadway musical, etc. And now, posthumously, thanks to HBO, these two collateral Kennedys have crossed over from a subcultural obsession to the full-blown stardom they so desired, perhaps delusionally, during their lives.

◆◆◆

LIKE JACKIE O, IF you'll allow a minor comparison to Little Edie's cousin, Barrymore has also been part of the public firmament for so long she seems a permanent part of the culture. Think about it: twenty-eight years ago, she played the adorable Gertie in her godfather's, Steven Speilberg's, *ET: The Extraterrestrial.* She was seven then. We've watched her grow up and go through well-documented trials and triumphs along the way. (And I'd certainly count her table-dance and boob-flash birthday gift to David Letterman back in 1995—a spontaneous eruption of the goofy, everywoman sexiness that is one of her trademarks—as one of her triumphs.)

She is the girl next door, who became a preteen megastar and substance abuser, who was institutionalized and went to rehab when most girls were just getting their periods. She emancipated herself at fifteen and before she could legally drink, she'd already gained the sort of perspective that would set her on the path to being a role model for female empowerment. Yes, I really said that. On the one hand, I'm talking about how Barrymore started her own production company, Flower Films, with partner Nancy

Juvonen when she was just twenty because she knew by then that she wanted to be in Hollywood but not of it.

"I loved all aspects of filmmaking. I studied it so much that I just kind of clicked and I was, like, *producing, producing, producing, hmm.* So, I decided to start a company and on a guttural instinct I asked this woman to start it with me," she explains. "She's very organized, and I'm very disorganized, but we had the same creative tastes and intentions and approach to life. I had all this background and experience, but we both said let's create like a college for how you [get to] be a producer. And we're definitely not going to read any books written on it because that's all going to come from, like, Hollywood people, and we definitely don't want to party with Tinseltown and wine and dine—we want to go to school for how we would make movies. And that's what we did."

So they logged years—really years—watching documentaries, studying film, reading scripts, meeting with agents, making lists of writers and directors they wanted to work with. After starring in and unofficially helping hits such as *Scream* and *Ever After* get made, Barrymore's Flower Films debuted as a full-blown production company with the modest back-to-high-school hit, *Never Been Kissed*. A year later, Barrymore also starred in the company's monster *Charlie's Angels*.

On the other hand, though, I'm talking about an underlying message discernible in most Barrymore films, going back to the Cinderella redux, *Ever After*, which says, basically, girls don't have to take shit.

"What excited me most about that movie was that [it showed] the way I feel about life," says Barrymore. "Don't wait to be rescued, rescue yourself. I was so excited to do that movie. I was, like, *yeah, man.*"

I confess that I still get verklempt at all the girl-power shit in the *Charlie's Angels* films.

"I'm so glad you feel that way," she says, delighted. "That's all I wanted to come across. I love people who love each other and have a lack of competitiveness, but when they band together, there's no stopping them. Oh, and P.S., if you can't laugh at yourself, yeck, vomit."

◆◆◆

IF HER ENTIRELY HUMAN, preternaturally approachable persona is a put-on, it'll take a keener eye than mine to discern how. For example, when I succumb to exhaustion and go prone on her leather couch seconds after introductions are made, the first laughing words out of her mouth are, "Please, make yourself comfortable." When I bolt upright, she insists that I stay down. Then, her ancient golden retriever, Flossie, who once rescued her from a house fire, ambles over and starts licking my hands.

I take that as a sign and from my back ask her about this movie *Whip It*, which she directed and is working mightily to finish up for a fall release.

"In a nutshell (and I can make a good story sound bad whereas my partner, Nan, can make a bad story sound good), it's about a girl, played by Ellen Page, who lives in a small town and is battling her world—her family has a sort of a set of ideas of what your life is supposed to be—and she finds this Austin roller derby team. The movie is really about finding your tribe out in the world. It's not about winning or losing. It's about being yourself and being okay."

When I tell her my grandmother, like the characters in *Whip It*, was a roller derby girl, she says, "Get the fuck out, that's awesome!"

Barrymore plays derby demon Smashley Simpson, and the story fits with a credo she's pursued in both her films and her life.

"It's a little bit of be your own superhero. I was a girl who never believed that girls couldn't do what boys can do. And

I don't believe in being repressed, or 'no,' or that your dreams have limitations. And whatever people told me or society or anything that got in the way, or was tearing away at that idea, I just never let it. I think that's very, very true to derby. It's, like, this is who I am. I don't care if it has to come out in another form and an alter ego, but I want to go out there and kick ass and have fun and be theatrical and capable while I'm fucking doing it and have a good time and party. It's this whole culture, and the metaphor of it is so beautiful and interesting, and I dig it and agree with it.

"That's just the derby part of the film," she says. "It's also got a lot of comedy and a lot of drama because if you're not laughing through life, you're fucked, and if you don't explore the heartaches of falling in love and getting your heart broken or the struggles you go through with your family in order to try and make it work. There's drama in life and there's bad-ass action and I just love all those things and I wanted to incorporate them all into one film."

In case you haven't noticed, with Barrymore, words come in waves and it's a testament to her charm that you want to put them in your pocket and take them home with you, like seashells after a day at the beach.

Meanwhile, the film playing now on HBO is a bit of a revelation. Barrymore's performance in *Grey Gardens* delivers on the depth and maturity she hinted at in her brief turn as the empathetic teacher, Karen Pomeroy in *Donnie Darko*. One of that film's most gripping scenes is when Pomeroy leaves her class to go outside to have a private moment with God during which all she can do is scream, "Yes, *fuck*."

"Richard actually took that from a moment I had after we met with a studio, because I was so fucking disgusted by what they said and what their vision of the movie was. I was just like *FUUUUUCK*. So, we finally got to make it with people who let us make it the way we wanted to, and God bless them for it."

I tell her that scene changed my perception of her as an actor. She gets it.

"I think for as much as I'm so supposedly accessible, people don't really know me. I think it's funny, and I'm kind of glad, because then I go and have my own private life, even though I don't really get to have one, and the *Donnie Darko* of it all, that's a huge part of who I really am."

Despite that, Barrymore had to do everything but stalk *Grey Gardens* director Michael Sucsy to get the part.

"I've beat down the door for every opportunity I've gotten, or I created it for myself. I love a good fight because I don't believe in things that are just handed to you. It doesn't feel right to me. Nothing's happened like that," she says. "This was that thing where I was, like, beyond crossing a line where I might, like, get arrested. I didn't want to personally upset this person too much, but I was, like, *I have to do this*. I hounded. I finally got a meeting with [Sucsy]—he didn't even want to take a meeting with me. I came with a binder this thick, annotated, highlighted, researched, on her, her life. I knew her school curriculum. I knew her class schedule at Miss Porter's. And I was, like, I've got an overriding theme of what she is and who she is and that is a walking contradiction. Everything in the next moment will totally oppose what she just did or said."

To prepare for the role, Barrymore took diction lessons for a year and half, transforming the ways she speaks from her natural mien ("...like Moon Zappa. If you want to cast me as Spicoli's girlfriend, I'm your guy.") to Edie Beale's more formal, Yankee diction. She also cut herself off from friends, family, and technology for months.

"I told Michael, I'll give up my life for this, and I'll do what's right for her, which is I'll shut out the world, because she decided to shut out the world. And I'm very outgoing. I love my friends, I'm totally social, and I want to live like her, so I understand what it really feels like."

To keep herself company, of sorts, she composed letters to herself on an old typewriter.

"I wrote manifestos about how I'm a fraud and I'm naked in a snowstorm and everybody's laughing at me because they see the fucking joke. I'm a joke," she says, laughing at herself. "I had nothing to do at night. I was going crazy."

◆◆◆

IF YOU HAVEN'T SEEN the film yet, I daresay you will also be taken aback by Ms. Barrymore. It's a powerful, transformative performance. One in which she busts through what you might think you know about her and what she's capable of.

When you think about it, Barrymore's lived a lot in her thirty-four years, and if you can imagine it, she just seems to be coming into her own. The Hollywood girl who put the girlie in girl power, who grew up in the public eye, turned into woman when we weren't looking.

"My struggles were the best thing that ever happened to me, just because they made me so humble and grateful, and I think that everybody should have it all taken away at some point so that they never forget it," she says. "When I was, like, thirteen and got locked up in an institution because my mother stuck me in it and all this bad shit happened and I went off the deep end and blah, blah, blah, that was my important lifetime revelation—that one must always conduct oneself with humility, grace, and gratitude."

Some would say that runs contrary to the prevailing Hollywood attitude.

"Well, fuck that," she laughs

Monster Out Of The Box
A Sandow Birk Omnibus

Originally published in The Surfer's Journal, *August, 2009.*

Author's note: Sandow Birk was in the middle of a major, global blasphemy when Scott Hulet, one of the West Coast's great cultural anthropologists, commissioned this piece. Birk's American Qur'an made a lot of people nervous when his gallerist, Eleana Del Rio, started showing the first of the suras he'd meticulously transcribed and then adorned with richly illustrated scenes from contemporary Americana. The Koran proscribes illustrations of its texts. Some wondered why do it? Why show it? American Qur'an has since traveled the world and been hailed as a masterpiece. Back then, Birk was hitting his stride as an artist of consequence. Now, he fits comfortably in the long tradition of major West Coast artists who follow their muse and damn the torpedoes.

THE GUEST OF HONOR is dressed in slacks, sensible shoes, and a button-down shirt that was possibly ironed. Handsome in a retro, California beach-boy way, with hair neater than a dry gin martini, he looks more like someone who stepped out of a Jan and Dean song than a heretic stoking the flames of fatwa. Still, the woman with the salt-and-pepper hair, turquoise jewelry, and the pack of American Spirit cigarettes in her overcoat pocket is palpably agitated. She's pretty much taken over the question-and-answer session.

She is one of a couple dozen Otis Art Institute alumni gathered on a comfortable autumn evening at the Koplin Del Rio gallery in Culver City. They're there to both celebrate their unlikely star graduate and, as it turns out, to confront his most recent project. The woman with salt-and-pepper hair wants to know some things about the guest of honor and this project, a third of which is hanging from the gallery walls. She wants to know how it came to be, what the hell he was thinking, and was he aware of the potential ramifications.

The guest of honor, the artist Sandow Birk, patiently and politely tells the story: His travels to Muslim countries—surf trips to places like Indonesia and Morocco—made him curious. This curiosity led to a personal exploration of a document that's played almost no historic role in our cultural and political landscape until fairly recently. Now it's damned near center stage. Birk simply wanted to know what the fuss was all about.

As for what he was thinking, Birk admits to having thought more about the consequences of this project than perhaps any other in his increasingly ambitious oeuvre. And yes, he's aware that some might find what he's doing here provocative. And yes, he knows that in many Muslim countries the consequences would be grave indeed.

"But," he starts to say, and something changes in the laid-back, unassumingly polite man. He straightens up a little—you notice he's tall, solidly built, and his eyes have some steel in them—and he continues, "I don't live in those countries. I live in America."

The throng of Otis Art Institute alumni falls silent while the weight of what he has just said hits the back of their throats like a shot of whisky. There is a short instant of recognition, then ingestion, and finally comprehension. Suddenly, this little celebratory event has turned into a referendum on the separation of church and state here in Los Angeles, here in California, here in the United States. Or, to put it another way, if R. Crumb can render the Book of Genesis as a comic book, can't Sandow Birk transcribe and illustrate the Holy Koran?

The short answer is yes. The longer answer is yes, but…

Begun nearly five years ago, Birk's *American Qur'an* is, in some ways, highly reverent. It endeavors to render each of the Koran's 114 suras, or chapters, in accordance with the traditional specifications for colors, margins, formatting, page illuminations, and adornment.

Trickier for some, especially the woman with the salt-and-pepper hair, is how Birk extends the source material with personal touches. The traditional calligraphy translating what Muslims believe is the word of God told through the angel Gabriel to the prophet Muhammad is done in a uniquely American idiom: cholo graffiti. More to the point, Birk illuminates the underlying context of each chapter—sometimes literally, sometimes interpretively—with scenes from life in contemporary America.

For instance, a stock-car race—that most American of indulgences—illustrates sura hundred, "Chargers," a Koranic verse about horses snorting into battle and god knowing the violent love for worldly goods that resides in men's hearts, etc. Sura sixty-five, "Divorce," provides fairly explicit (and relatively compassionate) instructions for the disposition of a divorce. Birk illustrates this chapter with a man leaning against his pick-up truck, a cooler at his feet, beer in hand, staring across the gulf of their front yard at his wife who has a toddler at her feet and a bun in the oven. A forsaken Big Wheel sits in the grass between them.

Thus, Birk's Koran is both personal and American. And herein lies the blasphemy, if it is such, where it was bound to be—in the art. The Koran, one could argue, isn't supposed to be personalized, editorialized, illuminated, or contextualized—unless, of course, one could argue back, one lives in America.

Either way, much controversy greeted the opening of Birk's *American Qur'an*. The *New York Times* and *The Associated Press* speculated on potential blowback from the Muslim community.

"Our families and people who know the gallery were scared," Koplin Del Rio owner Eleana Del Rio said. "Who knew what the outcome would be?" Still, she said, there was never any question about exhibiting the work. "We were one-hundred percent supportive."

For his part, Birk thinks all the Sturm und Drang is just a little off target.

"So far, it's been about how it relates to Islam—what are they going to think? But that's really kind of missing the point. The audience is Americans. That's whom I'm thinking this is for," he says. "It's saying look at yourself. It's saying this is how we live, this is the message from God, and how do those things fit together— sort of taking it at face value. Whether you're talking about the Bible or the Koran, when the guy tells you a flood's going to come or you're going to burn in hell, how is that supposed to affect you when you're just going to the grocery store today? It's the whole conundrum of religion, I think."

Birk pauses and laughs before finishing the thought. "That sort of putting two things together—the divine message and the really mundane of America."

Back at the Koplin Del Rio gallery, with the question-and-answer session waiting for some resolution in the wake of Birk's declaration, the woman with the salt-and-pepper hair finally breaks the silence. "I think you're a very, very brave man," she says.

At the reception that follows, the woman says her name is Diane and explains that aside from being an artist and an Otis alumni, she's a South African Jew. "I think I shouldn't tell him what I know about jihad and world history," she confides in a near-whisper.

Soon enough, though, it's something other than jihad and the modern Crusades and the banality of American culture or whatever else one might read into the subtext of Birk's *American Qur'an* that has caught her imagination.

"I can't believe through surfing he traveled the world and became fascinated with the Koran and this is what happened," says Diane, shaking her head, as mystified now with the impetus for Birk's intellectual journey as with the journey itself.

She's got a point. With Birk, you can't blame it all on surfing, but you can blame a lot.

◆◆◆

SANDOW BIRK, NOW FORTY-SIX, grew up in Seal Beach. He started surfing when he was eleven. Like a lot of kids around those parts, he rode his bike to the beach in the morning to get a session in before school. On the other hand, Birk's parents, who were refugees from Detroit, didn't acclimate well to certain aspects of the SoCal lifestyle as quickly as did Birk.

"They were totally not into surfing at all," says Birk. "They still don't really get it."

Birk says his parents invoked an every-other-day rule for surfing when he started succumbing to catnaps as a result of his morning sessions. Showing early signs of the motivation (and defiance?) he would later apply to some of his more ambitious projects, Birk skirted the rule by sneaking out at night and rolling the family car silently down the driveway. He and his friends would then make a break for some night surfing at the Huntington Beach pier, which was lit up to the end, "So you could see the sets coming in," says Birk.

Weekends were spent surfing in Mexico—"with no money."

Eventually, Birk started funding his surfing habit the old-fashioned way. "Me and my friends had a little surfboard company in the garage," he says. "We made our own boards, so I learned a little bit about how to make boards."

Birk came of age at a particularly pregnant time in Southern California youth culture, when surfing and skateboarding collided with the Orange County to Hollywood punk-rock nexus. "During the whole punk-rock years, all my friends were in bands, and we used to go to Hollywood all the time during high school and see bands play," he reminisces, "Black Flag and all that."

Not surprisingly, mainlining the LA punk-rock scene had an influence on the young man. "I was going to try to be an architect, but I was always that kid who drew on the folders and stuff at school and then painting surfboards in the factory and then…ah, I just didn't want to go be an architect," he says, "so I went to art school instead."

It just seemed like way more fun, like more punk rock. "My parents weren't happy about it," he deadpans. Asked if his artistic sensibility gestated out of the surf and skate culture he grew up in, Birk chuckles. "I don't think there was a surf and skate culture there," he says. "Surf culture was painting pinstripes on the rails and skate culture was, like, Magic Marker on your T-shirt." Back in the early eighties, Otis was located near MacArthur Park in the scrappy Westlake neighborhood just west of downtown Los Angeles.

Enticed by the availability of cheap spaces, artists, punks, and bohemians started the first wave of post-Watts downtown backfill. For Birk, his first year of art school was a seminal experience.

"I started hanging out with people who were artists and lived in lofts and painted and went to art shows," he says. "I was totally blown away. I didn't even know you could do that. I didn't know there were people who were, like, really artists, in the city in our time."

We're talking over lunch at a boisterous restaurant in downtown Long Beach near Birk's home. After a long time in Hollywood, Birk and his wife, the talented artist and sculptor Elyse Pignolet, whom Birk met in San Francisco, now reside in Long Beach. Their home is in the Masonic Temple, a beautiful 1920s building built by the Long Beach masons for their headquarters. It was converted to multifamily lofts a few years ago and is now called the Temple Lofts.

Their loft is an open, bright, work/live arrangement shared with a dog and a shit load of evidence of the artist's life—canvases, sketches, archives, books. Entering the loft, one is immediately greeted by a large, elaborate sculpture modeled on an offshore oil rig. Called "California Dreaming," it was constructed of detritus found on Southern California beaches. A close look reveals crutches, tubes, gas containers, egg crates, car parts, and the like. It inspires one to donate to Heal the Bay, Baykeeper, or Surfrider. A homey-looking living area waits in the rear, beyond the workspace.

After a morning surf session, Birk seems relaxed and in the mood to talk a little story.

"So then," he continues, "I really wanted to be an artist, but I didn't really like school. So I dropped out with my high school friend and had this idea to drive to Brazil. We took my car and just started driving. We drove all through Mexico and the car eventually blew up. So we took the bus all the way to Brazil."

To stay afloat, they worked with every garage-door board manufacturer they could find along the way. Birk's buddy would shape, and Birk would glass and paint.

"We were just out of high school, you know; we weren't very good or anything, but as we'd travel along, we'd work in all these different places, like in Mexico, Ecuador. We'd pull into town, and there'd be one guy making surfboards, and we were, like, straight from Huntington Beach," recalls Birk. "So the guy would be like, 'Oh, yeah, come and show me the newest thing.'"

It was when the transition from twin-fins to tri-fins was happening, and we'd show them how to make the tri-fin. And everyone would be, like, you can stay here for, like, a week, and we'd show them all the tricks and they'd say, 'Oh, call this guy when you get to the next town.' So we were able to work all the way down."

Birk arrived in Rio the day before Carnival with two hundred bucks in his pocket. In 1984 dollars it was just enough to make it through the five days of partying that greeted him. Luckily, when Carnival ended he and his friend had an audition with the head of the local surfboard factory.

"He was a really cool guy, Daniel Freeman, the first Brazilian on the World Tour in the seventies," says Birk. "Remember the Bronzed Aussies? He started the Brazilian version of that. They were called the Brazil Nuts. They had matching track suits of the seventies."

Birk spent the next half a year or so working in Freeman's factory, learning Portuguese, and surfing. Then, he met an expat Brit surfer who lured Birk and his buddy overseas with promises of traveling around Europe, surfing, and working in factories.

"He was, like, 'Yeah, I'll get you a job when you get there.' And we got there and no job, no nothing. That's when my buddy and I split up. We got in a big fight in a bar in Wales, and I haven't seen him since," says Birk. "It turned out he was smuggling cocaine in from Rio. That was part of his scheme to keep traveling, and I didn't know about it... And then it got ugly."

Stranded overseas with no money and no way home, Birk called his parents.

"They said, 'If you go back to college, we'll send you some money.' I didn't want to go home, so I went to college. I did a semester in Paris and a semester in England. I went to school in

Bath. From Bath I could take the train and go surfing at Swansea out in Wales and make it back to school."

Despite the cold water and temperamental swells, Birk says there was a whole scene out there at Swansea. ("The Brits are kind of hard-core.") But he spent more time honing his art-history chops in the museums of England and France than his cutbacks on the Irish Sea. The effects on his artwork were profound and lasting. From the outset, Birk defined himself as an artist who surfs rather than a surf artist. His inspirations and appropriations came from past masters, not just the lowbrow influences that typically inform surf and skate artists.

Before that, though, Birk would struggle to find the confidence to take himself seriously as an artist, a journey that took him back to Rio when he was done soaking up old-world art history.

"I had saved up money and bought a one-way ticket to Rio, and I was like, I'm going to go to Rio for the summer to see my friends and then I'll go to school. And then I got a full-time job, I got an apartment, and so then I stayed three years," explains Birk, chuckling a little at his obvious omission—that his parents weren't happy about it.

But for him, it was the good life on Ipanema Beach.

"It was insane. I was twenty-six; I was single. I'd ride a motorcycle with a surf rack on it, and I had a one-bedroom apartment a walk from the beach, and I was surfing every day in the tropics," he says. "Wow."

Up until then, Birk had been drawing "tons and tons of sketchbooks" but was daunted by the prospect of painting. In Rio, though, he finally confronted his self-doubt and began putting paint to canvas.

"I lived alone and started painting for the first time, you know, just getting a canvas and painting a picture—not a school assignment or something," he recalls. "For a year I did a whole series of like twenty paintings."

The experience taught Birk that he could motivate himself and not only paint but also have something to say as an artist.

"I didn't have it planned out that I was going to find my voice, but I think I did," he says. "I finally came back for a number of reasons, but one of the main ones was that I wanted to go back to school and become an artist."

◆◆◆

ONE OF BIRK'S EARLIEST painting series, featured in *The Surfer's Journal* some seventeen years ago, places surfers in the middle of paintings overtly referencing neo-classic masterpieces such as John Singleton Copley's *Watson and the Shark*. In Birk's fabulist concoction, it's called *Aggro Crowd at Lower Trestles*.

In a later series of urban paintings, Birk depicts a drive-by shooting (*Death of Manuel*) in the same heightened tone in which Jacques-Louis David, the nineteenth century neo-classical painter and revolutionary, portrayed the slaying of his friend, the radical publisher Jean-Paul Marat (*Death of Marat*). The subtexts are many layered. Marat was an associate of Robespierre and the Jacobins during the French Revolution's Reign of Terror. His killer was cliqued up, so to speak, with the more moderate Girondist faction.

In History Paintings, including the *Bashing of Reginald O. Denny*, *The Truce Between the Crips and the Bloods*, and *The Surrender of O. J. Simpson*, Birk gives the disposable icons of our modern media culture the same heightened status the old masters gave their subjects. The mock-heroic treatment instantly mythologizes contemporary events, infusing the paintings with a tone of irony and fable and freeing up Birk from the screeching didactics of so many contemporary artists attempting political commentary.

One of the best examples is the new-millennial *In Smog and Thunder: The Great War of the Californias*. Here, Birk elevates the banal kvetching of Northern Californians about philistine SoCal into a multimedia mock civil war between Los Angeles and San Francisco, referencing familiar war imagery from the Revolutionary War, the Civil War, and propaganda campaigns from the two world wars. *Smog and Thunder* meshes the contemporary and the classic—horses, motorcycles, Ironsides, helicopters, jet fighters, man-o'-wars—all find a place on this cultural battlefield. The effect is dizzying, hilarious, and certainly takes the piss out of the whole feud.

Prisonation: Visions of California in the 21st Century takes its cues from nineteenth century American landscape paintings to depict all thirty-three state prisons against their formerly idyllic backdrops. One is left with a sense of paradise lost one doesn't normally associate with prisons. Later, Birk would interpret Dante's *Divine Comedy* through the point of view of a South Bay slacker. The ambitious wood-etching series *Depravities of War*, finished just a couple of years ago, takes on the Iraq War and is inspired by seventeenth century artist Jacques Callot's *The Miseries of War*, which was inspired by Francisco De Goya's *The Disasters of War*. Tonally and formally, Birk recalls both in his series.

Birk's use of anachronism toys with parody, but more importantly gives perspective. How well, he seems to ask, does our media-intoxicated, self-absorbed culture match up against history? What, for instance, was the arrest of O. J., a celebrity-fueled circus, or a tragedy of Shakespearian proportions? Both? Birk's painting won't tell you, but it'll make you wonder.

Despite the tongue-in-cheek grandiosity, Birk confesses his style grew from humble beginnings. "That pretty much came from going to school in Europe, just seeing those old paintings," he says. "I just started copying them early on, I think as just sort of a way to learn how to paint better, stealing their ideas. That's the way it sort of grew."

If it was surfing that set Birk on his wandering path, it was also surfing that helped him define what he wanted to do when he finally returned to Los Angeles and art school in the late eighties.

"Back then, it was like to do anything serious you had to move to New York, and I totally didn't want to move to New York because I didn't want to quit surfing. So then, I was kind of pissed off that LA isn't bigger, so I sort of on purpose made LA the subject of everything. I wanted to make LA the art center... I was like, I'm going to paint my fucking city."

Birk stops himself and laughs at his hubris. But he is a bit of an anomaly. Outwardly, he bears none of the signifiers of the modern artist: no full-sleeve ink, no ironic facial hair, no contrived eccentricities. But the fact is, Los Angeles has become one of the important art centers of the world, and Birk has grown right along with it adding maturity to his ambition and grasp to his audacity. In the process, he's become one of the city's most significant artists.

"It's almost like he leads a double life," says writer and surfer Jamie Brisick, a friend and frequent flier with Birk for years. "He doesn't talk about himself a lot, then it comes to the end of the year, and you'll go to the show, and it's like, this guy's a fucking monster."

Now in a more mature phase in his life and work, the monster is coming out of the box.

"Well, one thing I've consciously done is choose ever-expanding topics," says Birk over dinner at an Ethiopian soul-food restaurant down the street from his gallery. "You know, I did the War of the Californias thing and I did the California prisons thing, and then the Dante thing spanned American [concerns], whereas the Iraq War project and the Koran thing are more international. We are consciously trying to take on the themes that are more globally relevant. I don't want to be just a West Coast California artist. Not anymore, anyway."

◆◆◆

IN AN HOUR OR SO, Birk will face those aforementioned Otis alumni and their anxieties. Speaking of which, since *American Qur'an* opened at her gallery, Del Rio tells me that despite the initial hysteria, the Muslim community has been mostly supportive, while the flack has come from the Christian right. Surprise, surprise. And while Del Rio believes Birk has "reached a new level of maturity for where he is in his artistic career," no one's betting he's going to fully give up board for brush.

"What's interesting about him as a surfer is that he's still as keen and hungry as any surfer," says Brisick. "He surfs really, really well."

Birk is more modest about it. "I don't think I'm getting better, but I don't think I'm getting worse. I'm right on that cusp where it's going to start going down-hill... I'm going to be frickin' fifty in like four years," he laughs, but admits, "I still haven't outgrown my boards. I'm still riding the same boards since high school."

Maybe, I suggest, it's time for a longboard, or even, yikes, a funboard.

"Yeah," says Birk while he ponders the inevitable, before rejecting it. "No! I just got a brand new four-fin."

The day after the reception, Birk and his wife fly to Lisbon for a long vacation. She's pregnant with their first child, a girl. Birk says he's thrilled at the prospects of being a dad. I ask him if he feels like he's settling down in his art and in his life, becoming...less punk?

"No, no. More punk," he laughs. "Do it yourself: that was the punk motto. Don't do what you don't want to do. Don't get a job, live every day... Hey, it goes with the surfing motto, too."

What's Wrong With Wes Anderson?

Originally published in the LA Weekly, *November 20, 2009*

Author's note: Ten years later, some things had changed.

I F WE WERE BACK in Wes Anderson's native Texas, the plate of
food he's showing little mercy might be called the Morning
Roundup or the Wildcatter's Special. Unfortunately for my
wallet, we're in a booth at Kate Mantilini on Wilshire Boulevard
in Beverly Hills, and here it's called Barry's Breakfast and costs
about four times more than it has any right to. Anderson spears
an Italian sausage link (butterflied and grilled), bites off a chunk,
holds the remains in the air for a moment, and confesses, "It's
my second breakfast." Despite that, he's more than game when
I suggest splitting a side order of pancakes. The thin man's
unexpected voraciousness reminds me of the last time I saw him.

It was a little more than ten years ago when I accompanied
Anderson on a road trip that started in Los Angeles on the
morning that his breakthrough movie, *Rushmore*, opened here
and in New York. With each mile marker on our way to Texas,
the first stop in a journey that would propel him to New York
and beyond, came reports from theaters on both coasts. The
reports were good. Anderson's quirky story of a love triangle
between a rich industrialist played by Bill Murray, an eccentric
prep-school rebel played by newcomer Jason Schwartzman, and
a first-grade teacher touched a nerve with a certain audience

that appreciated its postmodern updating of *The Graduate* by way of *Harold and Maude*.

As the miles passed and the momentum built, it became clear that the horizons of Anderson's future were expanding in ways that few people experience. Just two years earlier, his first feature, *Bottle Rocket*, had crashed and burned so badly that his panicked writing partner and muse, Owen Wilson, suggested they put as much distance as they could between themselves and the now-beloved cult classic. "When eighty-five people get up and leave the theater, you kind of get the message that something's wrong," says Anderson, remembering a particularly bad screening. That all changed in a day: *Rushmore* would soon be nominated for Independent Spirit and Golden Globe awards and placed on many critics' year-end Top Ten lists, not to mention relaunch Bill Murray's career. Suddenly, we were driving into a landscape of endless possibilities—terrifying in some ways, or so I imagined. Anderson, though, seemed poised and welcoming. Besides, the white Ford Explorer he had apparently convinced Disney to rent for him in perpetuity was stocked with a cooler full of sandwiches, sodas, and various snacking items. What could go wrong?

It wasn't yet noon when he asked if I wanted a sandwich from the cooler.

"In lieu of In-N-Out Burger?" I asked, worried we were going to blow past one of the few reasons to stop in Barstow.

"No, not in lieu of In-N-Out Burger. Let's stop at the next In-N-Out Burger!"

Anderson managed to talk, drive, and wolf down his burger, fries, and vanilla shake without missing a beat or a lane change.

◆◆◆

TEN YEARS CAN CHANGE some things. The guy driving the Ford Explorer had soft features, unstylish glasses, and a schoolboy haircut. He dressed in an oxford shirt and corduroys that looked like they were bought during a back-to-school sale at Kohl's. The guy across the booth at Kate Mantilini has a leaner body and a sharper face. The glasses are gone and the hair looks expensively trained. His oxford is crisp and monogrammed above the breast pocket in a delicate font that reads W. W. A, for Wesley Wales Anderson. His suit is a made-to-order burnt-orange corduroy number.

These clothes rest on wood hangers, not the floor. Sure, he looks a little overly art-directed, but who's to begrudge him? He's forty now, in love, lives in France, and is one of the singular voices in American cinema. He can dress how he pleases. But his eyes, arch then behind those nerd glasses, now seem like they're on the lookout, giving way only occasionally to the bursts of mischief that punctuate his often dolorous movies. Of course, not everything has changed. Anderson can still talk a blue streak while simultaneously gulping coffee and mashing up Texas-size gobs of food. There's another thing: now as then, Wes Anderson's future is at a critical juncture.

We meet up the day after his latest film, *Fantastic Mr. Fox*, kicked off AFI Fest at the Grauman's Chinese Theatre. It's not quite like a reunion of long-lost friends, but there is a certain familiarity. I ask him if he remembers leaving behind one chapter in his life and starting another during that trip a decade ago.

"I think, on that trip, without knowing it, I was moving permanently to New York, or moving to New York for the next seven years, or something like that," he says. "So to me, that was a big change, becoming a New Yorker."

We had departed from the house he shared with Owen and Luke Wilson on Citrus Avenue just south of Wilshire. It was the last place he lived in Los Angeles.

"I never particularly wanted to live in Los Angeles," he explains. "Owen liked LA a lot. Owen had been at USC for a year, and he loved it here, and I think he wanted to live here. I wanted to live in New York."

Why?

"I guess it's because of books and movies, and I love the theater and the idea of the theater," he says, "So that appeals to me more. Owen likes the ocean... Owen has a really nice way with the ocean and the sea."

Anderson tells me that throughout filming of *The Life Aquatic with Steve Zissou*, the entire cast and crew would be intensely focused on a scene until, inevitably, something just off camera distracted them—Wilson splashing around in the sea.

"It's like somebody who gets up and walks out of the classroom and you can look out the window and he's outside climbing a tree or something," Anderson says. "Owen would end up in the water, you know, in almost any circumstance."

Anderson now lives in Paris, an event that, like his move to New York, was less planned than just happened. He had been in Europe promoting *The Life Aquatic* and wound down the tour in Paris for a few days. Meanwhile, his friend Schwartzman ended up in town shooting *Marie Antoinette*. After a while, Anderson moved in with the *Rushmore* star for a couple of months.

"Then, I got my own apartment, and it kind of went from there," he says. "I didn't leave Europe for a year and a half. I didn't come back. I was supposed to go away for two weeks on this trip, and I didn't come back."

I wonder if the choppy waters his picaresque, big-budget Cousteau send-up was navigating back home encouraged the exile, but Anderson says it was simply a matter of wanting a new experience.

"For me, in France, I'm a foreigner all the time. If I'm walking down the street and I turn a corner that's not familiar to me, it's like going to a movie or something," he says. "I feel like I'm on an adventure and seeing something new."

Anderson has a measured, folksy way of telling a story— even when he's reading from cue cards, as when he introduced

Fantastic Mr. Fox at the sold-out AFI screening by reminiscing about "the last time I was in this famous movie palace."

It was in 1996 for a midnight showing of *Independence Day*, July third turning into the fourth. "You could tell this movie was going to be a hit," he deadpanned. "There was a lot of excitement. And unlike tonight, we paid money for our tickets. I don't think it was any more crowded than it is now, and I personally would like to believe that there is at least as much excitement here at this moment, at least for me."

It was impossible to tell whether or not he was poking fun at something—*Independence Day*, the American Film Institute, himself. He went on to thank lots of people involved with the production of the film. Pointedly, he left out his director of photography, Tristan Oliver, who, along with animation director Mark Gustafson, had been quoted in an October eleventh *Los Angeles Times* piece blaming Anderson for tension during the *Fox* shoot.

"He made our lives miserable," said Gustafson.

"I think he's a little sociopathic," added Oliver. "I think he's a little OCD. Contact with people disturbs him... He's a bit like the Wizard of Oz. Behind the curtain."

Any way you slice it, an animated film done entirely in stop-motion—an exacting process that employs puppets, figurines, and micro-scaled sets that are moved in tiny increments and shot frame by frame to simulate movement—is going to be a bitch. Anderson also insisted his animators refrain from using their favorite tool, computer-generated imagery. In other words, every shot in *Fox* was built from scratch. But the real issue for Gustafson and Oliver was that Anderson rarely set foot on the studio floor during principal photography. Instead, he called the shots from his Paris apartment via a system that allowed Anderson and his editor, Andrew Weisblum, to look through some thirty cameras on the film's London set remotely from their computers.

In effect, principal photography was directed via email and phone.

Tension between a strong-willed director and his crew on a long, complicated shoot (more than a year in production) isn't exactly news. Still, having two key collaborators go on the record with their grievances is uncommon, and the tone of the *Times* piece seemed to convey pleasure that Anderson was being thrown under the bus.

The controversy was then aired on a fanboy site called *The Rushmore Academy—The World of Wes Anderson*. Oliver posted twice apologizing for "a couple of careless, flip remarks" that he says were taken out of context at a press junket and stating that he has nothing but "the utmost respect" for Anderson. He also asked that the death threats stop.

For his part, Anderson says he initially misjudged how the movie would be made. His original plan was to write the script, record the actors' voices, work with the production designer to create the sets and puppets, draw some pictures, and plan the shots. Then, he would hand the project off to the animators, who would send him back the shots.

"That's not the way it happened," he says. "In fact, all those things were kind of happening at once. And in the process of animating, I realized I wanted to be more involved than I thought. So we kind of had to make a system. What ended up happening was, for two years, all I was doing was working on this movie. I thought when the animation would be going on, I could direct another movie. Instead it was all day, every day, all weekends, a continual thing. And it was fun."

◆◆◆

FANTASTIC MR. FOX'S UNVEILING comes after a lengthy gestation. Anderson, a huge fan of the original 1933 *King Kong* movie, had wanted to adapt the classic Roald Dahl children's story for years.

"The idea of doing stop-motion and doing this book kind of occurred to me together around the time when we met before—a long time ago," he says. "Before we did *The Royal Tenenbaums*, I'd already met with Roald Dahl's wife."

Various snafus, including the difficulties Anderson's *Rushmore* champion (and former Disney Studios chairman) Joe Roth was having getting traction for his startup Revolution Studios, put the project on hold. "So I did other movies in between," says Anderson.

Those movies have comprised an oeuvre saturated with droll humor, signature color palettes, and nostalgia for an often idealized past. His trademark moves—deadpan, retro, British Invasion, eccentricity, pastiche, a fetish for objects/artifacts, and, not least, characters in various states of arrested development—have formed a trademark aesthetic. Whether that aesthetic serves to leaven his films' pathos or hedge their emotional bets by creating a safe distance for both auteur and audience is debatable. What isn't, though, is that by the time *The Royal Tenenbaums* came out in 2001, the highly literate, postmodern, Prozac-popping kids who listened to Elliott Smith and read *McSweeney's* had made Anderson their Chosen One. And *Tenenbaums*, which more than tripled the box office of *Rushmore* while earning Anderson and Owen Wilson an Oscar nomination for their screenplay, was a generational movie.

Then, the air came out of the tires. Released in 2004, *The Life Aquatic with Steve Zissou* cost sixty million dollars and took in twenty-four million. The more modestly budgeted *Darjeeling Limited* grossed twelve million in 2007, five million less than *Rushmore*. These were commercial failures, sure, but the critics were also starting to pile on. Phrases like "too precious," "cloying," and "detached" popped up more and more in Anderson's reviews.

In one case of hipster cannibalization, *The Hipster Handbook* author Robert Lanham, writing for Viceland, said of *The Life*

Aquatic: "Wes Anderson doesn't make movies anymore. He creates overly precious paintings inhabited by emasculated man-children who knit sweater vests to the accompaniment of Belle and Sebastian while fantasizing that they're macho enough to skin a caribou with a pocketknife. The set pieces to *The Life Aquatic* are stunning, but watching this film is like visiting the Natural History Museum. It's a beautiful building, but most of its pleasures are filled with lifeless things."

More ominously, and more irresponsibly, *Slate* pop critic Jonah Weiner came just short of calling Anderson a racist after the release of *The Darjeeling Limited*. "Wes Anderson situates his art squarely in a world of whiteness: privileged, bookish, prudish, woebegone, tennis-playing, Kinks-scored, fusty," he wrote. "He's wise enough to make fun of it here and there, but in the end, there's something enamored and uncritical about his attitude toward the gaffes, crises, prejudices, and insularities of those he portrays. In *The Darjeeling Limited*, he burrows even further into this world, even (especially?) as the story line promises an exotic escape. Hands down, it's his most obnoxious movie yet."

It's hard to say why the criticism became so vitriolic or why audiences stopped going to his movies. One catches a whiff of schadenfreude for the wunderkind who could be seen on TV around the time of *Life Aquatic* paying homage to Truffaut while also lampooning himself and all directors in a hilarious American Express commercial. It's almost like someone in charge couldn't wait to serve Anderson his comeuppance for being given too much too soon. It probably didn't help that Martin Scorsese had singled Anderson out as the next Martin Scorsese in an *Esquire* article published after *Rushmore* came out.

Anderson admits he was a little taken aback by the failure of *The Life Aquatic*—his biggest and most beautiful film, brimming with mirth, mischief, and longing. It's also the most metaphysical of Anderson films, ending on a scene in which the mysteries of nature—symbolized by the heretofore mythological jaguar shark—swallow whole the existential angst and self-absorption of team Zissou, replacing them with a transcendent awe.

"When it came out, it seemed like it just sank, and I didn't really know what to make of it because I kind of thought, *Well, this is like a seagoing adventure, this ought to have an audience*," he says. "But, stepping back, it's kind of a big, very odd... Not deliberately odd... I don't know what movie to say it is like. It's just sort of its own thing. Maybe if it came out twenty years earlier in a different environment, it would have been fine...in a time when *MASH* is a huge hit, where a movie can be released on one screen and play for three weeks, and then it can move to another place and play for a year and people can process it in a different way."

Anderson also concedes that some of the recent criticism has gotten into his head.

"I think certain criticisms that I've heard about myself repeatedly start to linger," he says, looking out the window, almost embarrassed for exposing himself in this way. "The things that I think about are whether or not I'm telling the same kind of family stories and whether these movies are so meticulously art-directed or organized that people can't get into the story. I feel like with *Darjeeling Limited*, I got a lot of people saying I was repeating certain things. But for me, I was doing a movie in India about these three brothers and those things are different. I mean, it's in India. It's a completely different movie.

"In the end, I just do whatever I do, probably," he says.

◆◆◆

IN SOME WAYS, *FANTASTIC Mr. Fox* can be seen as a referendum on what Anderson does. As with Spike Jonze's *Where the Wild Things Are*, goodwill toward the source material isn't in question. And it's unlikely that studios will continue to fork over *Life Aquatic* or *Fox*-size budgets to Anderson without some evidence he can pay them off.

To his credit, Anderson hasn't let the pressure of dealing with either a sacred text or his recent track record cow him: *Fox* is a Wes Anderson movie through and through, despite the curious absence of the director's name from distributor 20th Century Fox's early marketing campaign. In fact, it might be the *most* Anderson movie to date, seeing as he designed every aspect of it from scratch, including the vulpine principals and their coalition of furry friends. To say the movie is meticulously art-directed is an understatement. In many ways, it *is* art direction.

"I liked the idea of just doing a movie where we could build the whole movie, and working in miniatures is kind of interesting because, in a live-action movie, you're not designing somebody's face, and you're rarely designing a tree, you know?" Anderson says. "That was something that appealed to me. Building landscapes and things like that."

To get the film's look and feel right, Anderson visited Dahl's widow, Felicity, at the late author's estate in Buckinghamshire, England.

"When I was there, it was really muddy. It was the fall, or maybe the winter, and it was not like a green, English wonderland at that time. And I started taking pictures around his house and said, 'Let's build this little bit of landscape,' and had this thing of keeping it really fall type of colors," he recalls. "So everything was [about] taking pictures of landscapes or objects, tons of things from Dahl's house, and making them in miniature."

Visually, the film is a masterwork, and all the justification anyone should need for Anderson's insistence on applying old-fashioned techniques to what has become filmmaking's most progressive idiom—animation. In *Fox*, the textured, burnished, autumnal hues evoke an endless pumpkin patch in a New England October. Fur bristles, wind blows across meadows, sunlight radiates—the whole thing feels as tactile and pregnant as a field ready for harvest.

To write the screenplay, Anderson moved into Dahl's house for two weeks with his friend and sometimes collaborator Noah Baumbach, the writer and director of *Kicking and Screaming* and *The Squid and the Whale*. But whom, I ask Anderson, did they have in mind for the film's audience when crafting the script?

"I don't know what our audience is," he says. "I certainly sat down to write it as a children's film, and we didn't do anything while we were writing it to make it more adult. We didn't really do much to try to make it more for children, either."

The film has gotten rave early notices, critics calling it a return to form. Personally, I was left scratching my head at the end, wondering what's so fantastic about a fox whose ego and narcissism damn his family and friends to a life eating processed grocery-store food in a sewer system far beneath the gorgeous landscape the director rendered with so much love. It seems no cause for celebration, yet that's how it's played. And the celebration feels forced and tacked on—a concession one wonders if Anderson would have made a few years ago.

◆◆◆

AFTER EVERYTHING HAS BEEN eaten, including the pancakes, and the sun is starting to set, casting a soft glow right out of *Fantastic Mr. Fox*, I ask Anderson what his biggest surprise and biggest disappointment have been over the past ten years.

"What is a nice surprise is to have with Jumon, my girlfriend, this sort of life in Paris, for instance, that we know how to do," he says. "We know how to survive and have a nice time there and function in what was once to me a distant, exotic place."

"Does it still feel romantic there, the way you thought it would be?"

"Yeah, and I feel like it always will, because of the history. That will not go away, the history of that place. A negative would be...for me, the hardest things are just the movies you spend years on. Not everybody's occupation in their life is [about] this moment where it's kind of yes, or no, where there's a kind of deciding moment for the three years you just spent. And when the movie comes out, it can go badly."

I'm not sure why Anderson's recent movies have gone badly. All seem like different expressions of an artist's singular voice— each unique in its own way yet instantly recognizable as an Anderson film.

There's a scene in *The Darjeeling Limited* that crystallizes that voice and the deep, inchoate weltschmerz Anderson seems to have been grappling with since *Bottle Rocket*. In it, the lovely train attendant with whom Schwartzman's Jack (as in Nicholson) has become infatuated asks him, "What is wrong with you?" as he and his brothers are being kicked off the train.

"Let me think about that. I'll tell you next time I see you," Jack replies, staring after her as the train pulls away.

"I feel like, 'What's wrong with you?'—that could almost be addressed to practically my entire circle of friends," Anderson says. "The world is saying that to us, 'What's wrong with you?' When you ask me, 'What are you grappling with?' That's more or less." He pauses and laughs. "Let me think about it, and I'll tell you the next time I see you. I don't really know, but it's kind of vast enough that you can sink your teeth into it."

We say our good-byes, and I wonder as I drive north on a tidy side street if it'll be another ten years before he can tell me. Then, I see a figure striding through the Beverly Hills flats with the late-afternoon sun reflecting off his corduroy suit like it would a shield. There are no people anywhere, and the trees are little and white, and the Spanish-style houses are little and white, and the yards are precisely manicured. There's nothing out of the ordinary going on here, other than somebody walking in LA. And yet, for some reason, the whole thing strikes me as the loneliest thing on Earth. I pull over and ask if he wants a lift.

He does.

Into The Wilde

Originally published as "A Romance of the Near Future,"
Flaunt, *December 3, 2010*

*Author's note: I didn't really want to do this piece as I didn't know
or care much about the subject. But I was freelancing and it's hard
to say no, especially when mags were slashing freelance budgets
to the bone. Feet-dragging and fretting about how to gin up some
professional interest, I drove down to Venice Beach where my
assumptions were quickly upended. Just say yes, I guess.*

OLIVIA WILDE, WHOSE LAST name used to be Cockburn,
may have chosen her stage name in honor of Oscar, but
it's also a double entendre that is betrayed by her eyes. Alert,
alive. Fierce and playful. Confident. Dancing, like a ballerina or
a boxer. Her eyes look like they are ready for war, peace, or just a
laugh—it's up to you, she's down for whatever.

At first I'm thinking I want war. To explain, the drive from the
eastside has been a bitch. I'm tired as fuck and missing a friend's
art show to do an interview with a fatuous, young Hollywood type
(or, so I think) because of...who knows? Plus, the whitewashed,
faux-boho stretch of Venice where she lives and where we're
having dinner gives me a rash. (Of course, like all good bohos,
Olivia and her husband were here when it was still____ etc.,
etc.). To make matters worse, the restaurant is one of those overly
crowded, overly clattering, celeb-heaven clusterfucks where you
couldn't slide an Olsen twin between tables.

If I sound like a hater, that's not it. I'm just old. And it's dark in here. And the menu is in six-point type. Oh, and did I mention that Wilde, with the cheekbones and the eyes, is happily married? To a guy named Tao (I'm not making that up) who is the son of an Italian prince (that either), with whom she eloped at eighteen, when he was twenty-seven (nor that). Okay, maybe I am a hater. But, really, given all that, where's the fun going to come from? That's what's up when I arrive at the restaurant to find Wilde already drinking a glass of red wine. The waiter asks if I'd care for some wine as well. I say no and ask for a double espresso and a nonalcoholic beer.

"What do you call that, espresso and beer?" Olivia asks.

"An ulcer," I say.

She laughs. It's a loud, natural, good-times gal laugh. And, well, damn it, she's already disarming. Since I can't read the menu, I ask her if she has any recommendations. "Well, you're not into wine, so already we're on different pages. I don't know if I can make any recommendations," she teases. Wilde orders okra and avocado salad and cauliflower and something called mushroom toast.

"So, you're a vegetarian," I astutely ask.

"Yes."

"How come you're not skinnier?"

"Ha," she snorts. "Umm, because I'm married to an Italian and every time I ask him to cook dinner, you can be a hundred-percent sure it's going to be pasta. Anyway, there are a lot of fat vegetarians out there."

"And angry ones, too."

"Angry ones, too. The angriest ones are the raw foodists. You'll never meet more anal, dogmatic people."

So, now I'm thinking I should pay attention, this could be fun. I might even learn something. And I know what a self-involved boor I sound like saying that, but please forgive. I can only provide my context to this matter, not yours, and I'm not a faker, and the truth is, until yesterday, when I saw the screening of a movie starring Russell Crowe called *The Next Three Days*, in which Wilde has a cameo, I'd never seen the young lady on either a big or medium screen.

A little surfing on the small screen, though, caught me up on a few things. I find that Wilde starred in *The Black Donnellys*, an ill-fated TV series by Paul Haggis, who also wrote and directed *The Next Three Days*, not to mention *In The Valley of Elah* and *Crash* and a shitload of TV shows from *Diff'rent Strokes* to *Walker, Texas Ranger*. Wilde also had a role on the much-missed *The O.C.* ("My Hilary Swank year," she jokes.), is on leave from *House*, and has been shooting a bunch of movies, one of them called *Cowboys and Aliens* and another called *Tron: Legacy*.

Also, I discover, Maxim magazine named her the hottest of its Hot 100 a couple years ago. And she appeared in various states of flexible undress for a *GQ* cover story called, "Why We're Wild About Olivia Wilde." Oh, and Megan Fox said she'd love to make out with her. All of which had—due to a generational slip, perhaps—eluded me.

Which is all fine and what you'd expect, but dig a little deeper, just past the glossy depths of commodification, and you come across a website for Artists for Peace and Justice, on whose board of directors sits Wilde, alongside Haggis, Ben Stiller, Dr. Bob Arnot, and Dr. Reza Nabavian. These guys are working with a saint of a man, Father Rick Frechette, who has been ministering in the slums of Haiti for more than twenty years. Father Rick, as Olivia calls him, started as a priest and saw that what the slums around Port-au-Prince, among the poorest places in the western hemisphere, really needed were doctors. So, he became a doctor, built orphanages, medical clinics, street schools, and a pediatric hospital. Folks like this still walk the earth.

With funding help from APJ, Father Rick is opening a new school for the poor in Port-au-Prince, and this is what Wilde is really excited about. "Two hundred kids, seventh grade," she says. "It's the first secondary school for kids in the slums of Port-au-Prince. Before, if you were lucky enough to get through the sixth grade through some free education program, there was nothing else for you."

The school will provide two meals, clean water, medical assistance, and a safe place for kids to learn in and maybe even learn to hope for a viable future. APJ plans to expand the school through grade thirteen, and hold classes in arts education, sports, agriculture, and vocational training using local resources and labor.

"Our goal is also to encourage a sense of nationalism and pride that will stop the brain drain so people can get educated, go to med school, or any other kind of school elsewhere, but have a sense of responsibility to come back there and help their own country. That's woven into the fabric of our curriculum."

Wilde gets increasingly animated talking about this, waving her hands frenetically as she speaks. And they are strangely big, sturdy hands—potato-picking hands we call them in the old country. I tell her I'm afraid she's going to swat me with one of those mitts.

"Ha," she laughs. "I know. I'm a hand talker. I'm surprised I haven't knocked anything over yet."

"That's what you get for marrying an Italian."

I ask Wilde how often she goes to Haiti.

"I go there any time I have time off," she says. "It's really an incredible place to go." She says she stays in the local hospital when she goes to Port-au-Prince and does whatever is needed—load rice onto trucks, distribute food.

"How long do you stay when you go?"

"As long as I can. To me, the longer you stay, the more helpful you can be, the better the experience. I encourage people to go there to see it for themselves," she says. "And I always feel safe there, by the way."

"And Sean Penn is there," I add.

"Yes," Wilde laughs. "Sean Penn is there to protect you. He's doing incredible stuff. I toured his camp and was really impressed."

Having spent some time with Sean Penn, it doesn't surprise me. He's really pretty amazing, I suggest.

"Quite brilliant," Wilde agrees. "I didn't realize how brilliant he was until I was in Haiti hearing him explain the politics of his camp. He's pretty fascinating, genuinely interested in the history of Haiti and Haiti's people."

Wilde is also quite active in domestic politics. She put serious work in on Obama's election and now is focused on the midterm elections, which, depending on when you read this article, may have already wreaked their havoc.

"I'm very concerned at this point about the midterm elections," Wilde says. "People generally don't vote in them. What is at stake is so enormous, and I don't feel people have a sense of that and it's scary."

I offer that people might be dismayed by how lame the Democrats have been with the "change" mandate they were handed in the last general election, choosing tame and watered-down policies over real progressive politics (like the administration's challenge of the court order striking down the unconscionable Don't Ask Don't Tell).

"It doesn't matter. We need to rally the way they rally. It's time to go gangster," she counters. "I'm worried the disappointment you feel might lead people to lose a sense of responsibility and not involve themselves and not vote."

To help counteract that, Wilde has been doing get-the-vote-out campaigns, including a video with MoveOn.org holding people accountable for what happens in the election if they don't vote.

Her activism really isn't that surprising given her heritage. Her mother, Leslie Cockburn, is a *60 Minutes* producer and journalist, and her father, Andrew Cockburn, is also a journalist. Both her paternal uncles are journalists as well, and all the lads contribute to the muckraking website CounterPunch.org. Wilde's paternal grandfather, Claud Cockburn, was a well-known novelist and journalist who covered the Spanish Civil War and was known to be sympathetic to the communists fighting for the republicans against Franco and the nationalist takeover of the Spanish Republic. His cousin was the British novelist Evelyn Waugh. It's a fascinating family of letters and activism. Wilde's older sister is a civil-rights attorney in New York. So, perhaps what's surprising is that Olivia Wilde ended up an actor first and an activist second. I ask how this happened.

"I don't know," she says. "It [acting] came to me. Acting, for me, as a kid, was like therapy. I was a really angry child."

I ask her what a beautiful, intelligent, well-educated woman with admittedly loving and supportive parents had to be angry about. But before she can answer, my lamb arrives and I immediately feel ashamed and apologize.

"What an asshole you are. I'm going to make lamb noises while you eat," she jokes and tells me the lamb is the restaurants' specialty, which is good because ambience certainly isn't.

"You know," she continues, "when I say angry, I think it was more—because I had really loving parents—when I was a kid, I had all this unfocused energy that would come out in bouts of excitement or rage or in the form of a really overactive imagination, constantly coming up with alternate realities. My energy was such that I think that if I had other parents, I quite possibly would have been medicated. I was really frenetic. (And, yes, those big hands are flying around as she speaks.) The theater really calmed me and focused me, and to this day, I don't think I could live without it. It's my therapy."

Therapy has been fruitful. Besides getting to work with Russell Crowe in the new Haggis movie ("At times it was distracting how good he is," she says of Crowe.), Wilde makes her sci-fi, action-movie, fanboy's fantasy debut in the forthcoming *Tron* sequel.

For the uninitiated, *Tron* was a little-seen, but highly influential, film released in 1982, starring Jeff Bridges. Its plot is too Byzantine and techie for me to comprehend, but it has something with computers taking over. Along with *Blade Runner,* released the same year, it's considered one of the wellsprings of such franchises as *The Terminator* and *The Matrix*, etc. *Tron* was also one of the first films to incorporate extensive computer graphics, and director Steven Lisberger's unique visual style influenced a generation of artists. Video games, a television series, and now the remake have followed in its footsteps.

But, most importantly, "Daft Punk based their entire aesthetic on *Tron*," exclaims Wilde. Almost as important, Daft Punk is scoring the new Tron. Wilde adds that the sequel has taken so long to get into production because Disney "wanted it to be as revolutionary as the first." Wilde plays the film's heroine, Quorra.

I ask her what she thinks about the action-movie world.

"I never thought I'd be in an action movie," she says, "but I gotta say, I love it. I love the stunts. I love the physicality. I love the imagination necessary for the green screen. I think the technology is brilliant. I'm completely inspired by the people behind it, meaning the artists who are tirelessly painting images. I think it's brilliant."

I suggest it sounds like being part of a theater group.

"Exactly," she says, adding that she's never seen such high morale within every department working on a film, "Because they felt like they were part of doing something revolutionary. It was mind blowing."

"Do you save the world?"

"Yep," she laughs.

The Pirate of Penance

Originally published in Slake: Los Angeles #1, *"Still Life,"*
summer 2010.

*Author's note: I'd long wished for a Los Angeles-based quarterly
that could sit on the shelf next to* Granta, Paris Review, Tin House
*and the like while flaunting its Los Angeles ethos, which to me
meant smart, sexy, and slyly subversive. When conditions on the
ground, as they say, made it possible for Laurie Ochoa and me to
attempt such a thing, we started* Slake. *We were fighting against
conventional wisdom, the economy, trends, and shallow pockets—
none of which favored a painstakingly curated, edited, and art-
directed print publication. But* Slake *shined brightly for a couple
of years before burning out. This piece on Eddie Padilla, one of
the founders of the Brotherhood of Eternal Love, helped anchor*
Slake's *best-selling debut. It gave us a foundation to build around.
Padilla's intensely personal odyssey also contains the sweep of
history, of the sixties turning into the seventies, and of the hard
reckonings that followed.*

Mystic Beginnings

WHEN LOREY SMITH WAS twelve years old, her father
loaded her and her brother into his black 1965 Mustang
and drove them down the Pacific Coast Highway to this cool little
shop called Mystic Arts World. The store sold arts and crafts,

organic food and clothing, books about Eastern philosophy, and other things, too. Lorey's father knew some of the guys who ran Mystic Arts, and he thought the outing would be a nice diversion for the kids. It was a short drive from Huntington Beach but an exotic destination, at least for the girl in the back seat.

The year was 1969, and Laguna Beach, once the sleepy refuge of surfers, artists, and bohemians of little consequence, was a center of counterculture foment after a band of outlaws and outcasts went up a mountain with LSD and came down as messengers of love, peace, and the transformational qualities of acid and hash. They called themselves the Brotherhood of Eternal Love, and Mystic Arts World was their public face, a hippie hangout where vegetarianism, Buddhism, meditation, and all sorts of Aquarian ideals spread like gospel.

Lorey says she felt like Alice in Wonderland when she crossed the threshold and entered Mystic Arts. "It was like walking into a different world," she tells me forty years later. "Everything from what was on the walls to the way people were dressed gave off this feeling of love, and, like, freedom."

Her father bought the kids some beads to keep them busy, and Lorey fashioned a necklace. She walked up to a big, handsome guy with long hair and handed it to him.

"He opened up his hands, took the beads and had this big, beaming smile," she recalls, "and I just felt like, love, and I thought, *Someday I want to marry someone like that.*"

Into the Gran Azul

SECURITY GUARDS ARMED WITH machine guns patrol the grounds of the Gran Azul resort in Lima, Peru. It's the kind of place you have to know someone to even get close. But on an early winter day in 1975, Eddie Padilla, one of the founders of the Brotherhood of Eternal Love, has no trouble booking a room. He is a familiar face on a familiar errand.

Checking in with Padilla are Richard Brewer, a Brother from way back, and their friend James Thomason. "I chose Richard because he's a good guy," Padilla remembers. "He'll get your back. He's not going to run away. That played out in a way that I never, ever expected." Thomason is along for the ride—to party and taste some first-class Peruvian flake.

As the manager walks the men to their bungalow, he delivers a strange message. "Your friend is here," he says.

"Friend?" Padilla asks. "What friend?"

As soon as the manager says the name Fastie, Padilla curses. He's known the guy since high school where Fastie earned his nickname because he always knew the shortest distance to a quick buck. As far as Padilla is concerned, Fastie is a flashy, loud-mouthed whoremonger—the worst kind of smuggler. Padilla told him not to come to Lima while he was there. To make matters worse, Fastie's girlfriend is with him, and she has a crush on Padilla. When they run into her, she complains that Fastie has been taking off and leaving her at the hotel.

"She knows he's been going to see whores and coking out," Padilla says. "We're like, Oh, god." Prostitutes and police are thick as thieves in places like Lima, Peru.

Still, there's no reason to be paranoid. *All I have to do is spend the night, pick up the coke, give it to a few people, and peel out in twenty-four hours*, Padilla remembers thinking. Everything was set up ahead of time; the deal should be an in-and-out affair.

Though they had agreed to keep a low profile, Padilla, Brewer, and Thomason decide to go to the compound's bar that night. It's an upscale place, and they get all dressed up. Fastie is there. Things are tense, and Padilla knows better than to dance with Fastie's girlfriend. But when she asks, something won't let him say no. Maybe he just wants to rub Fastie's face in it. Maybe he's the guy who has to let everyone know he can have the girl. Whatever it is, when they get off the floor, Fastie isn't amused.

"All of a sudden, in a jealous rage, he gets up, scrapes everyone's drinks off the bar, and throws a drink on [his girlfriend]," Padilla says. "The bouncer, some Jamaican dude, kicks him out."

Fastie returns to his room and tosses his girlfriend's belongings out the window. She ends up spending the night in Padilla's bungalow.

The next morning, the girlfriend leaves to retrieve her belongings. She never comes back. Fastie isn't anywhere to be seen either.

If they'd been reading the signs, they might have waited until things settled down to pick up the coke. Instead, Padilla and Brewer stay on schedule and head to a nearby safe house for their load—twenty-five kilos of cocaine worth nearly 200,000 dollars—and return to the bungalow without a hitch. Things seem to be back on track.

"It's so fresh, it's still damp," Padilla says. "So I've got it on these big, silver serving trays, sitting on a table. James is making a paper of coke [think to-go cup]. Bob Dylan's *Blood on the Tracks* is playing. Richard's doing something...I don't know what. And I'm writing down numbers. All of the sudden, the door opens. I look and all I see is a chrome-plated .32. Oh, shit. I just thought, wow, my life just ended."

The Making of Eddie Padilla

THIRTY-FOUR YEARS LATER, EDDIE Padilla emerges from Burbank's Bob Hope Airport into a balmy Los Angeles autumn night. He has a well-groomed goatee, a shiny, bald dome, and a nose that clearly hasn't dodged every punch. Wearing a black jacket and tidy slacks, Padilla is muscular and sturdy at sixty-four. He walks like a slightly wounded panther and offers a knuckle-crushing handshake. "Hey, man, thanks for coming to get me," he says with a lingering SoCal-hippie-surfer accent.

We grab a coffee. Padilla speaks softly, with an economy that could be taken for either circumspection or shyness. The circumspection would be mutual. I had been approached about Padilla through his literary agents; they'd been unsuccessfully shopping his memoir. Right away, I was skeptical. Padilla's story was epic, harrowing, and hard to believe.

Aggravating my suspicions was the memoir's aggrandizing tone. Plus, I'm not a fan of hippies and their justifications for what often seems like plain irresponsibility or selfishness. Still, I have to admit, if even half of his story is true, Eddie Padilla would be the real-life Zelig of America's late twentieth-century drug history. And as is apparent from his first handshake, he has Clint Eastwood's charisma to go with his tale.

I drop Padilla off at one of those high-gloss condo complexes in Woodland Hills that seem designed especially for mid-level rappers, porn stars, and athletes. His son, Eric, manages the place. Though Padilla lives a short flight away in Northern California, he has never been here before. Tonight marks the first time in nine years that he will see his son. For twenty years now, Padilla has been literally and figuratively working on reclaiming his narrative. Reuniting with his son is part of that effort. I may be too, and I'm not sure how I feel about it.

As we approach, Padilla falls silent, unsure of what to expect. Eric is waiting outside the lobby when we pull up. He looks like a younger, slightly smaller version of Padilla. They greet each other with wide smiles and nervous hugs. I leave them to it.

I pick Padilla up the next morning to go surfing. He's in good spirits. The reunion with his son went well. Plus, he hasn't been in the water for a while, and surfing is one of the few passions left from his earlier days.

Out at County Line, it's a crystalline day with offshore winds and a decent swell kicking in. For Padilla, I've brought my spare board, a big, fancy log that would be cumbersome for most on a head-high day at County Line. Padilla inspects the long board like it's a foreign object.

"I don't know about this," he says. "How about if I take your board and you use this one?" Worried about the danger I'd pose to others and myself, I refuse. "Okay, then," he smiles, and we paddle out.

Padilla's reservations disappear as soon as the first set rolls in. He digs for the set wave, a fat, beautifully shaped A-frame. He deftly drops in, stays high on the shoulder, slips into the pocket, and makes his way down the line, chewing up every ounce of the wave. It's one of the best rides I see all day. But he's not done. Padilla catches wave after wave, surfing with a fluidity and grace that puts most of us out here to shame.

Exhausted after a couple hours, I get out of the water. When Padilla finally comes in, he is grinning ear to ear. "Who'd have thought I'd have to go from Santa Cruz to Los Angeles to find some good waves?" he jokes.

Buoyed by the return to his natural habitat, Padilla lets his guard down and begins to tell me about his life, over lunch at an upscale chain restaurant in Santa Monica. Though Padilla is forty years her senior, the attractive waitress is definitely flirting with him. Whatever it is that makes women melt, Padilla has it. He's magnetic and likeable.

As for his story, it could stand as a metaphor for the past few turbulent decades—the naïve idealism of flower power, the hedonism of the 1970s and '80s, the psychosis and cynicism of the war on drugs, and the recovery culture of more recent times. It's a story that's hard to imagine beginning anywhere but in Southern California.

Edward James Padilla was born in 1944 in the same Compton house where his father, Joe Padilla, was raised. Joe, a dashing Navy guy of Hispanic, Native American, and African-American ancestry, married Helen Ruth McClesky, a Scots-Irish beauty from a rough clan of Texas ranch hands who moved to Southern California, near Turlock, during the Dust Bowl.

Both family trees have their troubled histories. Joe's mother killed herself when Joe was twelve. The family broke apart after that, and Joe had to fend for himself through the Depression. "He had no idea what it was even like to have a mother," Padilla says.

Helen's father turned to moonshining and bootlegging in California. Padilla recalls how his grandfather liked to show off the hole in his leg. As the story goes, federal agents shot him during a car chase. Padilla raises his leg and imitates his grandfather's crotchety voice: "That goddamn bullet went through this leg and into that one."

When his grandfather finally ended up in prison, the family moved down to south Los Angeles where work could be found in the nearby shipyards. Padilla says his mother and father met in high school, "fell desperately in love," and got married. This didn't please the old man, who didn't want his daughter mixing with "Mexicans and niggers." Helen found both in one.

As the son of a mixed-race couple before such things were in vogue, Padilla got it from all sides. He wasn't Mexican enough for the Mexicans, white enough for the whites, or black enough for the blacks. He was also a frail kid who spent nine months with polio in a children's ward.

Padilla would get beaten up at school, and for consolation, his father would make him put on boxing gloves and head out to the garage for lessons with dad, a Golden Glove boxer and light heavyweight in the Navy. "If I turned my back, he'd kick me," Padilla says about his father, who died in 2001. "He was trying to teach me how to fight the world. My dad was a different kind of guy."

The family moved to Anaheim when Padilla was twelve. There, he says, he became aware of the sort of prejudice that you can't solve with fists, the sort that keeps a kid from getting a job at Disneyland like the rest of his friends.

"That's when I started really getting ahold of the idea that, hey, I'm not being treated like everybody else. I'm sure I had a chip on my shoulder."

Padilla got into a lot of fights, got kicked out of schools, and wound up in juvenile hall where he received an education in selling speed, downers, and pot.

By the time he was seventeen, Padilla was making enough as a dealer to afford his own apartment and car. But it wasn't exactly the good life. He was doing a lot of speed, and one day he got arrested for what must have been an adolescent speed freak's idea of seduction. "I started taking handfuls of speed, and I got so crazy. I mean, I got arrested for exposing myself to older women because just do that and we'll have sex. That's how psychotic I was."

To make matters worse, he got in a fight with the arresting officer. The incident landed him thirteen months at Atascadero State Hospital in San Luis Obispo. He came out feeling like he needed some stability in his life, or at least an eighteen-year-old's version of it. "I need to get married and settle down and be a pot dealer. I remember clearly thinking that. So, I married my friend, Eileen."

Padilla and Eileen were eighteen when they married on August twenty-two, 1962. Marriage, though, didn't solve certain problems—like how to get a job, which was now even tougher with a stint in a psych ward added to his résumé. "It would have been really cool if I could walk in somewhere and get a job that actually paid enough to pay rent and live, but from where I was coming from, I'd be lucky to get a job sweeping floors," he says. "I tried everything. So it was easy to start selling pot."

He turned out to be good at it.

Mountain High

EDDIE PADILLA TURNED TWENTY-ONE in 1965. Cultural historians wouldn't declare the arrival of the Summer of Love for a couple of years, but for Padilla and a group of trailblazing friends, it was already in full swing.

He figures he was already the biggest pot dealer in Anaheim by this time. For a kid who grew up watching *The Untouchables* and dreaming of being a mobster, this might be considered an achievement. But something else was going on, too. The drugs he was selling were getting harder and his lifestyle coarser.

He started sleeping with several women from the apartment complex where he and his wife lived. He spent a lot of time in a notorious tough-guy bar called The Stables. "That's where I started being comfortable," Padilla says. "This is where I belonged. Social outcasts for sure."

Eileen eventually had enough and took off for her mother's. But it wasn't just the philandering. Padilla also had an aura of escalating violence about him. "I had a gun. I felt like I was going down the road to shooting someone, just like hitting someone is a big step for some people. So that's kind of insane. I was going to shoot someone just to get it over with. It doesn't matter who, either."

Then, early on the morning of his twenty-first birthday, one of his friends picked him up and drove him to the top of Mount Palomar. Joining them was John Griggs, a Laguna Beach pot dealer and the leader of a biker gang whose introduction to LSD had come when his gang raided a Hollywood producer's party and took the acid. On the mountain with them were several others who would soon embark on one of the 1960s' most influential and least understood counterculture experiments: the Brotherhood of Eternal Love.

They climbed to the mountaintop and dropped the acid. Padilla says he was changed immediately. "I was completely convinced that I'd died on that mountain," he remembers. "It was crystal-clear air, perfect for taking acid. I came down a different person. It was what's called an ego death. I saw the light. I can't ever explain it."

A birthday party was already set with a lot of his old friends for later that night. Back home, in the middle of the celebration Padilla says he looked around at the guests, some of the hardest-partying, toughest folks around, and realized he didn't ever want to see those people again. He took the velvet painting of the devil off his wall and threw it in the dumpster. He dumped the bowls of reds and bennies laid out like chips and salsa down the toilet. He kept his pot.

"I went up the mountain with no morals or scruples, a very dangerous and violent person," he says, "and came down with morals and scruples."

From that day on, a core group of hustlers, dealers, bikers, and surfers, who at best could be said to have lived on the margins of polite society, started convening to take acid together.

"Every time we'd go and take LSD out in nature or out in the desert or up on the mountain, it would be just this incredible wonderful day," Padilla says. They were transformed, he claims, from tough cases, many of them doing hard drugs, to people with love in their hearts.

Things moved fast back then. The Vietnam War was raging; revolution was in the air, and the group that first started tripping on mountaintops wanted to be a part of it. Under the guidance of John Griggs, by most accounts the spiritual leader of the Brotherhood, they decided they needed to spread their acid-fueled revelations. In the foothills of the Santa Ana Mountains, they took over a Modjeska Canyon house that used to be a church and started having meetings. Soon, they were talking about co-ops and organic living; they were worshipping nature and preaching the gospel of finding peace and love through LSD.

The Brotherhood of Eternal Love incorporated as a church in October 1966, ten days after California banned LSD. The Brothers petitioned the state for the legal use of pot, acid, psilocybin, and mescaline as their sacraments. They started a vegan restaurant and gave away free meals. They opened Mystic Arts World, which quickly became the unofficial headquarters for the counterculture movement crystallizing among the surfers and artists of Laguna Beach.

The Brotherhood proved both industrious and ambitious. Soon, they were developing laboratories to cook up a new, better brand of LSD and opening up unprecedented networks to smuggle tons of hash out of Afghanistan. They were also canny; they carved out the bellies of surfboards and loaded them with pot and hash. They made passport fraud an art form and became adept at clearing border weigh stations loaded down with surf gear and other disposable weight, which they'd dump on the other side so they could return with the same weight in pot stuffed into hollowed-out VW panel trucks. In their own way, they were the underground rock stars of the psychedelic revolution.

Soon, their skills and chutzpah attracted the attention of another psychedelic revolutionary. By 1967, Timothy Leary was living up in the canyons around Laguna Beach carrying on a symbiotic, some would say parasitic, relationship with Griggs. Leary called Griggs "the holiest man in America," and more than anyone else, the Brothers implemented Leary's message to turn on, tune in, drop out.

"The Brotherhood were the folks who actually put that command into action and tried to carry it out," says Nick Schou, author of *Orange Sunshine: The Brotherhood of Eternal Love and Its Quest to Spread Peace, Love, and Acid to the World*. "Their home-grown acid, Orange Sunshine, was about three times more powerful than anything the hippies were using. They were responsible for distributing more acid than anyone in America. In the beginning, at least, they had the best of intentions."

The group, Schou says, was heavily influenced by the utopian ideals of Aldous Huxley's *Island*. "There was a definite plan to move to an island," Padilla says. "We were going to grow pot on the island, and we were going to import it. We need a yacht, and we need to learn how to grow food and farm, and we need to learn how to deliver babies… We were just little kids from Anaheim. God, these were big thoughts, big thoughts."

The End of Eternal Love

AROUND THE TIME LEARY was setting up camp in Laguna Beach, the island ideal took on a new urgency for Padilla. No longer just a local dealer, he'd made serious connections in Mexico and was moving large quantities around the region. In one deal, Padilla drove to San Francisco in dense fog with five hundred pounds of Mexican weed. But something didn't feel right. Padilla thought someone might have tipped off the cops. He was right: he was arrested the next day. It was the largest pot bust in San Francisco history to that point. In 1967, Padilla was sentenced to five to fifteen in San Quentin.

With his son Eric on the way, Padilla was granted a thirty-day stay of execution to get his affairs in order. "On the thirtieth day, I just left and went to Mexico, went to work for some syndicate guys," he says. "I bailed."

Padilla's flight was also precipitated by a schism within the Brotherhood that some trace to its ultimate demise. Acting on Leary's advice, Griggs took the profits from a marijuana deal, funds that some Brothers thought should go toward the eventual island purchase, and bought a four-hundred-acre ranch in Idyllwild near Palm Springs.

Padilla never cared much for Leary, nor for his influence over Griggs and the Brotherhood. "He was a glitter freak," Padilla says. "A guy named Richard Alpert, who became Ram Das, told us, 'You guys got a good thing going, don't get mixed up with Leary.'"

Padilla saw the Idyllwild incident as a turning point for the Brotherhood.

"This is betrayal. This is incredibly stupid. You're going to move the Brotherhood to a ranch in Idyllwild? To me, it was like becoming a target."

The Brotherhood split over it. Many of those facing federal indictments or arrest warrants took off for Hawaii. Others moved up to the ranch with Griggs and Leary.

As the Brotherhood's smuggling operations grew increasingly complex and international, revolution started looking increasingly like mercenary capitalism. Any chance the Brotherhood had to retain its cohesion and its gospel probably died in 1969 with John Griggs, who overdosed on psilocybin up at the Ranch. "That was John," Padilla says, smiling, "take more than anybody else."

Not long after, Mystic Arts burned down under mysterious circumstances. It seemed to signal an end, though the Brotherhood would continue to leave its mark on the era. The group masterminded Timothy Leary's escape from minimum-security Lompoc state prison following his arrest for possession of two kilos of hash and marijuana. Funded by the Brotherhood, the Weather Underground sprung Leary and spirited him and his wife off to Algeria with fake passports.

To facilitate his escape to Mexico, Padilla raised funds from various Brothers and other associates to gain entree with a Mexican pot syndicate run by a kingpin called Papa. His Mexican escapades—busting partners from jail and other adventures—could make their own movie.

One time he drove his truck to the hospital to visit his newborn son, Eric, who was sick with dysentery. On the way, he noticed a woman with a toddler by the side of the road. The kid was foaming at the mouth, the victim of a scorpion bite. Padilla says he threw the boy in the back of his truck and rushed him to the hospital. The doctors told him the kid would have died in another five minutes. They gave him an ambulance sticker for his efforts.

"I put it on my window," he tells me. "I was driving thousands of pounds of marijuana around in that panel truck. When I'd come to an intersection there would be a cop directing traffic. He'd stop everybody—I'd have a thousand pounds of weed in the back, and he'd wave me through because of that ambulance sticker."

In Mexico, Padilla ran a hacienda for Papa, overseeing the processing and distribution of the pot brought in by local farmers. For more than a year, he skimmed off the best bud and seeds. Meanwhile, he kept alive his dream of sailing to an island.

The dream came true when he and a few associates from the Brotherhood bought a seventy-foot yacht in St. Thomas called the *Jaffe*. The *Jaffe* met Padilla in the summer of 1970 in the busy port of Manzanillo. From there, it set sail for Maui. "It was five guys who had never sailed in their lives," says Padilla. On board was a ton of the Mexican weed.

The trip should have taken less than two weeks. A month into it, one of the guys onboard, a smuggler with Brotherhood roots named Joe Angeline, noticed the stars weren't right. "He said, 'Eddie, Orion's belt should be right over our heads.' But Orion's belt was way, way south of us. We could barely make it out."

When confronted, the captain confessed he didn't know where the hell they were, but had been afraid to tell them. "There's a hoist that hoists you all the way up to the top of the main mast, and we hauled him up there and made him sit there for a day," says Padilla. "That was funny."

Eventually, they flagged down a freighter and learned they were more than a thousand miles off course, dangerously close to the Japanese current. The freighter gave them three hundred gallons of fuel and put them back on track to Maui. He'd made it to his island with a load of the finest Mexican marijuana.

"The seeds of that," Padilla says, "became Maui Wowie."

Spiritual Warrior

MAUI WOWIE? THE HOLY grail of my pot-smoking youth, one of the most famous strains of marijuana in history?

When Padilla tells me he played a major role in its advent, my already-strained credulity nears the breaking point. I spend months looking into Padilla's stories, tracking down survivors, digging up what corroborative evidence I can. And well, he basically checks out. But there are his stories and there is his narrative—how an acid trip on Mount Palomar transformed a twenty-one-year-old borderline sociopath into a man with a purpose, a messenger of peace and love. That one's harder to swallow. While sitting over coffee at the dining room table in his son's apartment, Padilla finally tells a couple stories that beg me to challenge him.

Back in the mid-sixties, he and John Griggs make a deal to purchase a few kilos of pot from a source in Pacoima. They drive out in a station wagon with eighteen grand to make the buy. But the sellers burn them and take off with their money in a black Cadillac. The next day, Padilla and spiritual leader Griggs go back armed with a .38 and a .32. Padilla goes into the apartment where the deal was supposed to go down and finds one of the men sleeping on the couch. The guy wakes up and makes for a Winchester rifle sitting near the sink. Padilla runs up behind him and sticks the barrel of his gun in the guy's ear and says, "Dude, please don't make me fucking shoot you." Griggs and Padilla get their money back.

"So that stuff went on. I've been shot at. People have tried to kill me. I've had bullets whizzing by my ear," he says. "But I've never had to shoot anybody."

Padilla tells me of similar episodes in Maui where the locals, understandably, see the influx of the hippie mafia as encroachment on their turf. They set about intimidating the haoles from Laguna, often violently. One newcomer is shot in the head while he sleeps next to his son.

At his house on the Haleakala Crater one night, Padilla opens the door to let in his barking puppy only to find "a guy standing there with a pillow case over his head and holes cut out, and the guy behind him was taller and had a pager bag with the holes cut out."

One of the men has a handgun. Padilla manages to slam the gunman's hand in the door and chase off the invaders. "I'm going to kill both of you," he yells after them. "I'm going to find out who you are and kill you."

Padilla discovers the men work for a hood he knew back in Huntington Beach called Fast Eddie. Like a scene out of a gangster movie, Padilla and Fast Eddie have a showdown when Fast Eddie, in a car full of local muscle, tries to run Padilla and his passenger off the road. They all end up in Lahaina, where Fast Eddie's henchmen beat up Padilla pretty good before the cops break up the brawl.

"Hey, bra, you no run. Good man," Padilla recalls the Hawaiians saying to him. When Fast Eddie emerges from the chaos, Padilla points at him and tells the Hawaiians, "I want him. Let me have him. I worked him real good and that was that. People robbing and intimidating was over."

I tell him it doesn't seem like his life had changed very much since that day on Mount Palomar. "You know, don't get the wrong idea," he laughs. "I'm still who I am. We're still kind of dangerous people. Just because we were hippies with long hair and preaching love and peace doesn't mean we became wusses."

"It doesn't sound like you had a spiritual awakening to me," I say.

"I was very spiritual," he replies. "I thought I was making a life for myself."

"As what?"

"A warrior. A spiritual warrior."

"What was your spiritual warring doing? What were you fighting for?"

He falls silent. "I never thought about it before... Remember, I grew up in South Central. I already had an attitude from a young age. So by the time I got to Maui, it was like, here's your job, dealing with these people. The warrior part was, like, we want to live in Hawaii. We're not going to accept you guys running our lives. This is what we were trying to get away from. So my job as a self-motivated warrior was pretty clear, but it's really difficult to explain."

"So your job was protection?" I offer.

"I was never paid."

It occurs to me that Padilla really wanted to live beyond rules, institutions, and hierarchy, like some romanticized ideal of a pirate. "So why," I ask, "feel the need to color it with this patina of spirituality? Why not just call it what it was—living young and fast, making money, getting the girls, fucking off authority?"

"Uh, wow... I mean, you're right; it was about all that. It was living fast and really enjoying the lifestyle to the max."

"Why the need to justify it?"

"Well, it just seemed to me that was what was moving me."

"It seems that way to you now?"

"Now, yeah now. But then, I felt more, and this sounds really self-righteous, that we were the people who should be in charge, not the ones who were beating people up and taking their stuff and shooting them. So spiritual warrior, maybe it doesn't look like that to anyone else, but it sure as hell looks like that to me now." His voice is soft and intense. "I didn't have a sign on my head that said spiritual warrior, but I definitely felt that's what was going on... Nobody else was standing up to them. Nobody else would pick up a gun, but I sure as hell would."

"You have a massive ego," I suggest.

"Massive."

"And that's been your greatness and downfall all along?"

"Sure, yeah, I see that."

I ask again, amid all the chaos, how his life had improved since his supposed awakening on Mount Palomar.

"My life was incredibly better. I was surfing, sailing, living life. All this other stuff was just, you know...I'm not in San Quentin," he says. "That was the healthiest and clearest time of my life."

Then, he met Diane Pinnix.

Pinnix was a tall, beautiful girl from Beach Haven, New Jersey, who came of age when Gidget sparked a national surf-culture craze. It's not surprising that a headstrong girl from New Jersey would catch the bug, and she became one of the original East Coast surfer girls. Legend has it that when Pinnix decided she wanted to get away from New Jersey, she entered a beauty contest on a whim. First prize was a luggage set and a trip to Hawaii. Pinnix, then eighteen, won.

Pinnix's mother, Lois, still lives in Beach Haven. When I call her, she has a simple explanation for her daughter's flight to Hawaii and her subsequent plight. "It was the times, it was the times. She wanted to spread her wings. Drugs were a part of the thing, but I was very naïve. I was a young mother and in the dark."

Padilla first ran into Pinnix when he went with a friend looking to score some coke from a local kingpin. Pinnix was the kingpin's girlfriend. "I looked at Diane, and she looked at me, and the attraction was so strong," Padilla recalls. "That was it."

He started making a point of showing up wherever Pinnix was.

"We're traveling in the same pack, and we started talking and flirting," says Padilla. "It came to the point of ridiculousness... and my own friends were saying, 'Why don't you just fuck her and get it over with?' But that wasn't it, you know. I wanted her. It was an obsession. A massive ego trip, for sure, but at the same time there was an attraction unlike anything I'd ever experienced before."

By all accounts, Diane Pinnix, a stunning surfer girl/gun moll, with a nice cutback and blond hair to her ass, was the sort of woman who could make a man do things he hadn't bargained for.

"One day, we're getting ready to paddle out, waxing our boards, and I say, 'So, you want to be my old lady?' And she says, 'You have a wife and kids.' And I say, 'Okay.' I was willing to let it go right there, and I start to paddle out, and she says, 'But wait a minute.' And that was it. It was all over. And that's pretty much when I lost my mind."

Pinnix was a committed party girl, and Padilla started doing coke and drinking excessively to keep up. After getting iced out of a big deal by a new crew on Maui who claimed Brotherhood status, Padilla decided to go out on his own. He made connections in Colombia and was on his way to becoming a coke smuggler.

"There was no more spiritual warrior," he says. "This was a guy on his way to Hell. I had gone against everything that was precious to me. I left my wife and kids. I wasn't living the spiritual life I was back when we had the church and it was the Brotherhood of Eternal Love."

"Why did you do it?" I ask.

"Money. For Diane and me. I probably knew deep inside that if I didn't have enough money and coke, that she wouldn't stay with me…whether that's true or not, I'll never know. The bottom line is I became a coke addict, plain and simple."

Paradise Lost

A FEW DAYS BEFORE he's supposed to arrive at Peru's Gran Azul with Richard Brewer and James Thomason, Eddie Padilla is thousands of miles away on a beach in Tahiti. He sits and looks out at the ocean, contemplating how far things have degenerated, both for him and for the Brotherhood. He thinks about the messages of love, the utopian ideals, and the notion that they could change the world. All that is gone. What is left are the 1970s in all their nihilistic glory. The drugs, money, women, and warring, spiritual or otherwise, are taking their toll, and damn if he isn't feeling beat already at just thirty.

In Tahiti, Padilla at last finds the island paradise that eluded him in Maui. And with Pinnix set up in style on the mainland, it's a rare moment of peace in his increasingly out-of-control life. He wants more of that.

"It was incredible," he says. "The best surfing and living, the best food on the planet. While I was in Tahiti, I really got sober, and all of the sudden, I was looking at what I'd been doing, and I didn't want to go back."

Smuggling coke isn't about peace and love; it's about money, greed, and power. He suddenly sees his life as a betrayal of his ideals, and he wants out. Feeling something like a premonition, Padilla decides that this next trip to Peru will be his last. Decades later, he remembers the conversation he had with a friend on that Tahitian beach. "She says to me, 'What are you doing, how did you get into coke?' And I just look at her and say, 'I don't even know, but I know right now that I don't want to go back there.'"

He's trapped, though. Too much money has already been invested in the deal. "I'm totally responsible, and there's a whole bunch of people involved. But I'll be back,' I told her. That was the plan. 'I'll be back.'" He books a return flight to Tahiti. He never makes it.

Back at the Gran Azul, just hours before Padilla and his crew are scheduled to leave the country, quasi-military police agents storm the bungalow. One slams Padilla to the floor, another kicks Brewer in the stomach, and quickly Padilla, Brewer, and Thomason are all in cuffs.

"At least ten or twelve of them come in through the door, and they all have guns drawn. I didn't have a chance," says Padilla.

A man they will come to know as Sergeant Delgado takes a hollow-point bullet from his gun, starts tapping it against Thomason's chest, and says, "Tell me everything."

In some ways, Padilla is a victim of his own success. While he's been hopping between Hawaii, Tahiti, Colombia, and Peru building his résumé as a coke-smuggling pirate, Richard Nixon has been marshaling his forces for the soon-to-be declared War on Drugs. It's the beginning of the national hysteria that will see Nixon pronounce the fugitive Timothy Leary "the most dangerous man in America," and today has more than 2.3 million Americans in prison, a vast majority of them for drug offenses.

Nixon's strategy in the drug war is announced with his Reorganization Plan No. 2. It calls for the consolidation of the government's various drug-fighting bureaucracies into the Drug Enforcement Agency. The DEA is formed, at least in part, to do something with Nixon's boner for the Brotherhood's members and associates, dubbed "the hippie mafia" in a 1972 *Rolling Stone* article. Congress holds months of hearings on the need for this new agency in the spring and summer of 1973. One is titled "Hashish Smuggling and Passport Fraud, The Brotherhood of Eternal Love."

After the DEA starts putting too much heat on his Colombian connections, Padilla sets up shop in Peru. But the DEA's budget shoots up from seventy-five to $141 million between 1973 and 1975, and Peru, the world's largest cocaine-producing country at the time, quickly becomes a client state in the drug war. Some of that DEA money goes to fund and train the notorious Peruvian Investigative Police, or PIP (now called the Peruvian National Police). The PIP operates with near immunity and is expected to get results in the war on drugs.

Sergeant Delgado heads the force. A mean-spirited thug with dead, black eyes, he is one of the most powerful men in Peru. An Interpol agent known as Rubio is with Delgado.

Before the DEA put Peru in its crosshairs, Padilla would have been able to buy out of the arrest. Naturally, his first reaction is to offer up the 58,000 dollars in cash he has with him. "Don't worry," he remembers Rubio telling him. "Don't say anything about this and when we get to the police station, we'll work something out."

The three Americans are taken to the notorious PIP headquarters, known as the Pink Panther, a pink mansion that the police confiscated (they are rumored to have executed the owners). With no tradition of case building, Peruvian detective work at the time pretty much consists of coerced confessions and snitching.

The PIP is famously brutal. During the two weeks the guys are held at Pink Panther, Padilla says they're surrounded by the sounds of women being raped and men being tortured.

The country's shaky institutions are rife with corruption, and there is little to no history in Peruvian jurisprudence of due process or jury trials. Prisoners wait for years to have their cases heard before a three-judge tribunal, only to see their fates determined in a matter of minutes. Their arrest immediately throws Padilla, Brewer, and Thomason into this Kafkaesque quagmire.

In a 1982 *Life* magazine story that details the horrors of the Peruvian prison system and two men who tried to escape it, a survivor tells of his time in the Pink Panther. "My god, I was in tears after they went at me," Robert B. Holland, a Special Forces Vietnam vet recounts. "I did a couple things in 'Nam I might go to Hell for. But Peru was a whole new day."

When their escape attempt fails, the two primary subjects of the *Life* story commit suicide by overdosing on sleeping pills. In a final letter to his wife, one of the men, David Treacly, writes, "I have no confidence in either their concept of justice, their methods of interrogation and inconceivable brutality, or in the bumbling incompetence and indifference of our embassy... So I'm going out tonight... John not only accepts and understands, but has decided he wants to go with me... Given the circumstances, I cannot think of anyone I'd rather go with."

In this atmosphere of brutality and corruption, Padilla and his friends strike a deal with Delgado. The deal is Delgado will keep the money and the cocaine, probably to resell, and Padilla, Brewer, and Thomason will say nothing to the DEA about the drugs or cash—it's their only leverage. When they go to trial, Delgado is supposed to testify that he never saw the coke on display until he opened a black travel bag. The story will be that a jealous Fastie planted the bag as revenge for Padilla flirting with his girlfriend. With Delgado's testimony, they are assured, they will be home in six months. In the meantime, though, they will have to go to San Juan de Lurigancho prison.

"'Don't worry,'" Padilla remembers being told. "'You'll be out in four to six months. And the prison is nice. There's basketball, soccer, a great pool.'"

La Casa Del Diablo

THERE ARE, OF COURSE, no pools or athletic facilities at Lurigancho. There aren't even working toilets. Built in the 1960s to house 1,500 inmates, Lurigancho has more than six thousand by the time Padilla is processed. (Today some estimates put the number of prisoners there at more than ten thousand.)

Going in, though, Padilla still has an outlaw's cocky sense of exemption. Besides, he's paid off his captors. "It's just like an adventure," he remembers thinking. "I'd been in prison. I'd been in jails."

That feeling doesn't last long. Padilla says the conditions are "like a dog kennel." Food is a bowl of rice a day—with beans on the lucky days. "People starved to death."

The running water, when it runs, comes from a community pump, which the prison often shuts down to clean rats out of the pipes. The water is full of worms and bacteria. Everybody has dysentery.

"If you got the runs, you better find a plug, because everybody's going to be real pissed if you shit in a cell," he says. "I had dysentery every day."

The toilet, a hole in the ground that prisoners line up to use, seems designed to make the most of this affliction. It constantly overflows with shit and piss, so the prisoners resort to relieving themselves onto an ever-growing mound of feces.

"The whole place smells like shit," says Padilla.

The American prisoners and some other expats live together in the same cellblock, a more modern facility built off the big hall, which is a real-world incarnation of Dante's *Inferno*, where murderers, rapists, and the destitute teem together in a bazaar of daily strife. There, Padilla says, you see people starving, drowning in tuberculosis, being beaten and stabbed to death.

Padilla's description of the prison is in keeping with interviews that a former human rights activist, who is familiar with Lurigancho, has conducted for this story with past and present volunteers in Lima. All have requested anonymity.

One volunteer says the guards have surrendered the place to the prisoners. Everything from cots to a spot in a cell must be purchased. Those with no resources are left to wander the outskirts of the cellblocks, relying on handouts and picking through garbage like zombies.

Another volunteer, who worked at Lurigancho when Padilla was imprisoned there, says, "There were always ugly things… We felt very powerless against the mistreatment." She says there are constant fights between prison pavilions, wars between inmates, and murders tacitly sanctioned by the guards, who are often paid off to look the other way.

As it becomes increasingly clear that his chances of getting out quickly are about as good as going for a swim in the pool, Padilla's days are given over to survival, often in a haze of pasta, a particularly toxic paste form of cocaine smuggled into the prison and sold by well-connected inmates. Nights are filled with the sounds of screaming and snoring, and the insane beating of drums from the big hall.

Padilla doesn't hesitate when asked to describe the worst thing he witnessed. "Watching a whole cell block get killed," he says. "Watching a .50 caliber machine gun, at least a dozen rifles and a half dozen pistols...until no one is moving. And then, they open up the door and storm it. They shoot everybody."

The massacre comes, Padilla says, after a handful of prisoners take some guards hostage and demanded better conditions. The inmates release the guards when the prison warden agrees to their demands. The next day, the military comes in and shoots the place up. Padilla believes hundreds of inmates are killed in the attack.

On another occasion, Padilla says confused guards open fire on prisoners returning on a bus from court, killing dozens. "One of the [wounded] guys was in our cell block. He came up to the cell block just covered in blood."

The prison's atrocities mostly escape international attention until December 1983, when police shoot and kill a Chicago nun being held hostage by prisoners attempting to flee. Eight prisoners are also killed. Lurigancho gains further notoriety when, in July 1986, police kill anywhere from 124 to 280 (accounts vary) rioting members of the Sendero Luminosa, or Shining Path, Marxist guerillas incarcerated at Lurigancho.

Lurigancho's tableau of evils, both epic and banal, earn the prison the name La Casa del Diablo, the house of the devil. It remains a hellish place; the *Associated Press* reports that two people a day still die in Lurigancho from violence or illness.

Despite being imprisoned in the midst of this, Padilla doesn't slip into despair. Not immediately. It takes something more potent. It takes Diane Pinnix.

Femme Fatale

QUICKLY AFTER THE ARRESTS, Diane Pinnix flies down to Lima, ostensibly to aid and abet Padilla's release. Before long, though, Peru's attractions prove irresistible and she starts partying. Padilla worries she'll get in trouble, the last thing he needs. He decides he has to get out of Lurigancho fast. His chance comes with a Colombian coke dealer named Jimmy, another inmate who's been supplying pasta for Padilla, Brewer, Thomason, and other cellies to smoke.

During a delivery one day, Jimmy tells the guys how he plans to escape Lurigancho. Jimmy's lawyer will bribe clerks to get him called to court, but his name will be left off the judge's docket. At the end of the day, in the chaos of transferring prisoners, Jimmy's lawyers will hand the soldiers in charge counterfeit documents saying the judge has ordered his immediate release. If the plan works, it's decided that Pinnix will give Jimmy what's left of Padilla's money to set up the same deal.

But Jimmy takes Padilla's money and never returns to Lurigancho. Nor does Pinnix. Word filters back through the prison grapevine that Diane has been seen on the streets of Lima holding hands and kissing someone who fits the description of Jimmy.

Padilla spirals into a rage. He thinks only of revenge. To exact it, he seeks out a violent man known as Pelone, the boss of a neighboring prison cell. Through Pelone, Padilla orders a hit on Jimmy, an expensive proposition for which he has no money. Padilla promises to pay up when Pelone's pistolero cousin brings back Jimmy's finger, the traditional token of a successful hit. Padilla knows that with no money, it might be his life he pays with, but he wants Jimmy dead. In the meantime, he needs pasta to numb his pain. Pelone is more than happy to supply on credit.

Months go by with no success in the hit and Padilla falls deeper into despair. In the back of his mind is an inescapable fact: the pain he is feeling is the same pain he caused his wife,

Eileen, and his kids, when he walked out on them for Pinnix. His spirit breaks.

"I gave up because of Diane. Not just because of Diane, but because I was betrayed and that brought on all the betrayal I gave Eileen, my kids. My dedication to God, you know it was just gone. I turned my back and betrayed all of it. Betrayed my soul."

Padilla rarely leaves his bunk. He interrupts his sleep and sobbing only to smoke pasta. When the pasta runs out, he turns to pills. In his bunk, he dreams of surfing, and of Tahiti and Maui. He gives up his battle with dysentery.

"That's how I got. I became absolutely disgusting. I stunk. I reeked," Padilla says. "Richard and James are pretty sure I'm going to die."

His death seems assured one night when Padilla turns over in his bunk and sees Pelone wearing a leather jacket zipped to the top. Padilla's cellmates aren't around, and Pelone has seized the opportunity to come calling for his debts. Pelone pulls a long shank from under his jacket and comes at Padilla. Using his boxing skills, Padilla manages to dodge the first couple of stabs, but Pelone is skilled with a blade, and Padilla soon finds himself staring defenselessly at a shank aimed for his midsection. Just as Pelone is about to thrust, one of Padilla's cellies miraculously appears, and grabs Pelone's shoulder before he can stab. The opening gives Padilla enough time to throw a left cross into Pelone's nose, breaking it, he says. They tumble to the floor, and by then, a group of Padilla's cellmates storm in and disarm Pelone. The guy who has saved Padilla pays off the four hundred dollar debt to Pelone—a prison fortune—on the condition that Padilla gets his shit together.

In order to survive, Padilla realizes he needs to get back to some idea of God, to find a way to live beyond his fear. He quits doing drugs and starts meditating. He trains in boxing again. But his biggest challenge is still beyond him: the big hall. If he can master that, he thinks, he can master his fear. But he's not ready. He needs something more than God to hold onto. For Padilla, that could only be a woman.

One day during visitation, a young, indigenous woman named Zoila catches Padilla's eye. Padilla sees something in her that he hasn't seen in what seems like forever.

"She was the purest, most wonderful thing that could happen to me," he says. "She was like a gift from God."

The note Padilla throws down to Zoila from his cellblock feels like a life preserver. When someone hands her the note and points to Padilla, she smiles and waves. After that, she becomes Padilla's regular visitor and something like a love affair unfolds.

"She helped me heal so much in the prison. That was grace. I crack when I think about that experience." And he actually does crack when he tells this story, reinforcing my suspicion that beneath the surface of every tough guy is a heartbroken mama's boy.

With his dignity on the mend, Padilla knows there's something he must still do to be worthy of Zoila. After jumping rope one day, he decides it's time. He asks a prison guard to open the door protecting his cellblock from the big hall. The guard smiles contemptuously and opens the door.

Padilla walks through the maze. He sees men lifting a dead body out of the way. Blood from tuberculosis stains the floors like abstract art. His journey through the hall is quick, but he survives. Before long, he goes back again, this time under the guidance of a man named Chivo, a leader in this strange netherworld of Lurigancho. After a while, Padilla is allowed to pass the big hall with immunity. Something has changed.

Escape

MORE THAN THREE YEARS after they were taken to Lurigancho, Padilla, Brewer, and Thomason finally have their day before the tribunal. As a matter of course, the Peruvian Supreme Court reviews cases after the tribunal renders its verdict—but guilty verdicts are rarely overturned. The tribunal will be the trio's biggest test. They have a couple of things working for them. First is Zoila, who packs the courtroom with family and friends. They also manage to secure the services of a sympathetic translator, without which they wouldn't stand a chance.

On the stand, all three stick to the story: Fastie planted the coke in their room and nobody saw it until Delgado opened the black travel bag. Thomason is just a friend who happened to be there. The key witness will be Delgado. Nobody knows whether he'll keep his bargain to back up the tale.

When Delgado walks into the courtroom, eyes as black and dead as ever, a visceral terror shoots through Padilla's body. But Delgado takes the stand and, to Padilla's surprise, gives a brief statement corroborating their account of the arrest. The tribunal has little choice but to render absuelto in all three cases—absolved. It's the first good news in years.

That evening, Padilla and Brewer are taken to a hotel while Thomason is held back at a holding pen in the Lima neighborhood of Pueblo Libre. He has draft-dodging issues. Jimmy Carter had pardoned all draft dodgers while the men were in prison, but that means little to the Peruvian authorities. There's no telling how long or how much money it will take to sort this out. The longer it takes, the more likely it is that Padilla's decade-old San Francisco conviction will turn up like an albatross around his neck.

There are other complications. Padilla and Brewer have recently been implicated in the arrest of a former associate who Jimmy and Pinnix tricked into doing a coke deal with them by saying the proceeds would go to help spring the guys. If that case makes it to court before they're free, they are done for sure. Padilla and Brewer have to decide whether to make a break for it or wait for Thomason. They stay.

When Padilla and Brewer return to Pueblo Libre the next day, bad news awaits. The Supreme Court will be reviewing the case. Their lawyer mentions Padilla's "FBI problems." Freedom is near, they're told, but it'll take money. Padilla, Brewer, and Thomason are put in a cell at the Pueblo Libre jail to await the Supreme Court's review.

Facing more than twenty years each should their verdicts be overturned, Padilla and Brewer know a return to Lurigancho is certain death. They start working on an escape plan. Thomason, facing just three years, wants no part of it.

Months go by in Pueblo Libre while Padilla and Brewer prepare for a moment that might never come. They ask an Episcopalian reverend, an Englishman who has started visiting them in Lurigancho, to bring them towels, maps of the city and the Amazon wilderness beyond it. He also brings them money. They scope out the jail and determine they can get over a wall on the roof if given a chance. They make an effort to befriend their jailers, to show they pose no threat. Brewer swipes a serving spoon and hides it in his shoe.

In June of 1978, soccer-mad Peru makes an unlikely run through the first round of the World Cup being held in neighboring Argentina. During Peru's match against Scotland to advance to the second round, the atmosphere in Lima is ecstatic, even in the jail. The guards bring in beer and booze and good food, which they share with the Americans. They leave the jail cell open believing the only way out is past them since the steel door leading to the roof is spring-locked.

The partying gets more intense as the game plays. The guards are rapt. Brewer wakes up Padilla, who is sleeping off some whiskey. It's time to go, he says. Padilla says he's ready if Brewer can spring the lock to the steel door. They are worried about the loud noise the lock makes when it releases. Then, something incredible happens just as Richards jams the spoon into the lock and springs the steel door open: Peru scores! It's pandemonium in the jail. Nobody hears the door or them as they scurry up the stairs and onto the roof.

On the roof, Padilla and Brewer scale the wall and look up at the barbed-wire-topped chain link fence. They throw towels over the barbs and hoist themselves up and over onto the freedom side of the two-story wall. They'll have to jump down onto another rooftop, scramble to the jail's outside wall and scale that to get to the street. Their plan is to split up and reconvene at the reverend's church in Miraflores.

At the outside wall, Brewer urges Padilla to jump. Padilla hesitates, and in a flash, Brewer is hurtling down into a patch of light, landing hard on the ground below. Brewer grabs a ladder propped against a shack and hauls it over to the outer wall. Padilla finally jumps into the dark and lands with a thud on a pile of lumber. Pain immediately shoots through his body. He tries to stand but crumples. His ankle swells up immediately. His heel is broken. Padilla crawls and hops to the ladder and pulls himself up, the lower half of his body dead weight. He makes it to the top of the second wall and lets himself fall to the ground.

Out in the street, Brewer tries desperately to hail a cab. Padilla calls to him. Seconds go by like hours. Finally, Brewer sees him and comes racing back, asking what the fuck happened; how did he get so dirty? Padilla tells him he can't walk. Brewer races back and hoists Padilla over his shoulder, carrying him across the street into the shelter of an alley. He flags down a car and they make their way to the reverend's church in Miraflores.

Thirty-one years later, the same reverend answers a call at his home in the English countryside. Retired for twenty years, he asks that his name not be disclosed while he recalls for me the night the two men he'd been visiting in prison for months showed up at his door.

"It was unexpected. One of them had broken a bone in his heel and was having a tough time getting around. I think there was a lot of adrenaline going," the reverend says with typical English understatement. "We gave them some food and clothing and moved them onto a contact they had... The police came around to find out what part I had in their escape and held my passport for awhile."

Padilla and Brewer next enlist the cousin of an inmate Padilla befriended in Lurigancho. He is a travel guide with the Peruvian tourism industry with access to an underground network of friends and relatives. The guide's family, like many others, has suffered at the hands of Delgado and the PIP as the War on Drugs has conflated with political persecution and the other abuses you'd expect in a police state.

A domestic flight, arranged through a sympathetic airline worker, takes Padilla and Brewer to the Amazon River city of Iquitos. They stay for weeks at the lodge of a man who used be a PIP agent, but quit over the agency's brutal practices. There, the natural beauty of the Amazon and their first taste of real freedom bring Padilla and Brewer to tears. The hum of jungle birds and the roar of big cats at night almost drown out the sounds of snoring, screaming, and drumming at Lurigancho, still echoing in their heads. Padilla thinks of Zoila. He feels she's out there in her village somewhere in the Amazon wilderness. It breaks his heart that he'll never be able to thank her enough.

After a close call with PIP agents in Iquitos, Padilla and Brewer acquire forged documents identifying the two as Peruvians going to visit family in Colombia. They fly to the Colombian border town of Leticia and reach a hotel owned by an expat. Padilla calls his ex-wife Eileen and she sends money on the next flight in. They pay off the Colombian equivalent of the PIP to write a temporary visa that gives them seventy-two hours to get out of the country or be arrested.

During their brief stay at the hotel, Padilla and Brewer befriend a group of college kids. One of them is a Colombian girl who rooms with Caroline Kennedy at Radcliffe. The friendship pays off in Bogota, the girl's hometown, when Padilla and Brewer can't get a hotel room there because they have no passports. They're terrified they've come all this way only to get picked up for being indigent. Then, Padilla remembers he has the girl's phone number. Their last night in South America is spent at the penthouse home of Caroline Kennedy's college roommate. The next day they get a flight to Mexico City, and then it's on to LAX.

Home.

As they exit the airport through a stream of people, Padilla puts his hand on Brewer's shoulder, and they stop for a minute. Padilla looks uncertainly at Brewer and his look is returned. Until now, they've known what they were running to. Now that they're here, they both realize the hardest part comes next.

Epilogue

Twelve years after she entered Mystic Arts World, Lorey Smith has grown into a woman already disappointed by marriage. She is cautious and jaded. To help get her out of her funk, Smith's sister suggests she come down to Corona del Mar for a party. A friend of her uncle is going to be there, and he can show her a good time. She hesitates, but when her sister tells her that the guy used to be in the Brotherhood, she softens.

"I had this thought, *okay, he's not anybody's who's going to harm me,*" Smith says. "I felt safe. So I said, 'I'll come down.'"

The party is in full howl when Smith arrives. Every time she turns around, she bumps into her uncle's friend. His name is Eddie.

"He was following me all over the house. I thought, *What is up with this guy?* My sister would say, 'Oh, he's fine. He's fine.'

I didn't know everybody had been partying for the last three weeks. She left that part out."

Little by little, Smith settles in. She and Eddie start talking. They dance, despite Eddie's obvious limp. Two days turn into four. Smith is compelled by this guy, but unsure. He seems haunted, hunted even.

"I didn't know he was blasted on coke and had drank who knows how much by the time I got there—I just knew something was wrong. But once we actually started talking, and it did take a couple of days, then, I was like, 'Wow, what's his story? All this pain.'"

At some point during the partying, Smith loses track of Eddie. "All of a sudden, I heard this noise, like moaning, like pain and moaning. And I opened the front door and he's out on the lawn, by this bush…just in this really, really bad place."

"I tried to get him to talk a little bit about it, and he did, and he shared enough with me sitting on the grass that one particular night that I was just…fascinated that he was even sitting there having been through what he'd been through."

Over time Eddie tells Smith more and more about what he's been through, about Lurigancho, a prison in Peru known as La Casa del Diablo. About how he escaped with his life, but wasn't sure about his soul.

"I was like, 'Whoa, you're kidding, you should write a book.'"

Smith tells this story at a small kitchen table in her small condo in Santa Rosa, California. It's the middle of December and a relentless, cold rain has been pounding for days. Smith serves up some sandwiches as she talks. The oven is on for heat.

Padilla comes in from the living room when he hears us talking about how he and Lorey met in Corona del Mar. "I wasn't fit for polite company," he jokes. Lucky for him, Smith wasn't too polite, and they kept seeing each other. It didn't take them long to figure out they'd met before, when a wide-eyed twelve-year-old handed a handsome man a handmade necklace and that man accepted it with a smile.

Eddie Padilla and Lorey Smith have been together since 1981. It's one of the few happy endings in this story.

Jimmy the dealer and Diane Pinnix stayed together until Jimmy beat her up badly, putting her in the hospital. Jimmy briefly went to jail before he bailed out and fled to Columbia. He was eventually gunned down in the street.

Diane Pinnix died a junkie's death seven years ago in Jamaica. "The unfortunate thing is she died alone," says her mother. "She was beautiful when she was younger."

Drugs and alcohol continued to dictate the life of James Thomason, the man Padilla says did his time with more courage and grace than anyone else. I visit Thomason at the Rescue Mission in Tustin. His shoulder bears a tattoo that reads "Lurigancho 75-78." His hard life has punched in his face. When I ask about his time in prison, he says. "I don't know what hell is, but Lurigancho is as close as I can think of."

Thomason tells me of the dysentery, the filth, the flies, people getting stabbed, and Padilla's descent into despair after Pinnix betrayed him with Jimmy. "That's when he really lost it," says James. "He was a lowly person in that Peruvian prison, and nobody cared. He wasn't Eddie Padilla anymore. He was a prisoner."

When I ask about the massacre, Thomason's eyes go distant, and his galloping speech slows to a near-halt. "They came in with rifles and the machine gun," he says.

These days Thomason dreams of being able to afford an apartment by the beach, watch TV, drink a few beers, and live out his days. Though he seems a poster boy for Post-Traumatic Stress Disorder, he admits to no lasting ill effects from his time in Lurigancho. It occurs to me that surviving Lurigancho is both the worst thing that ever happened to him and his greatest accomplishment.

Richard Brewer died a little more than two years ago. Upon his return from Peru, he quickly went back to his old ways. But he never lost his outlaw's code of honor. At Brewer's memorial, friends gathered to paddle his ashes out to sea. Afterward, they had a bonfire on the beach. Everybody had stories to tell, but Padilla had *the* story.

"I said, 'You guys know the story…but what you guys probably don't know is, he came back for me. We had agreed to go our different ways. He knew I wasn't going to be able to walk, and he came back for me.'"

We had just finished watching a documentary on Lurigancho and sifting through a kaleidoscope of memories—some better than others—when Padilla relates this. It's late in a long day and he starts sobbing.

"All those guys called themselves the Brotherhood for so long, but you know what? Richard was a real brother. He came back for me. He carried me… I always thought that if anybody came back for anybody, it would be me coming back for them."

As Padilla says this, embarrassed by his tears, it feels like a fresh revelation. In some ways, I think the simple fact that he wasn't the rescuer but the one who was rescued may have turned out to be the god Eddie Padilla was looking for his entire life—the ego break that neither acid, the Brotherhood, nor his misguided idea of freedom could provide. Perhaps this newfound humility allowed him to admit, where others didn't, that Lurigancho broke him. Maybe it gave him the strength to ask for help and to claw his way back after descending into a deadly alcoholism and drug addiction, fueled by his crippled leg and fractured psyche.

At death's door and living on the streets, Padilla finally made it into rehab and set about on the long road back to recovery. He went to AA meetings and therapy for years. He managed to earn a degree in drug and alcohol counseling and has made a career of working with juveniles and cons. He hopes his memoir will be useful in his work, both as a cautionary tale and a story of redemption. In the end, he just might have earned the narrative he seeks.

"You know when they first started telling me about the Brotherhood, that seems like what it was all about—it was people helping people," says Padilla's brother Dennis, who was instrumental in helping Padilla stay sober in those first crucial years of recovery. "It wasn't about money and things, and I think that's where he's at today."

Sergeant Delgado was killed in a shootout when a friend of one of the doomed guys in the *Life* article tried to bust them out. According to the report, it took eleven rounds to bring him down.

Lone Wolf

Originally published in Orion, *April 29, 2013*

Author's note: I'd blown all my money on Slake and was getting ready to pull the plug on the project. My mom was in the grips of advanced Alzheimer's disease. Occupy Los Angeles—the biggest and longest lasting of the Occupy movements—had finally fizzled. The Great Recession was hanging over life like a dark cloud and I was feeling broke, spiritually and financially. I needed something to believe in. Then came wolf OR7, insouciantly traipsing into Northern California, pissing on trees and claiming his birthright in the very place where the last wild wolf in California had been killed some ninety years prior. Bingo.

THE NIGHT IS DARK on a narrow slip of canyon floor alongside the North Fork Feather River. The mountains are big and close, their steep, tree-covered slopes tall enough to block out the moon and stars. Flashlight in hand, I follow the sound of roiling water toward the river, though my chances of finding what I'm looking for are slim. My objective is a moving target, one that's highly elusive by nature and even more so under the cover of a black night.

It is hard to tell at this point whether my path to California's remote Plumas County has been one of fortune or folly. Online, the "lodge" where I'm staying in Belden, population twenty-two, is an appealing, rustic western Sierra getaway. In real life, it's a trailer park hotel. But I may well be on the right track. When I checked in and asked about the object of my obsession, the thickly bearded innkeeper with the feral, blue eyes nodded and told me that his dog went crazy about a week ago. "I've never seen him like that before," he said, gazing out the window across the river and into the forest.

I hurried to my assigned trailer, where a large buck camped out front was munching on flower bulbs, and checked my laptop. I scanned back through the reports posted online by the California Department of Fish and Wildlife, and sure enough he was in the area when the innkeeper's dog went barking mad. And has been since.

Just being close to where he's been—may still be—is enough to send me out into the night. Maybe he is up on the bluff across the highway where the hydropower pipe climbs eight hundred feet up the mountainside like a giant snake disappearing into the trees. Maybe he's tracking that buck with eyes honed for picking up the slightest of movements from great distances, even in the dark. Maybe, just maybe, I'll catch a glimpse of him—the first wild wolf to enter California in more than eighty years.

◆◆◆

NEARLY TWO YEARS AGO, when I first read a small news item about the wolf with the blandly scientific designation of OR7—the seventh wolf collared in Oregon—crossing into California, I was caught off guard by the intense affinity I felt for him and his journey. It wasn't just the grand scale of his adventure, with the late summer and fall months spent traveling the length of Oregon, his Christmastime crossing into California, the subsequent seven-hundred-mile midwinter foray through the state's remote northern counties, only to cross back into Oregon in March before doubling back to the Golden State in April. Having logged thousands of miles in search of my own place in the world, I could relate. But the awareness OR7 sparked in me of a moment's wild possibility had to do with something bigger, deeper, and older than all that.

It was the winter of Occupy, a time for reckoning with the past decades' economic, spiritual, and environmental betrayals. I had hopes that bankrupt paradigms might fall and something new, better, and more honest might take their place. My own reckonings and rebellions had mostly left me out of money and ideas, and frankly I needed something to believe in. And then came this wolf—this long-toothed shadow of our bastardized best friends, a thing we tried our damnedest to eradicate— trotting insouciantly into California.

OR7's return struck me as a singular act of defiance—by god, nature, fate, whatever words you prefer. I rejoiced at his coming south, so far that he was now howling at the backdoor of our failing civilization, forcing us by his very presence to consider the question, how are we going to live? Can we surrender some of what we've taken? Can we accept that OR7, nature's foot soldier, the vanguard wolf of California from the clan of creatures we couldn't tame but could only kill, deserves some of this, too? Or will we continue to insist the land and all that's on it, under it, and over it is ours to do with as we please? Who better, I thought, to stalk our hypocrisies and upend our delusions than the most mythologized and demonized animal in history?

I felt compelled to try and get closer to this young wolf, formidable at 105 pounds, measuring nearly three feet at the shoulder, six feet in length, and possessing jaws that can crack an elk femur the way a nutcracker can crack a walnut. So early last September, I drove into Plumas County, California, following the North Fork Feather River, which begins auspiciously near Lassen Peak, the southernmost volcano in the Cascade Range. The river drains some twenty-one hundred square miles of western-slope Sierra into Lake Oroville, one of the largest reservoirs in the country. It has carried countless dreams downstream: gold dreams, ranching dreams, hydropower, rail, and timber dreams—each a tributary in the larger river of dreams that settled the American West and tamed wild California.

Many of these dreams are dead or dying, but I could still see their vestiges as I drove downslope through the Feather River Canyon where defunct railroad tracks cut into the hillsides, and shorn mountaintops peak through low clouds and fog. The occasional Sierra Pacific lumber truck rumbles along the Feather River Highway past mining cottages that dot the riverside and stare down diminishing prospects with the occasional splash of fresh paint and flower boxes.

Except for a few stubborn holdouts, the era of man seems just about done in Plumas County. It's an eerie, forgotten landscape, and there's a certain poetic justice in OR7's arrival. Bounty hunters killed OR7's last remaining California cousin near here in 1924, back when wolves were considered to be an enemy of Manifest Destiny. OR7, though, doesn't seem to have revenge in mind. He has yet to take sheep or cow from the descendants of those who shot, trapped, poisoned, and burned his kind to extinction in the West.

But this hasn't stopped some locals from greeting his arrival as if the devil himself were paying a visit. As soon as his epic trek signaled a wolf with Golden State aspirations, the hysteria began. To calm local fears of pending doom, the California Department of Fish and Wildlife conducted public meetings featuring wildlife officials, celebrity wolf experts, government resources managers, and a highly agitated public—all awaiting the imminent arrival of a solitary, thirty-month-old Canis lupus.

After one meeting, Marcia Armstrong, a supervisor for Siskiyou County, where OR7 dallied briefly before moving on, told the *Los Angeles Times* that she would like to see all encroaching wolves "shot on sight." Adding to the tinder were ranchers warning that a wolf repopulation would be "catastrophic." Other folks spread rumors of conspiratorial wolf smuggling by federal agencies and of a government out to trample rights and make it harder to log, mine, and dam the rural West.

Those sympathetic to OR7's plight had very different demands. Some even pleaded with officials to import a mate for the lone wolf, who was clearly looking for love in all the wrong places.

◆◆◆

BACK ALONG THE BANKS of the North Fork Feather River, the water is just a moving silhouette. I turn off the flashlight and crouch down at the river's edge, scanning the area without moving my head, trying to be as still as possible, looking for movement the way OR7 might, though at 120-degrees of arc, my visual field is only two-thirds of his.

Wolf stories, like ghost stories, emerge through insinuation and grow into their own kind of lore: large tracks in the mud, a moonlit howling that is too resonant to be the nattering of coyotes, a tingle down the spine. Or if you're an unlucky rancher, a hollowed-out rib cage where once was a sheep or calf. A wolf seen is a wolf seen mostly by accident, happy or otherwise.

I turn my back to the river and face the other way, toward the hillside, where that buck outside my trailer probably came from. The air is still. Nothing moves but gnats and mosquitoes. No sounds but the gurgling river. I feel exposed, not so much hunted as haunted. And I like it.

The next morning, I drive farther north, into territory OR7 may be claiming for himself. The road passes through Lassen National Forest and eventually skirts under the 14,179-feet-high Mount Shasta, just about an hour from where OR7 crossed over from Oregon. The route travels a California rarely seen by those who live within the clutches of the coastal megalopolises.

Here, salmon run in the rivers and bald eagles fly so low you can almost look them in the eye.

OR7 crossed this road and others many times as he traveled south. I scan the valley floors, farms, and ranches, picturing him loping along the edge of the highway at night, filled with the curiosity and the courage of one whose only experience of fear is that which he inspires. I see him stealing through private property where easy meals and misguided liaisons with canine cousins tempt his hungry soul. I imagine all the itchy fingers waiting for a shot at his shadow.

The air feels wild and dangerous and alive in a new way. So do I. And I begin to understand even more why OR7's incursion matters, why the land is so relieved to feel his feet pushing down into its soil once again. The land knows what I know driving into the untamed night—that we're less than we can be without him.

◆◆◆

KAREN KOVACS, THE WILDLIFE program manager for California Department of Fish and Wildlife's northern region, has agreed to meet me at her office in the coastal town of Eureka. When I arrive, it is damp and foggy and Kovacs says she's exhausted. OR7's arrival has put a mountain of to-dos in her threadbare department's inbox. Foremost among them is the petition filed by several environmental organizations to get gray wolves—this gray wolf—protected under the California Endangered Species Act. The petition triggers a taxing process of studies, peer reviews, hearings, and a series of votes, beginning with whether or not it is even warranted.

It's hard for Kovacs to imagine another animal getting this much attention. She points out that a wolverine, absent from California for as long as wolves, has recently made it into the Sierra with little fanfare. "People go cuckoo over wolves," she says. "We're not managing wildlife; we're managing people and people's perception of wildlife to a large degree. With OR7, you can almost draw the lines politically."

Those lines are basically drawn at how far we will go to accommodate wolves. How many entitlements—from hunting to heehawing in the backcountry on snowmobiles to grazing livestock on public lands—are we willing to forego to ensure that they are also part of the landscape?

From the beginning, the answer was the least number possible. Gray wolf reintroduction in the West was so controversial when the U.S. Fish and Wildlife Service began bringing wolves back into Yellowstone in 1995, that the agency had little choice but to define Northern Rocky Mountain gray wolves as an "experimental, nonessential species." That meant that no critical habitat would be set aside for them, and no restrictions on economic interests would accompany the recovery effort. The prevailing logic was that since wolves came with so much baggage—as fabled beasts revered and feared in folklore and fairytale, and as supposedly depraved killers of livestock—the species couldn't withstand the backlash against land-use restrictions the way the spotted owl could. But as apex predators whose domain once covered all of North America, wolves are indeed a land-use issue. We got rid of them and Native Americans at around the same time and for roughly the same reason: they were in the way.

It wasn't long after the questions of wolves (eradicated) and Native Americans (mostly eradicated) were resolved that settlers had license to do just about anything they wanted with the land. Not surprisingly, this led to the extreme overgrazing that culminated in the Dust Bowl and which spurred Franklin Roosevelt to sign the Taylor Grazing Act of 1934, a modest initial attempt at reining in free-range ranchers. This was followed by the establishment of the Bureau of Land Management, as well as nascent notions that public lands were for more than cattle,

logging, mining, and railroad interests. Then came expansions to
the National Park system, the creation of the Endangered Species
Act, and, from a rancher's perspective, lawsuit-happy tree huggers
making it harder and harder to earn a living off the land.

As wolves like OR7 move farther west from the Northern
Rockies, they do, in fact, give conservationists a powerful new
weapon with which to relitigate a number of policy wars over the
disposition of public lands. Returning wolves are the canaries in
the coalmine for other decimated species—brown bears, bison,
and the once-vast herds of ungulates that grazed the land before
cattle displaced them. As such, they carry much of the weight of
the past, and the fight for the future, on their backs.

It's a fight the US Fish and Wildlife Service evidently hoped
to duck out on as soon it could declare the gray wolf "recovered."
In order to do that, the agency determined there must be a
minimum of three hundred wolves and thirty breeding pairs
spread across Wyoming, Montana, and Idaho. Of course, how
many wolves are enough to ensure the survival of a species
practically wiped from the lower forty-eight states is a question
without a real answer. Nonetheless, based on those numbers,
federal protections on wolves in those states were lifted in 2011,
and responsibility reverted to state agencies.

Gray wolves still enjoy Endangered Species Act protection
in Washington, Oregon, and California, where their numbers are
negligible—or just one. But that may be fleeting as well. The Fish
and Wildlife Service recently announced its intention to lift all
federal protections for gray wolves, except for the tiny Mexican
gray wolf populations in New Mexico and Arizona, thus leaving
California to decide for itself how it wants to deal with OR7 and
his brethren.

Meanwhile, OR7 goes about his business. A prodigious
traveler, he has already covered roughly three thousand miles
in his peripatetic existence, indicating estimable strength and

endurance. He's a first-rate hunter who dines mostly on deer and small game and has now made it through two winters alone. When chasing prey, he can achieve bursts of nearly forty miles per hour, covering fifteen feet in a single bound. He has also shown a knack for taking over elk kills from mountain lions—a wise choice since a lone wolf is much more vulnerable to mortal injury than a pack wolf.

OR7 spends a good amount of time communicating with one leg lifted, marking trees, game trails, and carcasses, and covering other animals' marks—delineating a vast territory and sending out messages. Some are warnings, others invitations. Wolves are gregarious by nature and often monogamous, so OR7 is likely scattering calling cards of a sort, expressing his desire to settle down with a mate and start a pack of his own. Given the dearth of eligible companions, he's mostly talking to himself.

I ask Kovacs what might be motivating OR7's prolonged travels. "You were young once," she says. "What were you thinking? This is normal behavior for young wolves." But OR7 isn't exactly young anymore. He's creeping up on middle age for a wolf, and this wolf is without the safety, structure, and society of a pack. Kovacs doesn't deny that every day OR7 turns up on her radar is a surprise.

"It's a hard life out there," she concedes. "Wolves that move this great of a distance are usually a genetic dead end."

◆◆◆

A YOUNG GRAY WOLF stands on the Idaho banks of the Snake River on a fall day in a land where winter comes early and leaves late. The wolf contemplates taking the leap. What would make him or her plunge into the cold current and swim for the other side? It's what young, would-be alphas do. They disperse in search of new mates and new territory, thereby strengthening the gene pool and reducing habitat stress.

A wolf could do worse than Oregon's Wallowa County. It's a beautiful, rugged patch twice the size of Rhode Island with only seven thousand humans, dominated by the Wallowa Mountains, Eagle Cap Wilderness, Wallowa-Whitman National Forest, and the Zumwalt Prairie, one of the largest savannas on the continent. For an ungulate-eating apex predator, the area—with an estimated 22,400 mule deer, 2,500 white-tailed deer, and 15,600 Rocky Mountain elk—is a promised land.

If the wolves reintroduced to Yellowstone nearly twenty years ago were going to continue their westward expansion, that river needed to be crossed. But when it was, the other side was less than welcoming. The first known wolf to brave the crossing was captured in 1999, put in a crate, and shipped back to Idaho. The next year, two more wolves from Idaho were found dead, one hit by a car, the other shot.

Wolves, though, are nothing if not intrepid, and in January 2008, a radio-collared female wolf from Idaho, soon to be known as OR2, found a fellow traveler soon to be christened OR4. They crossed the river successfully, and together they started the Imnaha pack, named for a spot they favored along the Imnaha River. OR7 was born into their second litter in 2009, one of five pups in a family of immigrants. By 2010, the pack had at least fourteen members.

The usual howls of ruination greeted the arrival of Idaho's wolves in Northeast Oregon, even though the Imnaha pack averaged only about a cattle kill a month. In May 2011, two members of the pack were killed, and an order to kill two more was issued by the state's Department of Fish and Wildlife that September, until legal challenges put a stay on wolf executions in Oregon. Nonetheless, OR7 decided it was time to go and started off on his walkabout.

The Imnaha pack's territory cuts a vast, crescent-shaped swath around the small Wallowa County town of Joseph,

Oregon, nestled in the lap of Sacajawea Peak. It's one of the key battlegrounds in the wolf wars, and a local named Dale Potter, with a flair for the dramatic, has his sights set on OR7's relatives. Potter, who flew helicopters in Vietnam and says he still craves excitement, leads rallies encouraging folks to "smoke a pack a day" and to "shoot, shovel, and shut up." He posts signs around the area proclaiming wolves to be "sadistic killers" smuggled back into the area by their brothers-in-arms, the Nez Perce tribe, which, he says, wants to reclaim its land. "The wolf has kept me busy," says Potter. At the frenzied height of his wolf demonizing, a panicked local rancher reportedly got down on his knees in church and prayed that wolves wouldn't kill him and his family.

Potter's paranoia and demagoguery may seem practiced, but they articulate genuine anxieties that began in earnest when the sawmills started shutting down. The mills, says Potter, were the thread that stitched the fabric of this community together. When the jobs left, families left, schools closed, and things began to unravel in ways that cappuccino-drinking second-home owners couldn't quite put back together. For him, the reappearance of wolves symbolizes the sort of governmental interference and environmental regulations that he believes kill jobs and destroy a way of life he wants to preserve. "I don't hate the wolf," says Potter. "I hate the politics that brought this invasive species here."

I ask him if he's ever seen a wolf. "To tell you the truth," he replies, "I have not seen a wolf."

◆◆◆

AT FIVE THOUSAND FEET, Joseph is blanketed in fresh snow on the weekend before Halloween. With its quaint, Old-West ambience, the town already feels like a Christmas card come to life, and when Wally Sykes walks into one of the few restaurants open after eight p.m., he looks like an undersized Kris Kringle. We sit down for dinner at a wood table near the bar as burly men with thick beards give us the stink eye. Sykes is used to this by now. "It's strange to be actively involved in a schism within a community," he says.

Sykes is Joseph's most outspoken wolf advocate, and he has agreed to take me into Imnaha pack territory the next morning. Before he started trying to save wolves, Sykes rescued his Malamute, Kumo, who had wandered into a fur trapper's snare. The explicit cruelty of trapping spurred him to start TrapFree Oregon, and it was only a matter of time until he was dragged into the wolf wars.

Sykes became a full-fledged activist after coming upon tracks near his home at the base of the Wallowa Mountains. They were canine for sure, but the animal's gait and paw size dwarfed those of his hundred-pound dog. "I never thought I'd be seeing wolves in my lifetime," says Sykes. "I was thrilled."

Now, he spends a lot of time in the backcountry, tracking the Imnaha pack as it moves around the Wallowa Mountains, Eagle Cap Wilderness, and Zumwalt prairie. When he's not in the field, Sykes is often working on his Wolf News Update, a weekly newsletter from the frontlines of the wolf wars featuring news, studies, blogs, and, since states recently started issuing wolf-hunting licenses, the grim body count.

He is one of the few people to see Wallowa's wolves up close and is adamant they belong here. "Oregon is not a hunting preserve, it's not a game farm, it's a functioning ecosystem, and its wildlife is supposed to be managed as a public trust for all its citizens," he says. "Not just certain hunters and ranchers."

Sykes shares the belief of many ecologists and biologists that the absence of these apex predators resulted in a sloppy crumbling of the ecological pyramid that eventually trickled down to vegetation. This idea is one that wolf-hunter-turned-pioneering-conservationist Aldo Leopold expressed in his 1949 classic *A Sand County Almanac*:

I have lived to see state after state extirpate its wolves. I have watched the face of many a newly wolfless mountain, and seen the south-facing slopes wrinkle with a maze of new deer trails. I have seen every edible bush and seedling browsed, first to anaemic desuetude, and then to death. I have seen every edible tree defoliated to the height of a saddle horn.

The return of wolves to the West has indeed resulted in a trophic cascade of benefits to the ecological landscape. In Yellowstone, for example, the absence of wolves meant the park's elk and deer were fat, slow, and stupid. They destroyed streambeds, overgrazed grass, and over-browsed the shrubs and aspens. When wolves were reintroduced, the days of deer and elk lazing around riparian areas like hoofed couch potatoes were over. Yellowstone's aspen groves made a comeback, streambeds are in better shape, shady shrubs have increased oxygen levels in creeks and streams, thus improving fish habitats, berries are dropping, seeds are scattering, grasses are growing. A case can be made that wolves are far better wilderness managers than humans will ever be.

But for Sykes it's a moral issue as well. "For one hundred years, wolves were hounded, hunted, trapped, hacked, and poisoned until every single one was exterminated. They were extirpated in a brutal, vindictive, ignorant campaign," he says. "I would like to see this wrong righted. I would like to see some compassion and understanding for our most persecuted wildlife."

♦♦♦

THE NEXT MORNING WE'RE up early and packed into Sykes's car. Kumo is in the back, looking out the windows. We pass a large gravel pit on the outskirts of town that used to be a bone yard for livestock carcasses. Sykes says this may have been what attracted wolves to the area in the first place. The pile was removed and government agencies now work with ranchers to better dispose of bone piles, as well as to put up red pennants that seem to scare wolves, and other hazing programs to keep wolves away from livestock. When predation does occur, ranchers are reimbursed for their losses. Sykes is on the committee that doles out compensation.

We skirt the edges of the Zumwalt, "the wolf highway," and continue up into higher elevations to a spot Sykes won't identify. He points out deer tracks in the snow along the side of the road—a calving area for deer and elk. "In the spring and summer, there are wolves all over here," he says.

When the road runs out at the top of a hill, we get out of the car and trek into the snow wearing bright orange hunting caps. Even with a heavy sky hiding the highest peaks from view, the land is dramatic in white, green, and gray, marked by deep gulches, rolling hills, and formidable mountains. It doesn't take long for senses to sharpen. You see things you might otherwise miss—a rabbit darting into some shrubs, a tiny spider sitting on the snow crust, deer climbing the other side of a gulch. We inspect coyote and deer tracks in the snow.

This is where OR7 learned how to be a wolf. This is where he first saw deer like the ones I spotted on the opposite hillside. This is where he became part of the everything we've lost our connection to, the everything that we desecrate so casually. Sykes says he can see people transform when he takes them into wolf country, that simply being where wolves roam does something special to humans. "Wolves are good for our souls," he says.

We continue along the timbered edges of ravines and through meadows covered in shin-high snow periodically marked by tracks. Eventually, we reach a destination deep in the woods. It's the rendezvous point the Imnaha pack used for its previous summer's litter—where the alpha female nests with the pups and other members of the pack bring food or report for nanny duties. OR7 was likely nursed near here a few summers ago.

"I'm proud of him," says Sykes of the pack's current alpha, OR4, who picked this spot with its abundant game. "He chose well." At 115 pounds, OR4 is the biggest wolf in Oregon. In five breeding seasons, OR4 and his mate, OR2, have never failed to deliver a litter or keep their pups alive. "He's a helluva wolf," says Sykes, of OR4.

I wonder if Sykes thinks the same of OR4's famous offspring. He contemplates this for a minute and chuckles. "OR7's certainly determined, and he's certainly self-confident," he responds. I ask him why OR7 would leave such a beautiful, wild, and abundant place. "I think wolves have ambitions," Sykes explains. "They want to get out on their own. To a wolf, a land with no wolves is a vacuum. It's not unusual for a wolf to go into a vacuum and keep going."

♦♦♦

WHEN WE KILLED OFF all the wolves from the West, we told ourselves a lie—that we were separate from, or superior to, all that with which the wolf communes, that we knew better what to do with the land than did the wolf. The return of wolves to our landscape has delivered us with a rare opportunity to make amends with that lie and to embrace the simple truth: how we live with wolves is how we live with nature—either in harmony or discord. The choice is ours to make and, as this hyperactive era of floods, fires, hurricanes, and tornadoes shows, the stakes are high.

My search for OR7, I came to realize, was a quest for insight into what we'd do with the opportunity wolves presented. Right now, we're mostly killing it. Since the feds lifted protections, nearly twelve hundred wolves out of a population of almost two thousand in Wyoming, Montana, and Idaho have been slain by hunters and trappers. Hunters in Minnesota and Wisconsin, home to more than four thousand wolves, have killed nearly five hundred since hunts were sanctioned. Michigan became the sixth state to approve wolf hunting. It's scheduled to take place during the winter holiday season. Guns, crossbows, and foot traps are all permitted.

The hunting lobbies say the killings are necessary "management" to reduce livestock predation and to relieve pressure on game such as deer and elk; federal wildlife experts say there are enough wolves to withstand the slaughter. I don't buy either argument.

In the seventy-nine billion-dollar cattle industry, there were ninety-four million head of cattle tromping around the lower forty-eight states in 2010, the most recent year for which there are statistics. Wolves killed 8,100 of them, or 0.000086 percent. Even vultures killed two thousand more cattle than wolves. And while any livestock loss to an individual rancher can be significant, it's worth noting that respiratory illness, digestive issues, calving complications, weather, and plain negligence killed about 3.8 million cattle in 2010, costing the industry 2.35 billion dollars. By comparison, wolves cost it 3.6 million dollars, most of which was reimbursed by taxpayers.

Similarly, the cry from hunters that wolves decimate deer and elk populations isn't borne out by fact. Ungulate numbers are up in most game management areas across the West where wolves live and slightly down in just a few. Deer and elk are just harder to find. Wolves have made them more alert and elusive—made them better at being deer and elk, and us at being hunters.

As for the argument that there are enough wolves now to withstand the hunts, there were a hundred times more back when we almost exterminated them. These hunts wreak havoc on the highly developed social structure of wolves, tearing families and communities apart, and orphaning ill-prepared adolescents, who are then more likely to get in trouble. Hunting and trapping wolves serves no purpose for sustenance or profit. It's done for the basest of reasons, for a trophy that is nothing more than a token of shameful ignorance and folly. After all we've done to them, wolves deserve better. We deserve better, too.

◆◆◆

WHILE WOLF-HUNTING SEASON WAS just getting underway in neighboring states, California's wildlife commissioners met in Sacramento to vote on whether or not to consider protecting California's lone wolf under the California Endangered Species Act. The room was packed, and the battle for hearts and minds went on for hours. Conservationists, wolf lovers, ranchers, cattlemen associations all had their say, although neither side seemed much moved by the other. Not surprisingly, no one there had actually seen the wolf in question.

In the end, the commissioners agreed by a narrow margin that the petition to list the gray wolf, this gray wolf, as an endangered species did indeed warrant consideration. The vote triggered numerous studies, reviews, and meetings that should result in a decision any day now about whether to protect wolves in California. If approved, it'll be largely symbolic until more wolves wander across the border, prompting perhaps a new moniker to consider: CA1. But for anyone looking to make amends with the truth, it would be a welcome symbol, a small bit of progress in the tortured dance between humans and what's left of the wild.

Meanwhile, OR7 just keeps moving. In late February, he left Plumas County, where I crouched in darkness beside the river with naïve hopes of seeing him, and started retracing his long-ago steps north. By mid-March, he had crossed back into Oregon. Maybe he wants to know if you can, indeed, go home again. Or maybe he's hopeful yet that he'll find what he's looking for.

The only thing we know for sure is that time outruns even a wolf. And as every new day dawns unfulfilled, the epic story of OR7's journey to find a place for himself, to start a family and be the first of his kind so that others may follow, takes a turn toward a more familiar fate: that of a lonely middle age spent on the outside looking in while death does double time to chase you down.

The Farewell Tour

Originally published as "Driving Vince Donnelly,"
Los Angeles Times Magazine, June 16, 2002

Author's note: I first tried to write this when I was helping to care for my terminally ill dad during his final weeks. Upon seeing the mess of a first draft, Martin J. Smith, the fine editor for the long-gone, but still-missed, Los Angeles Times Magazine, told me to take care of business and come back to the piece later. As a result, this slice of life and death ended up being published on the first Father's Day after my dad died.

THE VALET AT THE Pittsburgh Airport rental-car office brings around our white Lincoln Continental, and Vince Donnelly raises his eyebrow slyly and says, "If I'm going to go, I'm going to go in style."

I appreciate the subversive humor. It helps alleviate the shock of how he looks. Prior to this trip, I hadn't seen my dad since I spent Christmas in Vail, Colorado, where he and my mother had moved several years ago. What a difference five months can make.

During the holidays, Vince didn't look so bad for a guy who recently had had a third of his pancreas cut out. I even dared to hope he was on the mend. Then, a couple of days after Christmas, he asked if I wanted to drive his new Cadillac STS down to the Eagle Diner where we'd find the best milkshakes in the county.

The weather was warm for the Colorado high country, the sky a saturated blue. It was not a day for bad news, and my dad tried to deliver it as gently as possible.

"The horses are out of the barn, Joe," Vince said as we gained speed and lost altitude cruising down the valley. "I don't think they're going back in. I can feel it. It's running wild."

My dad went on to explain that the cancer he'd been diagnosed with the previous summer had metastasized despite the drastic operation. His CA19-9 markers (cancer activity in the blood) were climbing the charts. He rattled off the meager survival statistics, the chemo protocols, and the grim prognosis. I stared out the diner's windows and told him he was going to be fine. There had to be some exception to these rules, and I was sure my dad would be that. After all, he'd lived his life being the exception. Growing up in a household weighed down by poverty, alcoholism, and old-world Catholicism, he still managed to get out, get educated, and become a successful business owner. He had survived colon cancer twice in his early fifties, and several years ago he'd brushed off prostate cancer as if it were the flu. I'd been conditioned to expect him to walk out of life's burning buildings.

As he spoke, my mind wandered back to Los Angeles, where my own trajectory away from the past had run out of turf. Vince had visited me there recently and appreciated all of the things that we residents take for granted–the light, the architecture, the action, the intelligence. We talked about spending more time together in LA. I thought better times had arrived for my dad and me. We had both survived near-death encounters with booze and the things that drive men crazy. He was lucky to walk away from a drunken head-on collision with a truck. I was lucky to have called a friend instead of pulling the trigger of the gun in my mouth. We'd both gotten sober since and had even become optimistic.

Now this: the two of us in the rain at Pittsburgh International Airport, loading three bags into the white Lincoln–one for my clothes, one for my dad's, and one for the syringes, saline solutions, antiseptics, enzymes, anxiety reducers, and chemo pills that have become my dad's constant traveling companions. Pittsburgh, the town where I more or less grew up and where my dad's working life finally paid off, is the first stop on our trip–a journey that will retrace our steps to Syracuse, NY where my family started.

As I navigate the rain and slippery roads toward the city, I wonder what the hell we're doing. The figure in the passenger seat is a hollowed-out version of my dad that is alien to me. His jokes help remind me that it's still him and that he is still alive. The white Lincoln radiates against the black skies and brown buildings of the city. I'm glad my dad chose white. It's heavenly.

Just a year before, my dad could bench press two hundred pounds, leg press five hundred, and swim, hike, and ski laps around athletes half his age. At sixty-eight, Vince Donnelly was in the middle of an astonishing physical renaissance when the cancer in his pancreas erupted.

His strength had helped him survive an operation at Johns Hopkins to remove a large chunk of his pancreas. Soon after, though, tests showed cancer in nearby lymph nodes. Opinions varied on whether my dad was treatable. The operating surgeon suggested that he just go home and live his life as best as possible, not concern himself with things such as CA19-9 markers, CAT scans, chemotherapy, and all of the other ways people try to corner and kill the beast. It was the doctor's way of saying that fighting probably was a waste of energy. But fighting is in my dad's blood. I didn't expect him to stop now just because cancer was in there, too.

The following spring, my dad's hopes for survival took a severe blow. PET scans ordered by my father's oncologist in

Vail showed cancer spreading throughout his upper spine and sternum. The images also indicated increased metastasis in his liver and near his kidney. The Vail oncologist told him he could reasonably expect to live four more months.

That's when my dad called and suggested this road trip through his past. The impulse surprised me. Although the Irish are given to singing weepy pub songs about heroic near-misses and might-have-beens, my dad was never the sentimental type. Vince justified the trip by saying he had business in Pittsburgh and wanted to "check out a few things relating to family history" in Syracuse. His voice told me there was something more to it, but I wasn't sure what. Maybe he needed to go back to own what he did, to see how far he'd come before he died. Maybe he needed to know he'd done enough, because even in these sober, looser, happier years of late, my dad still at times felt as if he should have earned more, done more, been more. That notion seemed preposterous to me, and my secret fear always had been that I could never live up to his legacy, that the deep ruts of his giant footsteps would swallow me.

I agreed to drive him. Truthfully, though, I was nervous. I was thirty-seven, sober, and alive but still dogged by self-doubt and not sure what I was doing with my life. Was I ready for this type of reckoning? God forgive me for thinking it, but my dad, facing death, could at least go back to where we came from as a conquering hero. What was I?

I told my dad we should call the trip "The Farewell Tour." He laughed and suggested we print T-shirts with a hot rod hearse on the front and the names and dates of the tour stops on the back.

A valet hails my dad like a close relative when we pull up to his beloved Duquesne Club, where he stays when he's in Pittsburgh for business. These places are the pinnacle of the social and business hierarchy of last-century towns such as Pittsburgh. In the past I'd looked down my nose at Duquesne Club anachronisms such as having to wear a coat and tie to dinner and the old, gold-framed artwork depicting fox hunts, steel mills, coal barges, and other bygone local customs. To me, the club was the kind of place where the Addams Family would be happy to room and board.

This time, however, I can't help but draw parallels between the club and my father. The club is irrelevant and fading. My father is fading and becoming irrelevant. Nature knows when you're dying, and the world politely moves on long before you're gone from it. Watching this happen to my dad hurts. The club no longer amuses me. It makes me uncomfortable.

Soon after arriving, Vince slips a previously undisclosed mission into the agenda of meetings with lawyers, accountants, and insurance people (death actually requires more precise planning than life). My dad is fond of an upbeat oncologist at the University of Pittsburgh Medical Center. If the four horsemen of the apocalypse appeared on the horizon, Michael Wong would say they were dressed nicely. Vince is attracted to Dr. Wong's positive outlook and wants him to provide a second opinion of the Vail oncologist's disheartening interpretation of the PET scans. I know a second opinion is ultimately meaningless, but I go along with the plan until I, too, get caught up in my father's hope that the lesions are actually arthritic football injuries that had been pestering him for years.

Dr. Wong meets us and tells Vince things that fall gently on his ears, including that blood markers are often unreliable, and PET scans are far from the industry-standard imaging technique. Wong says he will compare the CAT and PET scans and give us his assessment when we return from Syracuse.

The meeting buoys my dad. We're back on the initiative! That evening, we go down to the club's dim and mostly vacant dining room and eat pork loin and scalloped potatoes. Just to make sure things don't get too healthy, my dad orders chocolate cake and vanilla ice cream for dessert. Twice.

"I've got to keep my weight up," he says.

"Hey, this cancer [stuff's] not all bad," I offer.

"Not all of it."

Despite the joke, Vince is really desperate to keep his weight up. I can see he is terrified and scrapping to hold on to whatever life remains. I can't stomach the fight anymore. He's getting mauled. I don't want to see the champ getting pummeled while everyone's heart breaks—like when Ali fought Larry Holmes. I just want him to die gracefully. With every forkful of cake and ice cream I want to scream, "It's over! You're dying right here in front of me! Stop chasing false hope! Stop nuking yourself with chemo! Give up!"

I don't say a thing, because my dad wants to live and what can you say to that?

After the operation on his pancreas, I started hugging my dad—big, uncomfortable, loving hugs. This hugging thing was new for him. All of his life he could joke, pat a back, shake a hand, but he couldn't put his affection into a messy embrace. I also began to stroke his hair, to hold his face, to kiss him five times in a row. To his surprise, he liked it. He started asking for it. This cancer had opened up a new world of physical affection between us that didn't previously exist. I wondered what might have been different if we'd lived our lives like this.

Saying good night after dinner, Vince turns in his doorway and says, "Joe, come in here and wrap me up in your big, strong arms. I'll never forget how you held me in the hospital like I was a little baby." He cries and cries as I hold on and hold back my own tears. He's just skin and bones.

◆◆◆

IT'S HARD TO THINK of anything to look forward to in Syracuse. I was born there, but all I know of it are my dad's memories— of pulling my grandfather out of bars when he'd gone missing for days, of fighting with his father when he tried to "get at" my grandmother during a bad drunk. One story still haunts: the time my grandfather lined up my dad and his younger siblings with a shotgun and drunkenly threatened to blow their heads off. Vince talked the gun out of his father's hands.

Vince told these stories without bitterness. Things were just the way they were. At least through Vince's stories my grandfather was a real figure to me, not always horrifying, sometimes even funny and warm. I knew my grandfather loved to fish and dance, was faster with a quip than you were, that he worked hard and had a terrible chip on his shoulder. I knew that my dad's ultimately sobering head-on collision was an eerie and fortunate echo of an accident in which my intoxicated grandfather killed someone in a road accident.

I also knew that before he died, my grandfather had sought and received forgiveness from my dad, because, despite everything, Vince always hung the moon for him. But I knew almost nothing about my grandmother.

What little information I had painted a vague picture of a bent-knee Catholic, praying for deliverance from poverty and regret—a woman who lived on the edge of severe depression. The nature of that depression was shrouded in mystery. She kept my father at a chilly distance even though he was often thrown into the role of protecting her from her drunken husband. My dad could never quite explain this except to say, "She lived with a lot of disappointment."

We drive north from Pittsburgh in a barrage of cold rain relieved by frequent stops for coffee, doughnuts, and ice cream sandwiches. When we finally skate into downtown Syracuse, the afternoon sun appears briefly and barely. I ask my dad if he thinks it's somehow symbolic.

"It's probably happy to see me return to the scene of my many crimes," Vince jokes.

We park across the street from the little house on Teal Avenue where Vince grew up. He stares at it and tells a story about the woman who lived upstairs and sewed him a winter coat from the remnants of his father's overcoat. Vince laughs about how bad it looked. I suggest that he stand in front of the house for a photo. He does so without enthusiasm.

During the next couple of days we drive by my father's old haunts, rarely braving the miserable weather to get out of the Lincoln. Vince provides a constant soundtrack about friends, family, and history. We stop at the grim tenement where I was born. My dad seems embarrassed. I ask what the complex is called.

"The slums," he says.

Syracuse unfolds as a black-and-gray ghost town. I'd be surprised if there's a less attractive place in America. We cover the same ground again and again. It's clear that Vince is searching for something, some place or meaning that is eluding us. I want to go home to Los Angeles, return to the sun. This place spooks me, and I know it's because I can still feel it in me, like the memory of a close call.

Eventually we turn onto a shoddy thoroughfare that lights a flame in Vince's eyes. We park and walk. He's found the route along which he used to escort his mother to work at Woolworth. The store is gone, but Vince sees what he's been looking for. It's a small shop in a tidy Victorian set back from the street. It sells tombstones and once had one for sale with a lamb etched on it.

"We'd walk by the monument place every day because she worked up here, and we'd see that little lamb. How many times she must have looked at that stone," Vince says, his eyes going past the shop. "It probably cost fifty bucks. Fifty bucks to buy the stone with the lamb on it for the baby she thought she had killed."

Standing in front of the strange shop, Vince explains the terrible nature of the baby's death, which he had only recently learned from his sister. The baby was his older brother, "Baby

Paul," who died just months before Vince was born. Apparently his mother had given Paul a can of talcum powder to play with that she thought was empty. Somehow the baby got the top open and, his mother believed, some powder got in Paul's lungs and killed him. She carried that secret guilt her whole life until she told Vince's sister while on her deathbed.

"My mother, you know, she had that tragedy with her first child. I can't imagine what it was like. She loses a child in March and she has a second one in August," Vince says. "How she could transfer any immediate love and care to that second child was beyond me—that child being me."

Only then do I realize what Vince has been looking for. It wasn't the memories of his childhood, the ghost of his father, or the sled he rode in the winter. He was really looking for the tiny footprints of the older brother he never knew–forever just "Baby Paul" to him, a long-lost explanation for his mother's absent embrace.

On the day before we leave Syracuse, the sun shines. Vince and I go to brunch at one of those old-style inns that are landmarks of the aristocratic village of Skaneateles on Skaneateles Lake, about twenty minutes from Syracuse. The drive takes us past the cemetery where his parents and ancestors are buried.

The inn delivers mediocre food onto white tablecloths with an air of old-world gentility. Vince says little at breakfast. Something's brewing. Driving back, he suggests we stop and visit the cemetery, and I guess this has been the reason for his silence. The closer we get to the cemetery, the darker the skies grow, the stronger the wind howls. By the time we reach the gates, it is lightening and hailing. It's as if the gods have been warning us away for days and now are indignant at our persistence. I agree with them. What does any of this matter anymore?

I ask my dad if he thinks it's a coincidence that golf ball-size hail is bombarding us as we approach his family gravesite. "I doubt it," he says.

The family plot is on a little knoll. I can barely make it out through the rain-soaked windows. The stones are dark silhouettes lit by lightning, as if from a horror movie. My dad rolls down his window and looks out.

"I told you about my mother wanting the stone with the lamb on it, but she could never afford it. She felt bad about it. I don't know when I did it—a number of years ago—I got a stone with a lamb on it that said 'Paul' and put it in the ground. A flat one with a lamb on it," Vince says. "As soon as I pull away, we'll probably be the last family to ever go look in on it."

I realize he's right; I will probably never return here. I won't have to, though, because my dad has taken me all the way in. There is nothing left unsaid or undone between us. No ghosts to haunt my memories. I won't come back, but I will carry all of this with me wherever I go, even back to bright Los Angeles. It's part of who I am and who I always have been—my father's son, and for that I am grateful.

Back in Pittsburgh the news is bad. After reviewing the scans, Dr. Wong confirms the dire forecast of my dad's oncologist in Vail. "At least we know what we're up against," Vince says.

My dad died six months later, surpassing expectations by eight weeks, breaking everyone's heart in the process. I keep a vial with some of his ashes at home. Now and then I look in the container and think about the mystery of life and how something so complex can come down to something so simple.

[Handwritten notes at top:]
heralded filmmaker
2 films coming out on same day
(not documentaries
1st time in 8 yrs
old hurt both films
- great man is a real human being ~~weakness~~

*[Handwritten: * overall]*

Werner Herzog In Los Angeles

[Handwritten: ~~organizing~~ ∧ Organizing principles (Hope, America)]

[Handwritten left margin, vertical: Setting the scene — Camera zoomed out]

Originally published in the Los Angeles Times, April 12, 2017

Author's note: One of the best things about doing the Christian Bale profile was that it afforded me the opportunity to talk to Werner Herzog. As I recall, even on the phone, he was casually hilarious and incredibly endearing. Nearly a decade later, I got to meet the man in person when, after a long absence from narrative filmmaking, he had two features coming out on the same weekend. The films came and went quickly, but Herzog endures. A man fully alive.

WERNER HERZOG IS AT a booth in a Sunset Boulevard restaurant, just down the hill from where he once rescued Joaquin Phoenix.

[Handwritten right margin: telling anec... gets inter...]

The rescue happened eleven years ago when the freshly Oscar-nominated Phoenix flipped his car on a winding road in Laurel Canyon. The actor, upside down and out of it, reported hearing a gentle tapping on his window, then a voice with a thick accent telling him to relax.

"That's Werner Herzog!" the actor said to himself. "There's something so calming and beautiful about Werner Herzog's voice," he told reporters afterward.

What Phoenix didn't say, but Herzog did in the narration he provided for the 2010 animated short "When Herzog Rescued Phoenix" by Sascha Ciezata (of "When Lynch Met Lucas" fame), is that the upside-down Phoenix was trying to light a cigarette

while gasoline dripped into the cabin of his car—a Dodge Challenger, if the short is to be believed. Herzog "confiscated" the lighter, smashed in the back window, dragged Phoenix to safety, and then dashed off, like a Bavarian Batman driving a Volkswagen Beetle, before the sirens drew too close.

One of the short's more than 205,000 YouTube viewers commented, "God has the same voice as Werner Herzog… it's weird." To which another replied, "God's real name is Werner, but he's too shy to admit it."

" lens " zoomed way out

On this Friday afternoon of light breezes, mild temperatures, and unusual milestones even for a guy with a capacity for milestones, the voice of God is registering slightly apprehensive.

camera zoomed ~~out~~ in

"It's a little weird," he says, acknowledging mild anxiety, "because there are two films out on the same day."

The films—*Queen of the Desert*, starring Nicole Kidman, and *Salt and Fire*, starring Michael Shannon, Herzog's new Klaus Kinski, some might say—are the director's first narrative offerings in nearly eight years. If you didn't know any better, you might guess he'd ordered up the combo platter himself to trumpet his return to fiction after his prolific near-decade of making documentaries, including last year's *Into the Inferno* and *Lo and Behold, Reveries of the Connected World*.

"Oh, for God's sake, no. I wouldn't have such a crazy idea. I tried to prevent it, but, uh, my influence has been limited," the director says, dispelling the notion of an intentional Herzog double feature. "It might happen that the films obliterate each other… My output is too large. Too big."

Though we may think concerns about the commercial fates of his films too petty for visionary iconoclasts such as Herzog, he says he's not one to make art just for art's sake: "I make them for audiences, always. Not for my own pleasure."

Not that there isn't some fun in coming back with a bang, right? "Yes, I try to see the fun inside of it," he smiles.

◆◆◆

(handwritten in margin: Zoomed in)

HERZOG IS A FIT seventy-four, with eyes that actually twinkle and a traditional Bavarian Trachten jacket carefully placed on the chair next to him for a later photo shoot. Searching for the fun inside the mysteries of life, fate, and people's obsessions would seem to sum up Herzog's mission, whose arrival as a visionary filmmaker began in 1968 when his first feature film, *Signs of Life*, won a grand jury prize at the Berlin International Film Festival. That search has led him to death row, under Antarctic ice, into ancient caves, and up to the mouths of active volcanoes—usually with a sense of play about what he's doing, even in extreme conditions.

The new films are set in deserts on opposite sides of the world, and though *Salt and Fire* could be taken as a lament, it's still full of Herzog's idiosyncratic humor, a characteristic he feels the media often miss.

And if the media don't always get him, Herzog insists his audiences do. "They always laugh. It's sometimes a strange, dark unusual sense of humor. It's not the Eddie Murphy humor; it's something else."

Herzog says his humor has been buoyed over the past twenty years by his living in Los Angeles, which he turned to after things didn't work out with San Francisco. "My wife and I found it not the most exciting place in the United States, and we said we want to move to the city with the most substance, and it was immediately clear that Los Angeles, that's the place."

As for "the glitz and glamour of Hollywood," Herzog says, "that is a very thin crust. Behind it is an enormous intensity of culture and creative energy and things that ultimately decide the big things, the big internal movements of the planet. Things get done here."

Among those things: "The collective dreams of the world in cinema and acceptance of gays and lesbians as an integral part of a dignified civilization, and many, many other things that are just wonderful. You see the influx of the Mexicans, which I find very invigorating… If you can imagine California or Los Angeles without the Mexican population, it would be the instant end of California."

To Herzog, someone like Elon Musk epitomizes the spirit of Los Angeles, with his outsize ambitions to day-trip private citizens to the moon and eventually colonize Mars.

And yet Los Angeles, Herzog admits, has also contributed its fair share to the "big cultural stupidities," such as hippies ("The worldview was just not adequate to the real problems of the time," he says), children's yoga, <u>the choco-nut smoothies on</u> — ᴢoomed <u>the breakfast menu here,</u> and, despite his admiration for Musk, ⁱⁿ colonizing Mars.

"Mars is an ill-conceived idea. It's definitely ill-conceived, and it's not going to happen," Herzog says. "We should look after the habitability of our planet rather than making an inhospitable planet, Mars, somehow livable."

Herzog, though, might be willing to join Musk on one of his lunar jaunts—provided certain conditions were met.

"Well, I have said it to him, just to get some spark of a reaction out of him, 'Yes, of course, I'd like to go—only if I had a camera along. Sure, that would be wonderful,'" he says, grinning. "They always send technicians out into space, and they haven't sent a poet out there yet."

shows his character

The impulse to send civilians into space does strike a chord with Herzog, who thought the idea to give a seat on the space shuttle Challenger's doomed tenth mission to schoolteacher Christa McAuliffe was inspired. "My breath and my heart stopped for a moment, because all of a sudden there was some new idea…send somebody who would go back to her classroom and have some exciting stories for the kids."

Back on terra firma, Herzog says he's always seeing something new and inspiring in Los Angeles. "All the time, all the time," he says. "There's never been a dull day here in Los Angeles."

♦♦♦

HERZOG'S FIRST US CITY, however, was Pittsburgh, when, as a twenty-year-old student from the Bavarian Alps, he studied film at Duquesne University. "I had worked in a steel factory as a welder during high school to earn money for my first films. So I thought, that's the right men out there for me," he says. "But [the steel industry] was in decay already. It was in full decay and it was clear it would not recover."

In Pittsburgh, though, and in traveling throughout the Midwest, Herzog says he saw the best of the country. "I was picked up, literally, from the street by a family who gave me shelter when I dropped out of university... I was homeless, and I had lost the money of the scholarship—and all of the sudden, enormous hospitality. In all the difficulties I had at the time, Americans of the heartland had been the best of the best."

Herzog isn't surprised that the issue of Rust Belt decay has finally found its way to the top of the national conversation. "There's justice in it," he says, "because for years, I have been complaining to my friends, liberals, Democrats—men and women who have a lot of sense, make good observations, but they came to politics between Seattle and Boston and New York and Los Angeles and would speak about the rest of America as 'the flyovers.' And I said, 'That's a cynic way to look at the heartland of America.'"

Though Herzog thinks "it's good that the heartland found its voice," he knows all too well what can happen when that voice curdles. "In my childhood and in my adolescence, I saw the aftermath of what should have never happened. But let me say something about America. America, no matter what, always has this enormous, mysterious way to rejuvenate itself and pull itself out of crisis, and that is something that always gives me confidence in your country."

It's reassuring, perhaps, that Herzog, an artist who has mined as deeply as any the absurdities and pratfalls of our existence, is optimistic about the future.

"I'm not into the mood of Weltschmerz," he says, using the German word for world-weariness that describes how many are feeling these days. "I'm into the mood of joy of the world, absolute joy and curiosity. I'm full of projects. I'm full of joy and full of things that I see on the horizon."

Acknowledgments

WHEN I WAS A kid, the bathroom was sometimes the only place to get a break from a crowded and anxious household. When opportunity struck, I'd hide out there with the newspaper, *Time* magazine, *Sports Illustrated, Rolling Stone,* whatever was within arm's reach, and read with fascination about the types of people I've been lucky enough to grow up and write about—artists, athletes, and outsiders.

I'd be ecstatic if this book were to contribute to the tradition of fine bathroom reads and I want to thank Tyson Cornell and Rare Bird Lit for making it possible for the characters gathered here to fit neatly into our sanctuaries with us. And thanks, of course, to the generous subjects of this collection who shared more of their time and spirit with me than they had to.

I want to thank Trish Kiesewetter, Gary Rivlin, Tara Flanagan, Janet Duckworth, Manohla Dargis, Martin J. Smith, Scott Hulet, Gregory Blake Miller, Andrew Blechman, Scott Foundas, and all the great editors I've worked with for aiding and abetting my work and life. Thanks, also, to the many friends and family members who have helped me forge a path and leave a bit of a trail. There are too many of you to mention, but you know who you are and I am deeply grateful to you.

I especially want to thank Arty Nelson and Laurie Ochoa. There's not enough space to do it right, but, Arty, you've been a great friend and inspiration for more than forty years, and, Laurie, most of this would not have been possible without you.

Finally, I'm most grateful to my greatest collaborator, Ingrid Allen.